Dubai & Co.

Dubai & Co.

Global Strategies for Doing Business in the Gulf States

Aamir A. Rehman

New York   Chicago   San Francisco   Lisbon   London   Madrid   Mexico City   Milan
New Delhi   San Juan   Seoul   Singapore   Sydney   Toronto

The *McGraw·Hill* Companies

1 2 3 4 5 6 7 8 9 0   FGR/FGR   0 9 8 7

ISBN 13: 978-0-07-149413-7
MHID: 0-07-149413-8

McGraw-Hill books are available at special quantity discounts to use as premiums and sales promotions, or for use in corporate training programs. For more information, please write to the Director of Special Sales, Professional Publishing, McGraw-Hill, Two Penn Plaza, New York, NY 10121-2298. Or contact your local bookstore.

This book is printed on acid-free paper.

Library of Congress Cataloging-in-Publication Data

Rehman, Aamir A.
   Dubai & Co. : global strategies for doing business in the Gulf states
/ by Aamir A. Rehman.
        p. cm.
   ISBN-13: 978-0-07-149413-7
   ISBN-10: 0-07-149413-8
   1. Arab countries—Commerce.   2. Arab countries—Economic conditions.
3. Arab countries—Foreign economic relations.   4. International
business enterprises—Arab countries.   I. Title   II. Title: Dubai and
Co.
HF3866.Z5R44 2007
658'.04909536—dc22

                                                       2007042218

With love and gratitude to my parents,
Drs. Razia and Abdul Rehman,
whose countless gifts and blessings
could never be repaid.

CONTENTS

ACKNOWLEDGMENTS

This book is the work of many hands. I am deeply grateful to the large group of researchers, family, friends, and well-wishers who contributed to this work in innumerable ways. Their support, understanding, and kind wishes have enriched this book—and the life of its author—tremendously.

First, let me thank my wife Hina, my parents, my sister Naheed, and my entire family for their encouragement throughout the drafting process. Hina has been especially patient, sacrificing from the already scarce time we have together as I labored on the book. Her love and support are an endless blessing and source of joy and comfort. My gratitude to the family is eternal.

The efforts of Munir Zilanawala are the very heart of this book. Munir, whom we fondly call the "Chief Operating Officer" of the book project, recruited and led the research team, edited and revised each chapter, provided top-notch feedback and quality control, and masterfully managed a long list of operational details. He was also the lead researcher for Chapter 3, the core chapter on the GCC opportunity, and supported the research for all the other chapters. I cannot imagine producing this book without Munir's superb contributions, and collaborating with him has been a tremendous blessing. He has been a true partner in the venture.

The research team was dedicated, skilled, and diverse. Angel Leu led the research on two chapters—Chapters 4 and 7—and skillfully blended hard facts with qualitative interviews. Mohammad Usman Masood, lead researcher for Chapter 5, also contributed to other chapters and conducted a crucial GCC awareness survey. The quality of his work and passion behind it were outstanding. Osama Kazmi provided additional support for Chapter 5. Anaya Al-Nahari led the research for Chapter 2 and contributed immensely helpful local knowledge and input throughout the manuscript. Ahlam Aljasmi and Ryan Millikan provided valuable in-market research and perspective on marketing, supporting Chapter 6. Ryan also provided research for other chapters.

Zohaib Patel led the research for Chapter 8, on Gulf capital. He, like the entire research team, sacrificed evenings and weekends to contribute to these efforts. Mohamed Serageldin's research for Chapter 9, on the GCC's infrastructure, was comprehensive and rich. Ursula Jessee supported Chapter 10, on organization, and demonstrated drive and creativity through her research and management interviews. Masooma Hussain supported Chapter 1, producing thorough research on the market "clusters" within the Middle East. The research team's diligent efforts helped add a great deal of rigor and detail to the analysis.

Several advisors provided valuable feedback and support on the manuscript. I am grateful to Mohamed Ali Vaid, Omar Khan, Hassan Jaffar, Umair Khan, Imran Javaid, Rafi Shikoh, Imraan Mir, and Case Dorkey for the insight they provided throughout the process. Abdur-Rahman Syed, in addition to providing feedback and advice, helped recruit the research team. Seema Rathod and Amin Venjara provided similar support in recruiting our high-caliber team.

I am indebted to the great many mentors, colleagues, and well-wishers who have encouraged my decade-long passion for the GCC and global strategy. Many mentors at Harvard University, most notably Dr. S. Nazim Ali and Thomas D. Mullins, provided me access to Gulf business leaders very early in my career. Hatim Alireza, Taha Abdul-Basser, Abbas Kanji and Majid Jafar, dear friends from Harvard, have encouraged my GCC work tremendously. HSBC Amanah, The Boston Consulting Group, the Harvard Business School, the Monitor Group, and Creative Good were all pivotal in shaping a passion for strategy and for thought leadership. I am especially grateful to the Middle East leadership team of BCG—Tom Lewis, Zafar Momin, and Tom Bradtke—for enabling me to work with inspiring GCC clients on a fascinating set of strategic issues.

Iqbal Khan, founding CEO of HSBC Amanah, has been a cherished mentor and enabler of my Gulf-related efforts. Iqbal's values-based leadership has been a powerful source of inspiration for over a decade. I thank Iqbal for the countless lessons that his example and his words have taught me over the years. His enthusiasm for this book has been heartwarming.

Jeanne Glasser, editorial director at McGraw-Hill, was the catalyst of this book. From the day she suggested a much-needed "book on Dubai," her support for this effort has been unwavering. I thank her for the confidence she has shown in the book and in me, and for her kind guidance and feedback throughout the publishing process. I thank Herb Schaffner, publisher at McGraw-Hill, and the broader McGraw-Hill team, for the gracious support they have provided. Credit for the book is to be shared, while responsibility for any shortcomings is mine.

All who have contributed to these efforts—named and unnamed—have my deep appreciation and good wishes. It is our collective hope that this book help integrate the Gulf economies and their people more deeply into global business, in a spirit of genuine collaboration, shared prosperity, and mutual advancement.

Introducing Dubai & Co.

The economies of the Arabian Gulf states are among the most dynamic in the world today. Wealth is being generated at historic rates, driven largely—but not entirely—by a boom in oil prices. Gross domestic product (GDP) growth in the Gulf countries often approaches or exceeds the double digits, thanks in large part to these countries' rapidly evolving demographics; youth make up roughly half the population in these states and often lead consumer demand. Education levels, connectivity to the broader world, and business expertise are higher than ever before. Gulf governments are changing the regulatory environments of their states, with a closed-economy approach quickly yielding to World Trade Organization (WTO) standards and demands for open trade. Competition is increasing in every industry in the Gulf, where multinational corporations are finding themselves deadlocked in a tug-of-war with increasingly savvy local firms. And in contrast with some other emerging markets, the Gulf states have a superb infrastructure and sound banking systems. According to Transparency International, the global civil society organization that monitors corruption, most Gulf countries have about the same level of corruption as Taiwan and South Korea. Even Saudi Arabia, considered the least transparent, is ranked as less corrupt than both China and India.[1] To be sure, the states of the Gulf Cooperation Council (GCC)—the United Arab Emirates (UAE), Saudi Arabia,

Qatar, Bahrain, Kuwait, and Oman—have become exciting and promising places to do business.

BEYOND THE PUMP

Gulf economies are best known, of course, for their roles in global oil and gas markets. Saudi Arabia does, after all, control 25 percent of the world's known oil reserves. GCC economies affect our everyday life, however, at a lot more places than the gas pump.

If you shopped at Tiffany's in the mid-1980s or purchased a Gucci handbag in recent years, you bought from a business controlled by Gulf investors. Had a Caribou coffee lately? This second-largest US coffee chain is owned by a Bahrain-funded entity that is fully compliant with the investment guidelines of Islamic law. Stay at some of New York's finest hotels—including the W Hotel in Union Square and the Jumeirah Essex House overlooking Central Park—and you're at a property owned by Dubai investors. Stayed at a Fairmont Hotels & Resorts recently? The company is now largely owned by a consortium that includes the billionaire Saudi investor Prince Alwaleed Bin Talal—the Gulf's version of Warren Buffett. Alwaleed's large stakes in Citigroup, Apple, and other key multinational firms give him influence over companies with hundreds of millions of customers worldwide. And the low interest rates that make your mortgage and car loan affordable are due in part to over $110 billion in US Treasury bonds owned directly by oil exporters, including wealthy Gulf nations, plus many billions more owned indirectly via London.[2]

The list of prominent businesses with large GCC investors is extensive. Madame Tussaud's, the British wax museum that is a must-see for London-bound tourists, was once owned by Dubai International Capital. Another Dubai entity, Istithmar, has pursued about a 2 percent equity stake in Standard Chartered, the UK-based global banking institution. Abu Dhabi, the capital emirate of the UAE, is not to be outdone: its Mubadala Development Company has a 5 percent stake in the Italian luxury automaker Ferrari. Elsewhere in the Gulf, the Kuwait Investment Authority is, at 7.1 percent, by far the largest shareholder in Daimler AG (until recently, DaimlerChrysler)—the manufacturer of your Mercedes-Benz or Town & Country minivan.

The Kuwait Investment Authority, by the way, was also the single largest subscriber in the world's biggest IPO ever—the Industrial and Commercial Bank of China's offering in 2006, which raised $19 billion.[3] And if that were not enough, consider the fact that a large share of China's exports comes through Dubai's massive Port Rashid. The port is the home base of Dubai Ports World (DPW), a firm that runs port terminals from Hong Kong to Germany to Canada and would today be managing several US ports were it not for congressional intervention.

The impact of the GCC in the lives of consumers worldwide is not surprising, considering the interdependence and openness of today's globalizing economies. The crucial lesson, however, is that the GCC economies touch our lives in countless ways.

HARD FACTS: THE GCC IN THE GLOBAL ECONOMY

If the GCC's high-profile investments worldwide and the megaprojects at home—including the planned world's tallest building (Burj Dubai) and the world's first "seven-star" hotel (Burj al-Arab)—aren't enough to convince you of the rising importance of the Gulf states in the global economy, these facts and figures should capture the attention of any hard-nosed global executive or strategist:

- In 2006, GDP per capita in the GCC was close to $20,000—nearly 3 times that of China and more than 5 times that of India.[4]
- The GCC's current account surplus ($155 billion) is roughly on par with that of China ($161 billion). China achieves this, however, with a population over 30 times larger than that of the GCC countries.[5]
- The GCC's contribution to global savings is believed to be larger than China's—despite the fact that its population is only 3 percent of China's.
- Qatar, a small but resource-rich GCC country, reached a GDP per capita of $45,000—more than 10 times India's. If its economy grows according to expectations, Qatar may have the world's highest GDP per capita by 2011.[6]

- In 2005, the Saudi stock market's total market capitalization was greater than that of China or India.[7]
- SABIC, a major industrial conglomerate in Saudi Arabia, reached a market capitalization of $135 billion—a shade under that of Google and Honda, and greater than Coca-Cola.[8]
- Emaar, Dubai's leading real estate developer, had a higher market valuation than any other real estate company worldwide.[9]
- Over 28 million passengers fly through Dubai International Airport each year. That's more than 23 passengers per resident—twice the figure for London and four times the figure for New York.[10]
- A sign of the region's importance is that the 2003 World Bank and International Monetary Fund (IMF) meetings were held in Dubai, the first time the event occurred in an Arab country.[11]
- Dubai has 4 times more retail shopping space per person than the United States.[12]
- In a 2006 survey of consumer confidence, the UAE ranked ahead of the UK, France, Germany, and Italy.[13]

In today's world, no company with global aspirations can afford to ignore the GCC and the opportunities it presents.

HISTORICALLY OVERLOOKED

Most multinationals have overlooked the GCC in their global strategies. This oversight is in some ways understandable. For one thing, the founding of the Gulf Cooperation Council—the economic and political body linking the economies of the six constituent Arab countries—did not occur until the early 1980s. The very term "GCC" is therefore quite new to the language of business.

More important, the countries of the GCC did not enjoy their spectacular prosperity until the oil booms of the 1970s. At the time, global executives had almost no experience in the region. Even today, most senior executives have had little or no exposure to the GCC in their careers—their global dealings and postings having been more likely to occur in the United States, Europe, and Japan.

For the most part, this is because today's senior executives received their business education at a time when GCC markets had far less economic significance. In fact, hardly any Harvard Business School case studies before the 1990s even mentioned the Gulf economies.

With GCC economies—most prominently that of Dubai—now emerging in the business headlines, however, global executives are beginning to see the opportunity. The UAE, Saudi Arabia, Qatar, and other GCC economies are in the news to stay, as the fundamental conditions supporting their growth are likely to remain for the foreseeable future. Savvy corporations are therefore sharpening their focus on the GCC opportunity and developing thoughtful strategies to capitalize on those opportunities in order to bring much-desired growth to their top and bottom lines.

A STRATEGIC GUIDE

This book is your strategic guide to the GCC. It will not only provide the needed basics on the GCC, but it also will deliver in-depth explorations of a dynamic but sometimes misunderstood region that is proving itself to be vital to global business success. It will provide you with the market understanding and strategic insights you need to both formulate an effective approach to the GCC and integrate this region into your overall global strategy.

Dubai & Co. addresses the pressing issue of how global organizations can most effectively tap into the economic opportunity and promise of GCC markets. Throughout the book, I'll answer questions like:

- How are changes in the GCC business environment creating opportunity for multinationals?
- What are the essentials that global managers must know about the economies and private sectors in the GCC markets?
- Under what circumstances should multinationals consider distributorships or joint ventures with local GCC firms? Under what conditions are acquisitions and direct, organic entry advisable?
- To what degree should multinationals adjust their marketing messages, product portfolios, and branding to capture the market opportunity?

- What is the optimal human capital strategy for managing business in the region? How can multinationals find the right talent, and what are the key development initiatives needed for business leaders working in the region?
- Can the GCC be a source of capital for global businesses? What could multinationals do to make themselves more attractive to GCC investors?
- How can the GCC region be integrated into global companies' operational logistics and supply chains? Are there operational efficiencies to be captured by investing in the region?
- How should a GCC-specific business unit be organized and managed? How can multinationals foster awareness at headquarters of the strategic opportunity in the GCC?

This book will provide practical and concise answers to these questions and more. In addition to analysis of macroeconomic data and commercial information, you will find case studies and illustrations based on the real-life experiences of multinationals and leading local firms. Trend analysis and forecasts for the future will also draw on interviews with key business leaders and decision makers in the public policy and commercial spheres.

A STROLL THROUGH GCC MARKETS

Understanding the Opportunity

The early chapters in this book give you the essentials—the macroeconomic and historical background—needed to understand the business potential of the region. Chapter 1 describes the GCC's positioning within the broader Middle East. Although often viewed as a monolith, the Arab world is composed of three distinct clusters: the Levant, North Africa, and the GCC countries. Viewing the Middle East as a single, uniform bloc causes many business leaders to associate the entire region with stereotypical images of conflict, instability, and low standards of living, which causes them to miss out on attractive and dynamic markets.

The Levant, traditionally referred to as *bilad al-Sham* within the region, consists of Iraq, Lebanon, Israel and the Palestinian Territories, Jordan, and Syria. In recent years, many of these areas—especially

Iraq—have experienced a great deal of conflict and turmoil, leading them to be seen as unstable and largely unattractive markets. The Levant, however, boasts a rich commercial heritage that is renowned in the Middle East and beyond. Merchants from the Levant—particularly from Lebanon—have long been admired for their entrepreneurship and commercial savvy. These traits find their roots in the centuries of trade experience inhabitants acquired in their years living along the vital Arabia-Asia commercial route, as well as in the frequent contact that those living in the string of port cities had with commercial affairs. Fed by regular rains and large rivers, the Levant, unlike the GCC, has a robust agricultural sector that has been critical to its historical prosperity. Current-day Iraq is, after all, located on the site of ancient Mesopotamia and part of the zone known as the "Fertile Crescent," the existence of which enabled the transition from nomadic tribes to permanent civilizations. The economic promise of the Levant is today overshadowed by political conflict.

The second cluster of the Middle East—North Africa—consists of Egypt, Sudan, Libya, Algeria, Tunisia, and Morocco. These countries share a tradition shaped by Mediterranean trade, vast expanses of desert, a combination of agriculture and herding, and the experience of European (predominantly French) colonialism. Meaningful oil and gas reserves are found here, but GDP per capita and general standards of living are modest. Egypt, the largest Arab nation, whose population exceeds 80 million, has been a center of cultural heritage throughout ancient, medieval, and modern times. Egypt remains the cultural hub of the Middle East, with its thriving film industry and literary output serving as evidence.

The GCC nations make up a third, distinct cluster of Middle Eastern states. Their heritage is largely nomadic due to the region's harsh desert terrain. Prior to its accumulation of oil wealth, the GCC's facilitation of trade between Asia, Africa, and Europe was its core commercial activity with relevance to the outside world. Fishing, pearling, and other low-intensity maritime industries were also of local importance, as was raising livestock, which developed into a key form of wealth for the region. The past few decades, on the other hand, have seen fabulous oil booms, busts, and nowadays, significant economic reforms. Today, the prosperity and dynamism of the GCC stands out from the rest of the Middle East, making the GCC nations a natural destination for talent and entrepreneurial ventures within the Arab world.

Having placed the GCC in the broader context of the Middle East, Chapter 2 sheds light on some aspects of the GCC that are often misunderstood and can lead multinationals to overlook the region's strategic opportunities. One core misconception is that oil is the only meaningful business sector in the Gulf. While it is true that oil revenues comprise the bulk of government revenue in most GCC economies, it is also true that the liquidity created from oil exports is channeled into a broad range of economic sectors. All GCC economies are intent on diversification, and it's no surprise that service sectors, consumer goods, and other nonenergy industries often present the most attractive opportunities for multinationals.

Another common misconception about the GCC is that women play a passive role in the economy. The reality is that—like elsewhere in the world—women control the bulk of purchasing decisions within the GCC countries, and so ignoring female consumers would be a costly mistake for businesses targeting the region. Women's economic power extends beyond consumerism. Some readers may be surprised to learn, for example, that Saudi universities now produce, each year, more female than male graduates, and that Saudi women reportedly hold 40 percent of the total real estate assets in the country.[14] These educated women are actively recruited by leading firms that seek to have a workforce reflective of their customer base and of society at large.

Chapter 3 will discuss, in greater depth, the elements that make GCC markets so attractive for global companies today. The combination of prosperity, demographic change, and deregulation has made these markets among the most dynamic in the world. Not only does the GCC have a GDP per capita several times that of China; it also is a region full of young consumers, ready to form lifetime associations with brands and companies that know how to meet their needs. Young populations in GCC countries have had a profound impact on both the public sector—keen to build infrastructure, diversify the economy, and create jobs for young people—and the private sector in which firms compete for the youth market.

Deregulation in the GCC is occurring at a massive scale. The phenomenon is fueled by both inherent interest in economic growth and diversification and the demands of international trade agreements. All six GCC countries are now members of the WTO. Dubai has famously created deregulated free zones across a range of strategic industries, including financial services, media, the Internet, health care, education, and even the flower market. Qatar, Kuwait, and Bahrain have established investment parks in which 100 percent foreign ownership is permitted. Each country is on its own timeline for implementation of the required changes, but all have committed to opening up their economies to the broader world. This means, of course, unprecedented access to attractive GCC markets.

Tapping into the GCC opportunity, however, requires strategies based on genuine understanding of the region. Chapter 4 will provide some essential background information on the history and economies of each country within the region. Although they have much in common, each country within the GCC has taken its own historical path, has its own unique features, and faces its own distinct challenges.

The UAE—which includes the bedrock Abu Dhabi, high-profile Dubai, and five other emirates—has become a beacon of change and a trendsetter for the region through its economic reforms and strategic development of core industries. The UAE is, in several ways, the region's most admired economy, both internally and globally. In a nutshell, the UAE is a *trendsetter*.

Saudi Arabia, by far the region's largest economy by both GDP and population, is the GCC's *core market*. Saudi Arabia is a complex society in which the monarchy, religious institutions, and business interests continually balance and shift power and influence. The Kingdom is the birthplace of Islam and caretaker of Islam's holiest sites, and at the same time it is a staunch US ally since World War II. It is also home to a quarter of the world's known oil reserves and has experienced two oil booms that have transformed the economy and created substantial wealth. Social issues and tensions, however, are palpable—unemployment is high, social freedoms are deeply sought, and the government has been engaged in stamping out extremist groups that have threatened the Kingdom's stability for years now. Yet, considering its size and influence, Saudi Arabia cannot be overlooked. Any business that seeks a genuine GCC footprint must develop a sound strategy for the Saudi market—especially if the business has a consumer or retail element.

Qatar is, in some ways, the *upstart* of the GCC. Its wealth boom is relatively recent and is driven by an upsurge in revenue from natural gas, though it also has substantial oil resources. Qatar may, according to some projections, have the world's highest GDP per capita by 2011. In building its economy, Qatar has learned from the experiences of its neighbors and is actively promoting knowledge-based industries; several leading universities, including Cornell, have opened campuses in Qatar, and GE has a research facility there as well. Politically, Qatar is managing a balancing act, acting as a key US ally and locale of large military bases while also providing a home for Al-Jazeera, the outspoken media voice of Arab and Islamic perspectives on world affairs.

Bahrain has been the GCC's *Wall Street* for decades and is home to hundreds of financial institutions. Its offshore status and proximity to Saudi Arabia made it a natural home for capital in the wake of the oil booms of the 1970s—especially after Beirut, which had been the GCC's key banking hub since 1975, was shaken up by political instability. Bahrain's economy is diversifying into other sectors as well, including manufacturing and heavy industry. Kraft has even built a food-processing facility there. Like New York's own Wall Street, Bahrain is actively engaged in an effort to retain its banking hub status as competing financial centers pop up: regional competitors are in the UAE, Qatar, and Saudi Arabia.

Kuwait is a pocket of prosperity within the GCC—a country with a small population and large oil revenues. Since the first Gulf War, Kuwait has quickly rebuilt and undergone significant reform. Kuwait's parliament exercises a significant amount of influence in the GCC and is observed closely by other GCC countries as one example of the slow shift toward democratization. Kuwait's role in the globe is that of exporter—both of oil and of dollar-denominated capital. The country is therefore very important for financial institutions worldwide.

Oman, the sixth country of the GCC, has in some ways the most natural economy. Oman has a genuine and growing middle class, which has been exhibiting increased consumerism along the model of other emerging markets in recent years. Oman's economy is a mix of energy, services, retail, finance, tourism, and other sectors. As an attraction to visitors and global firms, Oman also boasts a range of natural beauty and diversity—from mountains to beaches to oases to historic forts—quite unique among the GCC countries.

Developing Corporate Strategies

The second half of this book provides perspective on how to craft regional strategies for the GCC, taking a functional (that is, department-by-department) approach to the challenge. To effectively capture commercial opportunities in the region, multinational firms must be prepared to adjust their business models, building on the elements that are well suited for the region and modifying those that are not. Chapters 5 through 10 explore strategies for multinationals across the range of functions and departments, providing both thematic advice and specific examples of how other companies have approached the opportunities.

Chapter 5 discusses the complex issue of market-entry strategies. As GCC markets have historically been protected by regulatory barriers and had relatively little commercial potential, the norm for multinationals seeking to enter these markets has been straightforward distribution agreements. Multinationals have struck deals with local distributors to sell their goods—and manage all the local issues—for a percentage of revenues. The world's major pharmaceutical and auto manufacturers, for example, have adopted distribution models within the GCC. These distribution agreements have allowed multinationals to profit from GCC markets with minimal risk; responsibility assumed almost entirely by the local distributor. The drawback of this approach, however, has been that it limits the foreign firm's share of the profits and its ability to control local strategies.

As the GCC becomes more important to firms' global strategies, joint ventures with local partners will become increasingly important for success. The financial sector offers an array of examples—including the Saudi Hollandi Bank (ABN Amro), the Saudi American Bank (formerly part of Citigroup), and the Saudi British Bank (HSBC). Choosing the right partners and managing the relationship well can be as important as capturing the right economics from the joint ventures. Looking to the future, organic and acquisition-based market entry strategies are becoming increasingly possible and attractive, and we will explore benefits and drawbacks of this model as well.

Chapter 6 explores the challenge of marketing to buyers in the GCC nations. In many foreign markets, the marketing function is often the area that needs greatest local customization, and this holds true in the GCC states. The good news for multinationals is that leading marketing and advertising firms now have a presence in the GCC and can help tailor a company's messages to meet local needs. The challenge, nonetheless, is far broader: effective firms go beyond superficial marketing messages and fundamentally shift their product mix and messages to their customers to reflect local customers' experiences, tastes, and preferences. Retailers such as Zara and Benetton, for example, adjust their product mix to reflect the demand for long sleeves and long skirts. Some firms, including McDonald's, have launched products specifically designed for the Middle East market. The "McArabia" sandwich, developed by McDonald's Kuwait, illustrates the fast-food chain's attempt to localize its menu for customers in the lands of the GCC.

Human capital strategies—critical to any business's success—take on additional complexities in the GCC environment. Chapter 7 addresses these, discussing how multinationals' reliance on expatriate talent to run GCC businesses must be reduced in favor of local and regional talent. Whereas expatriate talent from the head office or "home country" of the multinational has historically played a central role in building the business and applying the best global practices, shifts in demographics, competition, and regulations are now making it more and more important to engage the local and regional workforce. *Localization* is a major initiative in most markets, with governments crafting requirements and incentives for hiring local nationals for key positions in multinationals. This push, largely driven by demographic shifts and the scale of the young workforce, can be a source of competitive advantage for firms that successfully attract and retain local talent. Local and regional talent bring in-depth expertise and commitment to the region in order to build a level of authenticity that, along with world-class management practices, can drive business performance to a higher level.

The GCC's role in crafting firms' financial strategies, the topic of Chapter 8, is an often overlooked but highly promising area. GCC economies are enjoying an unprecedented level of prosperity and liquidity, profoundly affecting financial markets locally and worldwide. The GCC has long been a net exporter of dollar-denominated capital, and its 2005 current account surplus, according to the IMF, was $155 billion. GCC investors hold equity stakes in key companies worldwide, as well as huge quantities of US Treasury notes and corporate bonds. Some of the world's most influential investment agencies—including the powerhouse Abu Dhabi Investment Authority (ADIA)—are GCC based. ADIA does not disclose its assets under management, but estimates range from $250 billion to over half a trillion dollars.

Local equity markets in GCC countries experienced a tremendous boom from 2002 to early 2006, followed by a sharp market correction leading to more realistic market valuations. Local real estate has similarly boomed and, at the time of this writing, is yet to experience a serious market correction. Volatility in the local investment market has been both a reflection of GCC investors' increased preference for local assets and a reminder to US-based investors of the importance of investing abroad.

Multinationals should view the GCC as a source of potential capital, both for regional activity and for their firms globally. Local joint ventures or acquisitions, for example, can be largely self-funding if firms take on local partners or list on local exchanges. Savvy firms can find ways to locally fund capital-intensive activities, thereby reducing market risk for the global parent. Some firms can even draw on GCC capital for general, global activity. Road shows for global debt and equity offerings increasingly include visits to key GCC investors. Many firms are even offering Sharia-compliant structures—which comply with Islamic law—to attract GCC capital. Asian firms, particularly in Malaysia, have been doing so for years. In recent times, even Boeing has used Islamic structures in its global sales.

The GCC also offers interesting opportunities to enhance firms' operations and logistics strategies. As we discuss in Chapter 9, GCC markets offer superb infrastructures, including ports, air links, power, roads, and telecom facilities. Dubai, in particular, offers outstanding facilities at Jebel Ali, the world's largest man-made harbor. Managing the day-to-day operations of a GCC business does introduce a handful of logistical complexities. Weekends, for example, are on a Friday-Saturday or Thursday-Friday schedule, and companies need full-time staff just to deal with often-cumbersome government regulations.

The right business design—the topic of Chapter 10—is a critical issue that underpins multinationals' long-term success in the
GCC. Business organizations must be set up in a way that enables
them to become rooted in the market and must evolve from international structures like those of bygone eras, when the GCC mat-
tered little and most of the international community lent the GCC
but scant attention. Today, global businesses must ensure that their
GCC organizations are managed with the right balance of delegation and control—allowing the local organization adequate flexibility while ensuring global consistency and oversight. While Dubai is
a natural choice for regional head offices, as its business and social
environments have been adapted to suit expatriate needs and preferences, consumer businesses must extend a significant presence in
Saudi Arabia to truly capture the GCC market. Whereas the GCC
countries are often the appropriate region from which to manage
the broader Middle East (i.e., the GCC states plus the Levant and
North Africa), managing the GCC from a Middle East head office
elsewhere can be a fatal mistake leading to inadequate focus on the
region. For all GCC operations, it is critical that multinational firms
maintain their global quality, service, and human resources standards—watering down these operations will lead to an uncompet-
itive performance and put the global brand at risk.

The GCC at Global Headquarters

The GCC is too attractive an opportunity to be ignored by a firm's
global headquarters. Most firms, however, have little to no
awareness of the GCC at the global strategy level.

Chapter 11 offers a range of suggestions for ensuring that the
GCC receives the attention it deserves at your company's headquarters. Typically, the GCC area reports to the head office through
the broader Middle East and North Africa (MENA) region, which
itself may be part of the European or Asian business unit or an
amalgamation of international businesses. When this happens, the
GCC receives little or no "airtime" due to the size of the current
business there relative to the size of the current business in Europe
or Japan.

Irrespective of reporting lines, savvy businesses should develop
a GCC-specific strategy that is presented and discussed at global

headquarters. This strategy should be comprehensive and must be kept current, as the region is changing dramatically from year to year. A GCC initiative can be an intriguing and highly fruitful project for a chief executive or head of strategy interested in demonstrating a knack for innovative, high-impact growth initiatives.

FROM THREAT TO OPPORTUNITY

For years, global businesses and their executives have viewed prosperity in the GCC countries as a threat. For many, the oil booms of the 1970s meant nothing but higher input costs, inflation, and frustrating lines at the gas station. GCC markets were relatively small and disconnected from the rest of the global economy, and their regulatory barriers were high and often felt insurmountable. Local infrastructure was underdeveloped, with hardly any culture of free zones or initiatives designed to attract international businesses. Global firms did not see how they could build genuine businesses in the GCC region.

Today, the game has changed, and business in and with the GCC countries is now a remarkable opportunity. The region is home to a young, growing, and prosperous consumer base hungry for global brands at the same time that it is exporting capital and looking for investment opportunities worldwide. Markets are deregulating, and the Internet and global media have created unprecedented connectivity between the GCC and the outside world. Doing business with the GCC has never been easier, and deregulation is proceeding further each day. Savvy multinationals will recognize these trends and act on them before their competitors do.

This may be the first book you read about the GCC and global strategy. If you manage, advise, or serve a global business that is looking for fast growth, it may not be the last.

PART 1

Understanding the Opportunity

CHAPTER 1

Lines in the Sand: The GCC in the Broader Middle East

INTRODUCTION

In my corporate career as a strategist, I have seen a broad range of reactions when I tell people—especially my fellow Americans—that I help companies do business in the Middle East. The term conjures a set of images that relatively few outsiders equate with economic opportunity, and I am often dealt the question "Is the Middle East safe?" The impetus of this inquiry stems from years of seeing war in the region: a series of conflicts with Israel, war between Iran and Iraq, Saddam Hussein's invasion of Kuwait and the first Gulf War, and other occasions of violence. The long and drawn-out second war in Iraq, in which the United States and a small set of allies easily defeated Saddam Hussein in 2003 but struggled to manage the subsequent occupation, has left deep scars and deeper impressions of the Arab world. "Is there really any business there?" is another frequent question asked of me. Clearly, those who ask this have missed or ignored the series of corporate acquisitions undertaken by Middle Eastern firms, not to mention the images of sleek office towers in Dubai and elsewhere. Another interesting query: "Do they care about corporate strategy?" I'm baffled by the

ongoing assumption that Middle Eastern businesses lack sophistication; as in any emerging market, there is a range of savvy that
includes a number of top-notch global firms.

A large part of this confusion occurs because the term *Middle
East* has always been a fuzzy one. Its definition varies widely
depending on whom you ask, and its perimeter is redrawn as political sentiments shift. As historian Roger Adelson and others have
rightly pointed out, the term is an invention of the Western powers—in particular, the UK—whose purpose was to define a region
to their east but less remote than China and the Pacific. Whereas the
French had coined the term "Near East" for the Ottoman Empire,
the term "Middle East" first appeared in the UK's *National Review*
magazine in 1902, in an article authored by an American military
strategist. A 1903 work used the term in its title—*The Middle East
Question of Some Problems of Indian Defense*—but used it for a broad
swath of territory including Tibet, Afghanistan, and other nations
near India that few would count in the "Middle East" today. After
this use in 1903, the term was no longer novel and ceased to appear
with quotation marks.[1]

The term also includes a very diverse set of countries that
share some common elements but are in many ways vastly different. Some are mainly desert, others have abundant agriculture.
Some are riddled with conflict and are "hot spots" for war; others
are highly stable. Some are wealthy; others are not.

In political circles, too, the term continues to be ill-defined. One
classic definition of the "Middle East" is that it includes all Arabic-
speaking countries plus Israel. Iran and Turkey, depending on
whom you ask, can also be thought of as peripheral "Middle
Eastern" states. In recent years, language referring to the United
States' "War on Terror" has often included Pakistan and
Afghanistan—long seen as parts of South and Central Asia,
respectively—within the rubric. Academic centers, including
Harvard University, are not spared the confusion: Harvard's academic department covering the region is called "Near Eastern
Languages and Civilizations," while an interdisciplinary center that
studies the area (created later on) is called the "Center for Middle
Eastern Studies." Adding to the complexity, the Bush administration
has introduced the term "Broader Middle East and North Africa,"
for which it has defined policy initiatives.[2] The United Nations,

whose work in the social sector varies widely among Middle Eastern and North African (MENA) countries, uses the terms "Southwest Asia," "West Asia," and "North Africa."

A more genuine approach, rooted in the indigenous differentiation within the region, is a three-cluster model. One cluster is the Levant—known as Bilad al-Sham in Arabic—which includes the Arab countries on the northern edge and northeast side of the Arabian Peninsula: Jordan, the West Bank and Gaza, Syria, Lebanon, and Iraq. A second cluster is North Africa, which spans from Morocco to Egypt and, for our purpose, includes the Arabic-speaking Sudan. Most countries of this region fall into the territory traditionally called al-Maghreb, which means "the West" and the place where the sun sets. Egypt is, in some ways, a cluster of its own due to its size, history, and complexity—but as our focus is elsewhere, we will include it in North Africa. The Gulf, called al-Khaleej, or "the Peninsula," consists of the Gulf Cooperation Council (GCC) states and Yemen. Figure 1.1 shows the stark differences in income that characterize these three clusters.

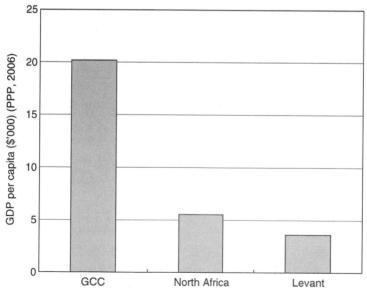

Figure 1.1 GDP per capita varies greatly by cluster (Source: IMF data, *CIA World Factbook* estimates [Iraq, West Bank, Gaza])

The three-cluster model is indigenous to the Arab world, effectively grouping the MENA region into broad categories each with distinct histories and environments. Each region has its own characteristics—geographic, social, political, and economic—that create very different business environments. The Levant is well-endowed but (in recent times) rather volatile. North Africa is large and populous, with moderate GDP per capita. The Gulf is oil-producing, wealthy, and relatively stable, with the highest standard of living in the Middle East. As the Arabic language—the glue that binds the Arab world—originated in the Arabian Peninsula and spread east and west, the three clusters have become part of a single cultural complex while at the same time each has evolved its own unique identity (see Figure 1.2).

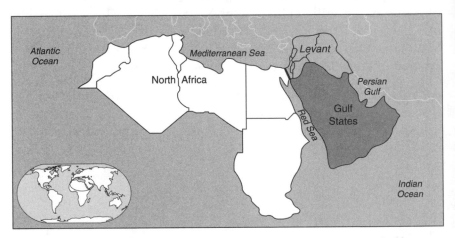

Figure 1.2 The Middle East and North Africa (Note: Yemen, a Gulf state, is not a member of the GCC.)

THE LEVANT: WELL-ENDOWED BUT CONFLICT RIDDEN

The area known as the Levant is home to one of the world's oldest and richest civilizations. The ancient civilization of Mesopotamia, admired by historians for its institution of the world's first known written legal system, is often the starting point for the study of human cultural and political history. The Levant includes the area known as the Fertile Crescent, where flowing rivers, rich soil, and human technology enabled early farmers to harvest crops in excess of their needs. The excess crops could be stored, traded, and used to support artisans, officials, priests, and other groups of people who helped craft this early civilization.

The Levant is also home to the "Holy Land," where many of the most revered religious sites of Jews, Christians, and Muslims are located. Many prophets of the monotheistic tradition, including Abraham and the prophets of Israel, are believed to be from the Levant. In the Jewish tradition, the Levant is home to the Promised Land, and it is also where Jesus is believed to have been born and preached his message while facing Roman persecution. Jerusalem, a sacred city for the three great monotheistic traditions, is the spiritual center of the Levant. The region is the birthplace of the world's—and the West's—religious systems and value frameworks and, as such, has shaped Western and global civilization at the core.

Quickly after the spread of Islam into the Levant in the seventh and eighth centuries, it became the seat of the Islamic caliphate. Damascus (under the Umayyad dynasty) and then Baghdad (under the Abbasid dynasty) had the political, commercial, and educational infrastructures needed to sustain leadership of the Muslim world. Both cities were renowned for their scholarship, art, sophistication, and cultural development. In fact, the sack of Baghdad by Mongol invaders in 1258—during which the rivers reportedly ran black from the ink of books that had been dumped there by the uneducated invaders—is considered one of the greatest losses of human knowledge in history. To this day, the Levant has a relatively high level of literacy, averaging almost 80 percent, comparable to the far-richer Gulf's level of 82 percent.[3]

Iraq is the most important—and certainly the most prominent—modern state in the Levant. Iraq's population is close to 27 million and includes Shiite Arab, Sunni Arab, and Kurdish populations.[4] The three communities were united as a single modern state in the wake of World War I and held together under a monarchy and then under Saddam Hussein's military dictatorship. Hussein's dictatorship was marked by much violence, both domestic and international, and after a decade-long war of attrition with Iran in the 1980s, during which Hussein enjoyed US and Arab support,

Iraq took an expansionist posture. Hussein's 1990 invasion of Kuwait—an oil-rich region to which Iraq had laid claim for decades but which was upheld as a separate, sovereign state by the UN—led to the first Gulf War. Iraq was defeated by a United States–led coalition that included all six GCC member states. Claiming that the Hussein regime had weapons of mass destruction, the United States, the UK, and a limited number of allies invaded Iraq in 2003, quickly defeated the regime, and began a long and complex occupation that has been characterized by sectarian violence and a lack of national unity. The future of the Iraqi state, at the time of this writing, remains tenuous.

From an economic perspective, however, Iraq is well-endowed. Its oil reserves are vast, and potential for prosperity is high. Unlike other oil states—in particular Saudi Arabia, whose population is roughly the same size as that of Iraq—Iraq has an education system that has been well developed for decades. The Iraqi intelligentsia—including physicians, lawyers, teachers, and other professionals—has long been an important pool of trained talent in the region, and many expatriate Iraqis have been successful in other Arab (and in GCC) countries. Iraq also enjoys substantial industrial and agricultural successes that were fostered under internal state direction and have not been directed outward for decades. As astute observers have noted, a stable Iraq has all of the qualities of a highly attractive market; namely, natural resources, a well-endowed economy, a large domestic market, and a sophisticated consumer base. Expect to see hot competition for market access in Iraq when it achieves some measure of stability.

Syria, with a population close to 20 million, is another large market that would be highly attractive for multinational firms if not for its political turmoil.[5] It has a large domestic market and has achieved a degree of industrialization under a state-controlled economy. Like Iraq, Syria spent many years under the secular dictator Hafiz al-Assad and is now so under his son Bashar al-Assad. Syria is on the watch list of Western powers as a potential security threat, and investor confidence in the country is very low. Although Syria lacks the massive oil reserves that Iraq has, it does have some oil capacity, as well as a Mediterranean coastline that gives it access to European Union (EU) markets. More important, it could be a reasonably favorable market for business and for international investment pending political reform and a shift in global sentiment.

Lebanon is a unique state in the Levant and plays a pivotal role in the broader MENA region. With its temperate climate and Mediterranean atmosphere, Lebanon has long been a popular tourist and business destination for the Arab world. Lebanon was a strong banking and financial center as well—especially in the 1960s and 1970s—before the outbreak of a devastating civil war, which lasted from 1975 to 1991 and was an extremely complex conflict among numerous religious and secular factions. Although it significantly rebuilt its infrastructure during the 1990s, Lebanon still is undergoing reconstruction efforts to return the country to its previous strength. Lebanon is religiously diverse—about 60 percent Muslim (of various sects) and 40 percent Christian—and its constitution has built-in mechanisms to ensure the representation of various religious communities.[6] Lebanon, with its social liberalism, has thriving nightlife and beaches, and it is also a source of much Arab popular culture—especially food, music, and music videos. While its domestic population (about 4 million) is limited, Lebanon has been a trade center for centuries, and Lebanese entrepreneurship is renowned within the MENA region. Many ethnic Lebanese live abroad, and the Lebanese often speak English and French in addition to Arabic. Many of Lebanon's most talented nationals work in the GCC, where openings at burgeoning businesses provide them with greater opportunities to apply their skills. The 2006 war between Hezbollah and Israel caused significant damage to Lebanon's infrastructure (estimated at $3.6 billion)[7] and devastated the tourist season, but in the long term, Lebanon is expected to recover strongly and to continue to be a prime tourist destination, especially in the summer months that make the Gulf's heat almost unbearable. Jordan, a monarchy that seeks to play a conciliatory role in the Israeli-Palestinian conflict, has a population of around 6 million. The kingdom, whose ruling family traces its roots to the clan of the Prophet Muhammad, has many cultural, familial, and social ties to the Palestinian people. Jordan is an importer of many natural resources, including oil (for which it relies on trade with the Gulf), but it is fast developing its services sector, including Arabic-speaking call centers and business process outsourcing (BPO) providers. Jordanians' level of education, neutral Arabic dialect, and lower cost of employment places them in a favorable position to receive much of the work that the MENA region's service sector is outsourcing.

NORTH AFRICA: VAST AND POPULOUS

Within the North Africa cluster, Egypt is the preeminent economy. With a population of over 80 million (a third of whom are below the age of 15),[8] Egypt's consumer base is more than twice the size of the entire GCC. Egyptians refer to Cairo as Umm al-Dunya, or "Mother of the World," a reference to the importance they place on Egypt's contributions to global civilization. Aside from its remarkable ancient civilization, which prospered due to the abundant resources of the Nile delta and Egyptians' sophisticated society, Egypt was the seat of the Fatimid and Mamluk caliphates for several centuries. In the tenth century CE (two centuries before Oxford University was founded), the Fatimids established Al Azhar University, which has been one of the finest seats of Islamic knowledge ever since.

Egypt is about 90 percent Muslim and 10 percent Christian, making it more religiously diverse than the indigenous populations of the GCC countries.[9] Egypt is renowned as the center of Arabic culture, producing not only the region's most popular films and entertainment media but also a rich and deep literary tradition that turned out writers like Nobel laureate Naguib Mahfouz. Under Gamal Abdel Nasser, who led Egypt from 1952 to 1970, the country was the center of Arab nationalism—a postcolonial ideology asserting the independence and strength of Arab civilization. Although Nasser's aspirations for pan-Arab unity were not realized, his perceived strength in standing up to foreign powers (particularly during the Suez Canal crises of the 1950s) made him a hero in the Arab world and among newly independent nations everywhere. Egypt at present is enjoying the fruits of the modest economic reforms that have been enacted in recent decades, but true prosperity remains elusive. Egypt in many ways remains a poor agricultural economy.

Sharing some common characteristics is a group of other North African states—Morocco, Algeria, and Tunisia—all of which were French colonies, use French in educated circles to this day, and have a significant expatriate community in France. Like their neighbor Libya (once under Italian control), they consist of coastal cities and very sparsely populated desert and countryside regions. Algeria enjoys significant natural gas reserves, providing about a quarter of the EU's gas imports,[10] and Morocco's tourism industry is the strongest in the group, boasting the popular vacation destinations of Tangiers, Casablanca, and Marrakesh. As illustrated in Figure 1.3, the states of the North African cluster have modest—but respectable by developing market standards—GDP per capita.

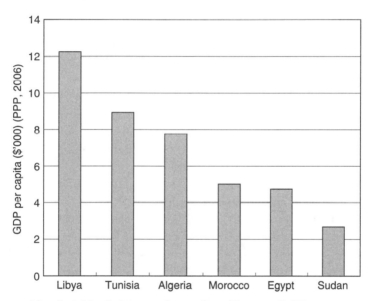

Figure 1.3 North Africa's income is modest (Source: IMF)

Libya's high GDP per capita is boosted by its sizable oil exports. Like other countries in the cluster, Libya's income distribution (especially of oil wealth) is highly uneven. Libya's socialist economic orientation and closed political system have limited the capacity for broad-based economic development. It is also noteworthy that the countries with the largest populations—Egypt and Sudan—have the lowest GDP per capita.

Table 1.1 presents an overview of relevant historical, demographic, economic, and other facts about the broader Middle East.

T A B L E   1 . 1

The Broader Middle East

Region	GCC	North Africa	Levant
GDP Per Capita, 2006	$20,100	$5,500	$3,700
Population, 2006 (millions)	36	190	60
Area (thousand sq. km)	2,572	8,259	728
Population Makeup	Small indigenous populations, large expatriate populations	Large indigenous populations, large immigration to Europe	Large Lebanese, Palestinian, and Iraqi diasporas; Iraq is very ethnically and culturally diverse
Colonial History	Britain maintained varying degrees of control between 1763 and 1971. Currently strong US influence.	Largely influenced by French colonialism. Libya has a history of Italian colonialism.	Influenced by periods of British (Iraq, Transjordan) and French (Lebanon, Syria) colonialism.
Political Systems	Monarchies	Monarchies and dictatorships	Mixed: democracy (Israel); monarchy (Jordan); dictatorship (Syria); unstable democracy (Lebanon); no sovereign government (Palestinian Territories); low-intensity civil war (Iraq)

Political Stability	Mostly stable	Mostly stable, but some succession issues	Significant pockets of instability, especially Iraq and between Israel and the Palestinian Territories
Economic Systems	Oil and gas are the bedrock of the economy. Revenue from nationalized oil companies fuels government budgets and consumer spending.	Agriculture is the significant source of income. Modern export agriculture produces Mediterranean products while traditional agriculture produces cereal crops. Foreign trade is highly concentrated in the EU. Economic growth is hampered by large populations and low human development.	Traditionally driven by trade and agriculture, the region has been negatively impacted by political and civil conflict. This holds true for the tourism sector. Reconstruction efforts pose opportunities, but political risk is very high.

THE GULF: TREMENDOUS WEALTH WITH
SMALL INDIGENOUS POPULATIONS

The economies of the GCC countries represent the most attractive cluster of markets in the Middle East. These markets are character-ized by oil wealth, small indigenous populations, relatively stable monarchies, desert climates, and modest origins. As we discuss in length throughout this book, the GCC represents a set of dynamic, opportunity-rich economies with much to offer multinational com-panies. A combination of sustained prosperity, attractive demo-graphic shifts, and regulatory reform make the GCC an increasingly appealing place to do business.

When viewed as a collective whole, the economies of the GCC form an impressive collective entity. Consider the following:

- All together, the GCC economies would be the seventh-largest in the developing world: twice the size of the economies of Turkey, South Africa, or Argentina.[11]
- In the five-year period ending in 2006, the GCC's GDP per capita rose 80 percent.[12]
- The region's combined central government surplus, driven by gushing oil revenues, stands at over 20 percent of GDP.[13]

In addition to their economic similarities, the GCC states share common political environments. All are monarchies, and although some do have consultative (often elected) bodies, ultimate power in each rests firmly with the sovereign. All trace their roots to simple desert tribes and retain some elements of traditional tribal culture. In fact, the ruling families of multiple GCC states trace their origins to the same part of the Arabian Peninsula. Most of the GCC states signed treaties with the UK during the colonial era that included the provision that the states and their rulers would be protected in exchange for exclusive ties with Britain. All are members of the WTO, and—like new WTO members everywhere—struggle with a delicate balance of protecting local businesses while opening up to the global economy.

While the Gulf states share core attributes that make them a common cluster, each of the six countries is unique. Table 1.2 pro-vides, at a glance, a comparison of the six states along a few key dimensions.

TABLE 1.2

GCC States

Similarities	Differences
Small indigenous populations	While Saudi Arabia, the UAE,
Wealthy relative to Levant and	Qatar, and Kuwait have large
North Africa	reserves of oil and gas, Bahrain and
High population growth	Oman have a very limited supply.
Major religion is Islam	Bahrain and Oman are markedly
Arabic is the unifying language	less wealthy than the other four
Ruled by hereditary monarchies	members.
All are WTO members	Bahrain, Oman, and Saudi Arabia
GCC Customs Union	have double-digit unemployment,
All are US allies	while the UAE, Qatar, and Kuwait
Peninsula Shield (regional	are in the 2 to 4% range.
defense force)	The UAE, Qatar, and Kuwait are
	more than two-thirds expatriate,
	while the other nations are in the
	20 to 35% range.
	Bahrain and Oman are the only
	two GCC states with free trade
	agreements with the United States.
	Kuwait is the only GCC currency
	not pegged to the US dollar.

In subsequent chapters, we will discuss each country in more detail, but suffice it to say at this point that the GCC states are by no means a monolith.

THE GULF COOPERATION COUNCIL: MEANINGFUL BUT INCOMPLETE UNION

The Gulf Cooperation Council (GCC) is officially named the Cooperation Council for Arab States of the Gulf. Its charter, signed in 1981 and 1982,[14] brought the six member states together on a common regional platform. Of interesting historical note is that a joint security pact among a group of Gulf states—including the present-day GCC members, plus Iran and Iraq—was explored in 1976 but could not be agreed upon as Iran and Iraq were not trusted and did not fit with the six others.[15] Talks about forming a common Gulf union occurred as early as 1971, but did not materialize until a decade later.[16]

It was common security concerns—and the emergence of common threats—that were the catalyst for the formation of the GCC. One such threat was the Iranian revolution of 1979, which created a theocratic Shiite state too close for comfort. Many feared that Iran would attempt to export its political ideology or, at a minimum, would incite Shiite minorities in the Gulf states to rebel against the Sunni monarchies. A second cause for concern materialized after the Soviet invasion of Afghanistan, also in 1979, which raised fears that the superpowers of the time (the United States and the Soviet Union) might take direct military action against nonaligned states to strengthen their global standing. The Gulf states—small, separate, and increasingly wealthy due to the 1970s oil boom—saw themselves as potential targets of both regional (from Iran or Iraq) or global (from the Soviet Union or another power) aggression. To protect themselves in what at the time was a climate of heightened security concern, the Gulf states chartered the GCC.

The document itself, however, acts as more than a mere safety shield; it outlines a broad mandate for collaboration. Some of the stated goals in the GCC charter are to:

- "Effect coordination, integration, and inter-connection between Member States in all fields in order to achieve unity between them.
- "Formulate similar regulations in various fields including . . . economic and financial affairs; commerce, customs and communications.
- "Stimulate scientific and technological progress.
- "Establish joint ventures and encourage cooperation by the private sector for the good of their peoples."[17]

The phrasing of the charter is broad and flexible, reflecting the gradualist approach toward collaboration that its drafters envisioned. The document calls, for example, for "similar" regulations and not "uniform" laws. The GCC's central administration is quite light: there is a small Secretariat-General, a Ministerial Council that gathers quarterly, and a Supreme Council of heads of state that meets annually. There is a Commission for the Settlement of

Disputes that meets if and when it is needed to adjudicate cross-border issues. The Secretariat-General is based in Riyadh. Unlike the EU, whose central agencies and departments play a more crucial role in the lives of member countries, the GCC is a relatively flexible association that reflects a spirit of cooperation and common identity.

The GCC union has been strongest so far in its economic actions. A common Customs Union over time was agreed to be phased in 2003, stimulating the free flow of goods among the GCC member states. Tariffs on non-GCC imports were envisioned by the Union to be standardized. Nationals of GCC member states travel freely between the six countries. Capital and investment flows are facilitated through relaxed regulation, and GCC nationals may often invest in equity markets outside of their own. During the stock market boom that ended in 2006, for example, it was common to find Saudi vehicles in the UAE camped out so that their Saudi owners could be among the first to invest in the latest IPO. GCC companies, although required to apply for licenses to operate in states other than their home, increasingly are able to branch out across the Gulf. The year 2007 had been identified as a target date for creating a truly common market—though, in reality, some barriers persist.

In 2003, the GCC expressed a commitment to creating a common currency by 2010. A GCC Monetary Union would, according to its proponents, aid in creating a common market, standardize monetary policy, and create greater efficiency in the intra-GCC flow of capital. In practice, however, the path to a common currency has been fraught with roadblocks. One key barrier to integration is that the constituent economies of the GCC have different macroeconomic needs to consider in forming monetary policy. Another fundamental challenge is that a common currency would require a common central bank—something that does not exist today and would be a delicate entity to create. Oman has publicly stated that it is not pursuing monetary union with its fellow GCC entities, and other states have expressed reservations about the timeline. To complicate matters further, in May 2007 Kuwait abandoned the practice of pegging its currency's valuation to the dollar, a practice which the other five GCC nations still maintain. The GCC may one day have a common currency, but it is unlikely to reach that stage by 2010.

In the realm of defense, the GCC has shown meaningful collective action. In addition to a stated commitment to the collective security of GCC member states, each GCC country (with the exception of Kuwait) has signed bilateral security agreements with Saudi Arabia. During the first Gulf War—following Iraq's 1990 invasion of Kuwait—all GCC states were part of the international coalition to liberate Kuwait and defend Saudi Arabia. As early as 1984, a joint military project called the Peninsula Shield was launched with a force of 7,000 troops.[18] Although the number of troops was later increased, in 2006 the troops returned to their home countries. King Abdullah of Saudi Arabia reportedly wants the common force to be increased but be based in their home countries and collaborate occasionally under joint command.[19] In December 2006, the GCC member states announced their intent to study the possibility of a peaceful GCC-wide nuclear energy program. The Saudi foreign minister asserted that the GCC has no intention of developing nuclear weapons.[20]

Although clearly not yet a single economy or political unit, the GCC has made significant strides toward standardization and a common market. Security and defense may have been the catalysts for bringing the GCC states together, but economics and global competitiveness create compelling reasons for increased integration. As a common unit, the GCC has greater scale, diversity, and strength than its constituent members have as separate markets, as the states—with the exception of Saudi Arabia—are too small to have the global economic impact to which they aspire. A more tightly connected GCC is good news not only for the region, but for multinational businesses that seek to do business there as well. The challenge, however, will be applying the most far-sighted and strategically sound policies to govern the economic unit, even if this pushes some member states outside their comfort zone.

KEY LESSONS

- The "Middle East" is *not a homogeneous region*; in fact, the very term lacks a consistent definition and represents a very diverse set of countries.

- A *three-cluster model*, indigenous to the region, fits better: the Levant, North Africa, and the Gulf states (GCC).
- *The Levant* is well-endowed, but its economic development has been hampered by conflict and strife.
- *North Africa* is large and populous, with modest GDP per capita.
- *The Gulf* is wealthy, dynamic, and an increasingly attractive place to do business.
- The GCC is a *meaningful but incomplete union*, most relevant in economic and defense matters and less standardized in other areas.

CHAPTER 2

Think Again: Addressing Misconceptions about the GCC

INTRODUCTION

Although GCC countries appear more frequently in the global media and business press today than ever before, misconceptions about the region persist. It's fair to say that many global business leaders nowadays have no formal training pertaining to the GCC; the region has become highly relevant to global business only in recent decades. These leaders rarely have direct contact with Gulf-based individuals or institutions. Therefore, they rely on coverage in the news and entertainment media that is often anecdotal, rarely analytical, and usually not focused on business opportunities.

Perpetuating these misconceptions is bad for business. Without a more fact-based understanding of the region, global business leaders are likely to misinterpret the opportunities—and risks—that exist there. They may miss out on large areas of opportunity, such as marketing to the large and growing pool of university-educated women in the GCC with high disposable incomes and discerning consumer tastes. They may misallocate resources based on false assumptions about the region's markets, relying, for example, on Arabic-language promotions alone when the bulk of their firm's potential customers may be more comfortable with English. Most fundamentally, many global leaders may overlook the region entirely—believing that the only "real" opportunities in the GCC are those linked directly to oil and gas. In truth, the region's growing population, broad prosperity, and increased diversification make it attractive across a much wider range of industries.

This chapter addresses five of the most common misconceptions about the GCC. For each misconception, factual counterpoints are presented to provide a more informed and nuanced understanding. Since any successful strategy relies on sound assumptions, this chapter is critical for ensuring that multinational concerns avoid common misperceptions and approach GCC markets with a more accurate understanding.

FIVE "DEADLY" MISCONCEPTIONS

When many global business leaders think of the Gulf and its economies, exotic images come to mind. They recall the film *Lawrence of Arabia*, with its images of vast deserts, harsh terrain, and tribal warfare. They think back to the first Gulf War of the early 1990s, and remember an occupied Kuwait and a threatened Saudi Arabia, defended by a US-led international coalition. A more distant—but still painful—memory is of the oil crises of the 1970s, with long lines at the gas pump and steep price hikes leading to stagflation. Many business leaders have been following the rapid rise of the region in the 2000s, which brings to mind Dubai's opulent Burj al-Arab (the world's first "seven-star" hotel) and similar high-profile projects.

As curiosity about the region abounds, so do the misconceptions. While there are many that could be addressed, we will focus on five of the most critical. These five "deadly" misconceptions—if allowed to persist in your organization—can lead to a great many lost opportunities and misallocated resources.

The five "deadly" misconceptions are:

1. It's all about oil—the region is only relevant to the interests of energy-related companies.
2. Everybody's rich—only high-end products and services are relevant.

3. The GCC customer "hates us"—global brands and businesses cannot succeed.
4. Women don't matter—female consumers, employees, and decision makers are marginal to the economy.
5. The markets are entirely Arab—the Arab consumer is the only target market in the Gulf.

Like most misconceptions, these five are the result of misinterpretations of the facts or incorrect generalizations based on anecdotal data. We address these misconceptions in detail, providing a more comprehensive and accurate picture of the issues involved in each.

Misconception 1: It's all about oil—the region is relevant to energy-related companies only.
Reality: Oil and gas drive wealth creation, but the range of economic activity and growth includes far more than just energy.

WEALTH CREATION THROUGH OIL AND GAS

Without a doubt, the energy sector is the most important economic engine in the GCC. For example, the six GCC countries control the following proportions of the oil and gas markets:

- 40 percent of the world's known oil reserves
- 22 percent of global oil supply
- 23 percent of global natural gas reserves[1]

Global energy markets, therefore, rely heavily on the GCC economies. Another remarkable statistic underscores how this reliance is likely to continue as the demand for oil increases worldwide: 90 percent of global spare oil capacity is in the GCC.[2] This means that the GCC is the single most important region in the world with respect to oil production, having the greatest capacity to meet the continually growing demand for oil.

Just as world energy markets rely on the GCC for oil and gas, GCC governments—which control their nations' natural resources—rely largely on oil and gas for their fiscal stability and for maintaining their high GDP. Energy income provides over

70 percent of government revenue in all six GCC countries. Oil and gas income has enabled GCC governments to maintain extremely attractive tax regimes—without, for example, any personal income tax.

The sustained rise in oil prices since 1998 has led to unprecedented levels of government surpluses in the GCC. In 2004 dollar terms, oil prices in late 2006 reached a level roughly six times their 1998 price ($60 a barrel versus $10). As a consequence, GCC government surpluses in 2006 were close to $175 billion in total.[3]

FROM ENERGY WEALTH TO LOCAL ECONOMIC DEVELOPMENT

The story does not stop there, however. Oil revenue is today, more than ever, being channeled into nonenergy sectors. Governments across the GCC have recognized the importance and urgency of developing other sectors, such as infrastructure and services, that will lead to more competitive and sustainable economies. Simply put, GCC governments know that they must diversify their economies if they are to survive in the long run.

The GCC's oil reserves—plentiful as they are—will not last forever. The reserves of Bahrain, for example, have been estimated to last for only another 10 years. Dubai's position is similar. Oman's outlook is a bit brighter—its oil has been forecast to last about 30 years.[4] Saudi Arabia, Kuwait, and the UAE (Abu Dhabi, in particular) have more abundant reserves but have compelling reasons to diversify: the necessity of creating jobs and stimulating economic competitiveness being the chief two of these. Qatar's natural gas reserves promise the tiny state a long stretch of prosperity, and the government is actively channeling some of its wealth toward the creation of a more knowledge-based economy.

Figure 2.1 provides a conceptual illustration of how oil and gas revenue stimulates GCC economies.

Oil and gas income brings prosperity to governments and to private entities, such as petrochemical firms and oil-shipping firms that are related to the energy sector. Government surpluses and private wealth create excess capital, which is deployed through a range of mechanisms. A large part of this capital is invested internationally, principally through governments or government-linked

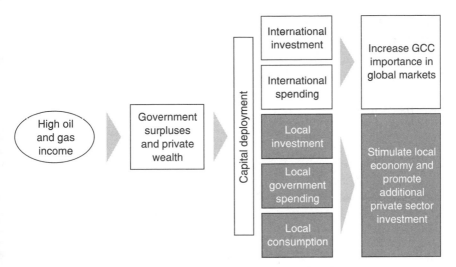

Figure 2.1 High oil and gas income is stimulating local economies

companies such as the powerful Abu Dhabi Investment Authority (ADIA) and the Kuwait Investment Authority. Some capital is used for foreign spending, both by private individuals and by the government.

An increasing amount of capital, however, is being allocated for local purposes. Local investment in sectors such as real estate, infrastructure, and heavy manufacturing is occurring at an unprecedented level. Local government spending is also high, as population growth and other factors fuel increased demand for social services. Local consumption—evident in the region's sprawling shopping malls, large supermarkets, luxury retailers, and booming tourism industry—has reached historic heights. These factors play a direct role in stimulating the high growth and dynamism of the GCC's local economies.

MASSIVE REAL ESTATE AND INFRASTRUCTURE PROJECTS

In every GCC market, large-scale real estate and infrastructure projects are under way. According to the International Monetary Fund (IMF), over $600 billion in infrastructure investment will be needed in the GCC through 2010.[5] While many GCC projects under way are lavish and reflect high levels of prosperity, the core motivation for real estate development and infrastructure investment is rooted in more fundamental factors. Oil windfalls in the 1970s and 1980s led to a "baby boom" in the region—in Saudi Arabia and Oman, for example, over 50 percent of the population is below 25 years old. For the other GCC states, the figure is between 30 and 45 percent.[6] Rapid population growth has put a strain on local housing and infrastructure. Visitors to Dubai—where many commuters spend hours each day stuck in traffic—will quickly appreciate the need for more roads and public transportation facilities.

The infrastructure needs of Saudi Arabia, which has the region's largest population by far, provide a telling example. Upgrading the country's electricity infrastructure to meet the needs of its growing population may require over $120 billion in investment. Managing the water supply in a parched desert environment may call for another $90 billion or more.[7] Such large-scale requirements for meeting basic needs reflect the critical importance of infrastructure investment to the region.

Airports across the GCC are being upgraded. Abu Dhabi, Bahrain, and even Dubai—whose airport is already a global hub used by 100 airlines—are planning or already in the midst of large-scale airport expansions. Qatar is building a new airport in Doha with a whopping price tag of $5.5 billion. The first phase is expected to be completed by 2009.

One unique real estate trend is the creation of man-made islands, typically for high-end housing and hotels. Dubai was the pioneer of this phenomenon in the region, announcing the construction of the lavish Palm Islands in May 2002. The self-declared "Eighth Wonder of the World," these islands are designed to be an archipelago in the shape of a palm tree and to include housing, hotels, shopping malls, and even theme parks. Dubai has since announced the creation of the "World Islands"—300 small, private islands with prices beginning at around $7 million each. Among the purchasers of World Island properties is Sir Richard Branson of Virgin, who snapped up the island representing Great Britain. Bahrain has announced a $1.2 billion artificial-island development called Durrat al-Bahrain ("the Pearl of Bahrain"), and another multi-island project called Amwaj Islands (the "Wave" Islands).[8]

INDUSTRY AND MANUFACTURING

GCC governments have identified industry and manufacturing as critical to long-term economic competitiveness, and investment is flowing into these sectors through both public and private channels. Perhaps the most prominent current industrial project is the King Abdullah Economic City, off the Red Sea in Saudi Arabia. The initiative, considered Saudi Arabia's largest private-sector investment, is a massive project costing over $25 billion. The Economic City is designed to include industrial, financial, educational, tourist, and residential areas. The first stage of the project is expected to be ready in two to three years.

Industrial "free zones," allowing full foreign ownership, freedom from certain regulations, and no taxes, have appeared in several GCC countries. The UAE, renowned for its free zones across multiple sectors, has spawned a remarkable number of light manufacturing and distribution firms in its Jebel Ali Free Zone (Dubai). Plans for Abu Dhabi's Saadiyat Island free zone are focused on commodities trading, storage, and transportation. Sharjah's free zone concentrates on heavy industry and airline cargo. Bahrain has an industrial free zone in North Sitra, a free port called Mina Salman, and plans for another industrial free zone in Hidd. The Kuwait Free Trade Zone offers industrial, commercial, and service licenses to foreign investors, along with facilities such as on-site banking and 24-hour support designed to attract foreign industrialists.

Direct investment in industrial projects is significant. Aluminum Bahrain (Alba) has recently completed an expansion estimated at $1.7 billion. Dubai has also signaled its ambitions in the aluminum sector through Dubai Aluminum (Dubal). Oman has announced a $2 billion aluminum smelter project in Sohar. These investments leverage the region's core industrial advantages: cheap energy, low-cost labor, access to shipping lines, central location, and attractive tax regimes.

TOURISM AND HOSPITALITY

The tourism sector is a strategic industry for the region. Dubai today has over 300 hotels—including the world-famous Burj al-Arab—and attracts over 6 million visitors each year.[9] Dubai has become a major destination for tourists from Europe—especially the UK, Russia, and Germany—as well as Asia and Australia. In a remarkable testament to its drawing power, Dubai attracts around four visitors for every one resident of the emirate. Investment in Dubai's tourism sector continues at a rapid pace, most notably through the "Dubailand" initiative. Dubailand is projected to be the largest theme park in the world—twice the size of Disney World in Florida. The project will take over 10 years to complete, with a first phase ending in 2010 and the final phase in 2018, and will include over 200 tourism, leisure, and entertainment subprojects. The Dubailand project is seeking to establish Dubai as a major tourist destination with appeal to visitors of all nationalities and markets.[10]

Other GCC countries have undertaken large-scale tourism and hospitality initiatives as well. Oman has announced the creatively named "Omagine" project—a beachfront complex designed to mix cultural, tourist, commercial, educational, and residential elements. The project even includes a theme park boasting seven pearl-shaped buildings. Kuwait has announced a major project to develop its Failaka Island into a tourist destination through a 10-year, multibillion-dollar investment initiative. Even Saudi Arabia, which hosts over 2 million religious pilgrims each year for the Hajj (the required Muslim pilgrimage) but is not positioned as an over-all leisure destination, is trying to develop a broader appeal to stimulate general tourism.

RETAILING

Dubai's retail sector caters to visitors from the GCC and beyond. The emirate has 30 shopping malls and is developing the world's largest mall. In fact, according to an AC Nielsen study, Dubai's shopping space per person is an astonishing four times the amount found in the United States.[11] This huge amount of retail space is one of the core attractions of the emirate, and Dubai business leaders have striven to create retail experiences that continue to draw regional and global visitors. The annual Dubai Shopping Festival,[12] a 32-day event in which the emirate creates a "Global Village" featuring goods from around the world, draws nearly 3 million local and international shoppers. The massive Mall of the Emirates, located along the route between Dubai and Abu Dhabi, includes an indoor ski slope to attract tourists and locals.

Most major real estate projects in the GCC, as mentioned above, include retail components. The GCC retail experience seeks to combine access to global retailers, such as major US and EU chains, with specialist categories such as shops offering jewelry and accessories of gold and pearls that reflect the traditional crafts of the region. A stroll through a mall in the GCC will take you past American retailers such as the Gap, European chains such as Zara, a food court full of cuisine from the United States, Asia, and the Middle East, and a handful of specialty shops focused on regional categories such as local clothing and perfume. The experience is designed to offer shoppers the best of all worlds and has succeeded in attracting a large and diverse set of consumers.

SERVICES

All GCC governments are actively promoting the development of the service sector of their economies, including financial, health care, IT, and food, among others. Dubai's strategy of creating free zone "cities" reflects its ambition of remaining the leading knowledge and services economy of the region. In addition to the massive Jebel Ali Free Zone—central to the emirate's industrialization strategy—Dubai's flagship "cities" include Dubai Internet City, Dubai Media City, and Knowledge Village. Collectively, these three comprise the Dubai Technology and Media Free Zone and have attracted leading global firms such as Microsoft, Oracle, and CNN. More recent "cities" include Dubai Health Care City, Dubai Metals and Commodities Centre, and a Gold and Diamond Park. Among the long list of other free zones under development are Dubai Outsource Zone and, as part of Dubai Investment Park, DuBiotech for life sciences research, development, and commercialization. True to form, Dubai has secured partnerships in these "cities" with leading global institutions such as Harvard Medical School.

Financial services is another industry actively being developed. The Dubai International Financial Centre (DIFC), a free zone with a planned 22 million square feet of office space, has attracted leading financial institutions such as Goldman Sachs, Merrill Lynch, Deutsche Bank, and Barclays Capital. It includes an exchange DIFX (Dubai International Financial Exchange) that seeks to position itself as a world-class trading center located between the global markets of London and Hong Kong. Bahrain, long the financial hub of the GCC, is responding to increased competition from Dubai and elsewhere by investing heavily in its Bahrain Financial Harbor project. The project is estimated to require $1.3 billion of capital.[13] Qatar launched its own Qatar Financial Centre in 2005, with similar ambitions of regional leadership.

The crucial lesson from these and other initiatives is that business in the GCC is about far more than energy. Multinational businesses in almost any sector can find relevant opportunities in the region, and few companies that seek global growth can afford to ignore the GCC.

> Misconception 2: Everybody's rich—only high-end products and services are relevant.
>
> Reality: Although some GCC consumers are wealthy, many are not and unemployment is a serious issue.

The international media is rife with images and caricatures of oil-rich Gulf Arabs with Rolls-Royce cars and private jets. While certainly some GCC nationals are very wealthy, the bulk of GCC consumers are not. In fact, global business leaders do themselves a disservice by promoting such stereotypes, since they lead to the false assumption that the only products and services in demand by the GCC consumer are high-end goods. The truth of the matter is that GCC society contains the full spectrum of social classes, and businesses that meet the needs of the numerous middle- and working-class consumers can enjoy significant success. The purveyors of midmarket mobile phones, for example, are just as relevant to the GCC as are its high-end jewelers. In fact, one reality that usually escapes international attention is that unemployment is in fact a serious issue and that some people—typically unskilled foreign workers—have a low standard of living.

To put this issue in perspective, consider the GCC's GDP per capita in purchasing power parity (PPP) terms. In 2006, the region's GDP per capita was around $20,000. Certainly this is a respectable figure—almost three times that of China ($7,600) and more than five times that of India ($3,700). From the perspective of emerging markets, the GCC's prosperity is, without a doubt, remarkable.

For the same year, however, GDP per capita in the United States was $43,500—more than twice the figure in the GCC. The EU average, almost $30,000, was about 50 percent higher than the GCC. Japan's was higher even than that of the EU—$33,100. In fact, the GDP per capita for the entire GCC was roughly that of Portugal, the poorest Western European country. Saudi Arabia, in the popular imagination a land full of oil-rich sheikhs, had a GDP per capita under $14,000—half the EU average and broadly similar to Eastern Europe's.

Figure 2.2 compares the Gulf's GDP per capita with other regions and nations, showing it to be far below the world's most developed economies and much higher than those of China and India.

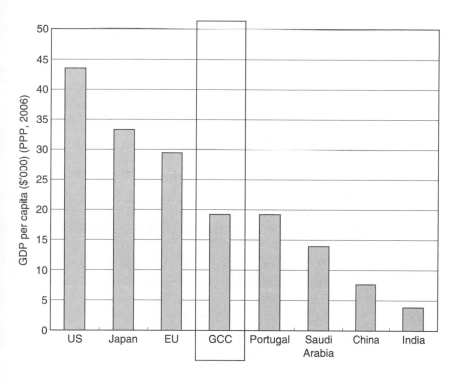

Figure 2.2 GCC GDP per capita is half US level, but five times India's (Source: EIU, *CIA World Factbook*, 2007)

Multinationals that consider these figures can tailor their product mix and service levels more appropriately. Certainly, the GCC has its share of millionaires, and some skilled expatriates have substantial disposable income. At the same time, mid-market propositions have a great deal of potential. It is not surprising, therefore, that IKEA has enjoyed success in the GCC with its moderately priced furniture, that Carrefour (the French equivalent of Wal-Mart) is expanding substantially in the region, or that low-cost Chinese-manufactured goods are highly popular.

Another humbling economic reality in the GCC is unemployment. Half the GCC states have unemployment figures in the double digits despite their strong oil and gas income. These countries—including the most populous one, Saudi Arabia—face the urgent challenge of creating millions of new jobs and bringing large segments of their citizens into the workforce. Unemployment in some GCC states, like unemployment anywhere, can be a cause of social frustration and unrest. In fact, job creation has been a central goal for GCC governments as they craft their economic diversification strategies. Industry, manufacturing, and services jobs are seen as a key requirement for ensuring widespread prosperity and continued social and economic stability and averting political extremism.

When it comes to unemployment, GCC states fall into two distinct categories—very high and very low. Bahrain, Oman, and Saudi Arabia have unemployment rates between 13 and 15 percent—far above the rates for the United States and EU. Kuwait, Qatar, and the UAE, by contrast, have remarkably low unemployment rates—below 3 percent. Figure 2.3 illustrates this phenomenon.

As the free flow of GCC citizen workers across borders becomes more common, one can expect some shifts in the above figures. The growing number of young nationals below the age of 20, however, has rightly concerned leaders in the GCC that large-scale unemployment could hit the region in the years ahead. Multinational firms that are sensitive to this pressing issue and play an active role in creating local jobs can expect a favorable reception from GCC governments and regulators.

Worse off than unemployed nationals, who typically receive government benefits, are many low-skilled foreign workers, typically from Asia. Long hours, meager wages, and crowded living conditions—often provided by their employers—result in a fairly poor quality of life for these workers. Although their wages are

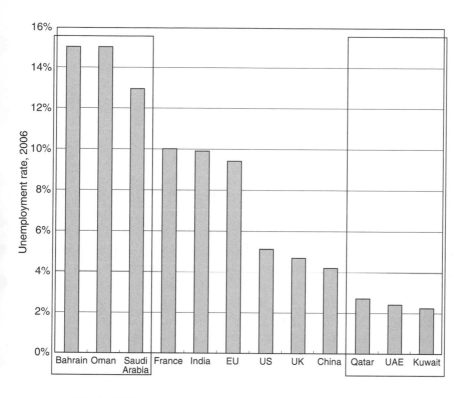

Figure 2.3 Half of GCC states have double-digit unemployment (Source: *CIA World Factbook, 2006*)

significantly higher than what they might earn in their home countries, unskilled workers often need to take on debt to fund their migration to the Gulf states. In recent months, these workers have begun organizing in protest of delayed wage payments by development and construction companies. While the labor laws on the books protect workers' rights, compliance has been imperfect and enforcement a challenge. Although for most multinational companies, these low-skilled workers are not the core target segment for selling goods and services, they do comprise a meaningful proportion of the GCC population and have some disposable income to spend on basic products such as food and packaged goods.

Misconception 3: The GCC customer "hates us"—global brands and businesses cannot succeed.

Reality: Gulf consumers embrace global brands and
       products. They will buy from a multinational if its offering
       best meets their needs.

Another common misconception about the GCC—and about
the Middle East in general—is that consumers are somehow averse
to global brands, especially those from the United States. Some
business leaders, subscribing to the view that most people in the
Arab world "hate us," assume that Western brands will not be
accepted and therefore attempting to enter the market is futile.
These executives wrongly equate distaste for US foreign policy with
dislike of US brands.

The truth, on the contrary, is that many US and other Western
brands have been extremely successful in GCC markets. This can be
noticed immediately by anyone who walks into a major GCC shopping mall or supermarket. Consider, for example, Dubai's popular
Deira City Centre mall: of the shopping center's 347 stores, nearly
80 percent are multinational brands with Western roots, and over 40
percent are American. At City Centre, one can find core American
retail chains, including DKNY, Polo, Calvin Klein, Forever 21, and
even a RadioShack. The signs are in English and the store logos are
the same as those one would find in an American mall. For those
with more European tastes, there are the United Colors of Benetton,
NEXT, Zara, Burberry's, and more. Should you fancy something
more risquè, try the trendy Bebe. These retailers and dozens more
have been brought to the GCC by local partners who recognize their
markets' taste for such merchandise. These savvy businesspeople
understand that GCC consumers do not reject Western brands, as
long as those brands are managed responsibly. Later in this book,
we will discuss the complexities involved in "responsibly" marketing to GCC buyers.

Western-brand fast-food restaurant chains are another
type of business that is highly successful throughout the GCC.
McDonald's, Burger King, KFC, Pizza Hut, and a host of other
American food chains are prevalent in major cities, shopping
centers, and airports. Many readers may be surprised to learn that
there is a prominent KFC just steps away from the Sacred Mosque
in Makkah, frequented by pilgrims from the Muslim world and
beyond. Influential business families secure franchise agreements

with these American-based fast food chains, identify strategic locations, and ensure that global standards are maintained.

Another interesting sign of the growing appetite for Western goods in the GCC is the development of formal and informal methods for customers to procure global brands that are not marketed in the GCC by foreign retailers.

Aramex: Shop & Ship

The shipping company Aramex began as a wholesale delivery service supporting US-based courier companies such as FedEx and Airborne Express. In 1997, Aramex became the first Arab-based international company listed on the Nasdaq. It subsequently went private and then listed publicly again, this time in Dubai. Aramex is a cofounder of the Global Distribution Alliance, a network of 40 distributors with almost $8 billion in revenue worldwide.

For the GCC, Aramex has developed a novel service called Shop & Ship, through which GCC customers can set up a mailing address in the United States or the UK to receive online purchases, as well as ordinary letters, magazine subscriptions, and any other items that can be sent through the mail. This allows the GCC consumer to purchase online from vendors like Amazon, DKNY, and Fendi. Aramex then forwards the goods on to the GCC-based purchaser, three times a week, and even calls or sends a text message to the purchaser's mobile phone when the goods arrive. Packages can be tracked along the way.

The rationale for this service is simple: buyers want the goods but many online vendors won't ship them to the GCC directly—or will do so only for very high prices—while others will not accept the Gulf consumer's credit card. The company profits by levying a one-time setup fee for establishing two mailboxes (one each in the United States and the UK); there are no annual fees. Aramex then charges for individual shipments by weight, with tariffs varying by destination.

As an illustration, consider a resident of Dubai shopping on Amazon.com who wishes to purchase three books, each costing $10 (£5.00) and weighing one pound (about half a kilogram). As its cheapest option, Amazon would charge $30 for shipping—equal to the cost of the goods—and deliver in 15 to 40 business days.

However, Aramex's charge for a 1.5-kilogram shipment to Dubai is $19, and it will arrive in far less time than will the Amazon shipment; the GCC consumer gets his or her books faster and cheaper.

Further, when one considers that electronic and software products are sometimes unable to be shipped internationally, the handicap faced by multinationals without a GCC presence becomes apparent.

Hawaa World: Help Me Shop!

Informal networks also exist that allow GCC shoppers—usually women—to connect with other shoppers based in the West or in Asia and that arrange purchases for them and bring items back on their behalf. On the popular women's portal Hawaa World ("Women World"),[14] which has over 150,000 members, consumers can make requests for others to shop on their behalf for items they cannot order online themselves: for example, if the online retailer does not ship to the GCC, if the product cannot be found online, if the retailer does not accept foreign credit cards, or if there is a risk that goods will break during shipment. People also discuss the merits of products and help each other find them locally. Some participants even offer products (often foreign) for sale. For example, consider Figure 2.4.

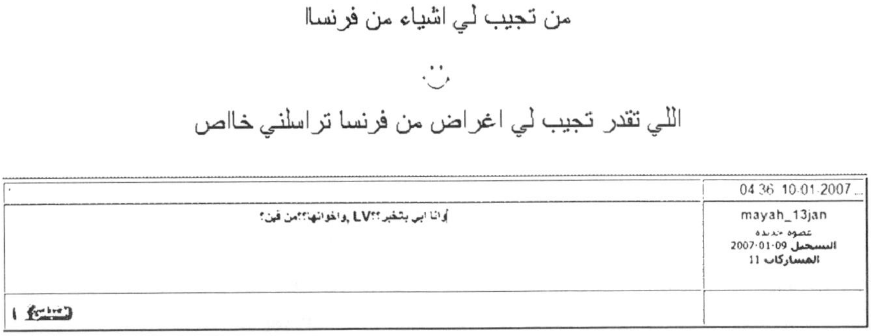

من تجيب لي اشياء من فرنسا

:)

اللي تقدر تجيب لي اغراض من فرنسا تراسلني خاص

	04 36 10.01.2007
أوانا ابي بتخبر؟؟ LV؟ واخوانها؟؟من فين؟	mayah_13jan
	عضوه جديد
	السجيل 2007-01-09
	المشاركات 11
(تشبيه) 1	

Figure 2.4 Hawaa World posting

The posting shown asks: "Who can send me some things from France? Whoever can send me items from France, please e-mail me privately. In Al Khobar [a large eastern Saudi Arabian city] I also want LV [Louis Vuitton] and her sisters [a slang term for other luxury brands such as Chanel, Dior, etc.]."

Examples like this should cause global marketing managers, who may have assumed that there was insufficient demand in the GCC for their products, to start wondering how many of the items purchased online and shipped to US or European addresses, or purchased by foreign visitors to the United States or Europe, ultimately end up in the GCC. In addition, the words of GCC consumers themselves demonstrate keen awareness of—and desire for—Western products, turning the "they hate us" misconception on its head. Another, deeper question is: How much revenue are multinationals losing from customers who lack the extra motivation to use Aramex or Hawaa World to arrange their purchases?

POLITICAL CRISES AND BRAND RISK

While the dominant reality is that GCC consumers embrace global brands when they suit their needs, political crises can—and do—lead to boycotts that have a negative economic impact on exporters to the region. The most notable recent boycott was that of Danish products in early 2006, following the publication of a cartoon depicting the Prophet Muhammad that was deemed offensive by Muslims around the world. The boycott strongly affected the sales of individual Danish companies and Danish exports in the Muslim world.

Consider the following figures:

- Denmark's exports to Saudi Arabia—its largest Muslim market—fell 40 percent during the cartoon-related boycott.[15]
- Arla Foods, a Danish dairy cooperative with over $400 million in Middle East sales each year, suspended production in Saudi Arabia because the boycott against its products was nearly total.[16]
- Denmark's worldwide exports fell 15.5 percent between February and June 2006 as a result of the boycott.[17]

The clear lesson from the Danish boycott is that multinationals must recognize that political crises, if not managed carefully, can expose their GCC business to serious risk. What's most striking about the Arla Foods example is that the decline in sales was not related to anything the company had done *itself*—the boycott was related to a cartoon published in Denmark. Fortunately, the crisis passed after a few months, and Danish products slowly returned to store shelves.

Yet the long-term question remains: How can a firm operating in the GCC countries manage risks associated with the politics of its home country? Savvy business leaders will work diligently, independent of any crisis, to build authentic franchises in the GCC that build trust in the local community. They will ensure—as we discuss in Chapter 6 of this book—that marketing messages and branding show respect for the local culture while maintaining the global "edge" at the core of their value proposition. Firms that are seen to be genuine partners, invested in the region, are less likely to suffer in the event of a politically motivated boycott.

No global executive should assume that his or her firm is not relevant to the GCC simply because it bears a foreign or Western brand. Abundant examples show the success of global brands in the region when they are managed effectively. Realizing that a global brand can be an asset and not a liability should propel more firms to explore making a deeper commitment to GCC markets.

> Misconception 4: Women don't matter—female consumers, employees, and decision makers are marginal to the economy.
> Reality: Female consumers are key decision makers. Ignoring the economic power of these savvy consumers can be a fatal mistake.

Around the world, marketers are increasingly crafting their strategies with a deeper understanding of a market reality: that female consumers control the bulk of purchase decisions. This fact has long been understood in the realm of household products such as groceries, home maintenance and decoration items, appliances, and children's clothing and toys. Recently, many firms have observed that women's purchasing power and influence extend far beyond the above categories and well into stereotypically male sectors. In a 2006 article, a spokesperson for the Ford Motor Company asserted that women influence 85 percent of auto purchases and make 45 percent of car purchases directly.[18] In consumer electronics, women outspend men, and influence 90 percent of purchases.[19] Gone are the days when companies could assume that men made the majority of major purchase decisions.

Some global executives, however, are under the impression that females in the GCC are marginalized out of purchase decisions. This impression may be driven partly by stereotypical images of Gulf women dressed in the traditional outer gown (abaya), which remains the norm for GCC women. There is a broad assumption, in many circles, that women who wear an abaya must be oppressed and disenfranchised. The international media has come to associate the abaya with exclusion and a denial of rights, leading observers to feel that traditionally dressed women lack the power to make economic decisions.

The reality, however, is that female consumers are enormously powerful and influential in the GCC. The evidence in the marketplace is overwhelming: far more stores cater to women than to men, more women are visible in shopping centers than men, and women are making hefty purchases with credit cards and cash, often outspending men. Billboards and television ads confirm this reality, with messages clearly targeting female consumers. Newsstands have plenty of women's lifestyle magazines—replete with sections on fashion and cosmetics—as many as one finds in the West or in Asia. Marketers who understand the region have grasped that females are driving core purchasing decisions.

GCC women—especially the younger ones—are becoming savvier and more sophisticated. University-educated women are a key, growing demographic with increasing disposable income and discerning taste. Each year, for example, over 40,000 UAE citizen women matriculate into university-level degree programs. What may surprise many readers, however, is that the number of female students is *twice* that of males.[20]

Consider Figure 2.5, which shows female students as a percentage of total first-year students at higher colleges and universities.

Savvy marketers target young, educated consumers because they represent the high-value customers of tomorrow. In the case of the GCC, this category is largely female.

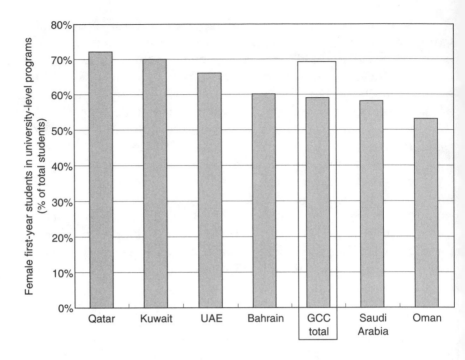

Figure 2.5 Most GCC college students are women (Source: GCC government data)

Another factor that makes young, educated women a crucial customer segment is their relatively high level of disposable income. Like their counterparts in Japan and unlike in the West, GCC women are less likely to live alone and are more likely to live with their parents or husbands. Female professionals will therefore be able to spend more of their disposable income on discretionary purchases such as clothing, accessories, and cosmetics. According to a recent article in an Arabic-language magazine, it is not uncommon for female citizens of UAE countries to feel pressure to own designer handbags costing over $1,500—and more of these women are taking out loans to support such status-driven spending.[21]

WOMEN IN THE WORKFORCE

As the data on university enrollment suggests, female professionals are becoming an increasingly important part of the GCC workforce.

Like women everywhere, GCC women look to strike a balance between their careers and their families. Having earned their degrees and developed their skills, these women are keen to contribute to the world outside the home and will seek challenging and fulfilling professional opportunities.

Far-sighted multinationals will recognize this fundamental trend and actively recruit female GCC nationals. These young women will be drawn to firms that provide a chance to grow, to make a difference, and to progress in the organization. Like women (and men) everywhere, they will prefer firms that honor their commitments to both family and work and will gravitate toward nondiscriminatory environments. Multinationals with experience recruiting, developing, and managing female executives worldwide should draw on this experience and apply the relevant best practices to help them tap into this promising and growing segment of professional talent.

WOMEN IN POSITIONS OF LEADERSHIP

Historically, it has been rare to see GCC women in positions of leadership in the corporate and government spheres. This is changing rapidly, however, and more women are emerging at the forefront of GCC institutions.

Sheikha Lubna al-Qasimi: Woman Steering the Economy

One key female leader in the GCC is Sheikha Lubna al-Qasimi, the UAE's minister of economy. Sheikha Lubna, a member of the Sharjah royal family, is the most senior female government minister in the history of the UAE. Educated in the United States, she has a strong background in technology management and business leadership. Her position is an example of the importance of family ties in driving social change, it was her uncle, the ruler of the Sharjah Emirate within the UAE, who supported her all along and encouraged her to complete her education. The fact that Sharjah, one of the UAE's most socially conservative emirates, is Sheikha Lubna's home is an important sign that even traditional societies have begun to understand that they can benefit from the advancement of women to positions of leadership and authority.

Sheikha Lubna began her career as a programmer at a software company in the emirates, being the only local and only woman on the team. Her progress was swift—five jobs and six years later, she joined Dubai Ports World, where as a senior executive she drove the IT strategy needed to expand the enterprise to its central role in global port management. Prior to her appointment as minister of economy, Sheikha Lubna also led Dubai's e-government initiative and served as CEO of Tejari.com, an award-winning business-to-business e-commerce portal in the UAE.

In addition to her corporate and government work, she serves on the board of a number of educational institutions, as well as the Dubai Chamber of Commerce and Industry. Her achievements have received recognition the world over, including mention in *Forbes* magazine and her receipt of the 2004 Entrepreneurship Award from the British House of Lords. Sheikha Lubna is widely admired as a role model by GCC women. Having met Sheikha Lubna personally in 2006, as the UAE Ministry of Economy was undergoing significant change, I can attest to her drive, professionalism, and commitment to results. Look for her to go far.

Expanding Female Power

Another role model in the corporate sector is Maha Al-Ghunaim, who is founder, vice chairman, and managing director of the Kuwait-based Global Investment House. Al-Ghunaim established the firm in 1998, and she had grown its assets under her management to over $6 billion by 2005. In 2006, she was ranked number 91 by *Forbes* magazine in its ranking of the world's most powerful women.[22]

While certainly there is much progress to be made in terms of female leadership in the GCC, and social freedoms for women are particularly constricted in Saudi Arabia, some degree of precedent has been set, and the trend is toward more women in positions of authority. Women in the GCC cannot be ignored: as consumers, as potential employees, and—increasingly—as leaders in business and society.

Misconception 5: The markets are entirely Arab—the Arab consumer is the only target market in the Gulf.
Reality: The expatriate market within the GCC is crucial.

One basic—and reasonable—assumption one might make about the GCC is that these markets are entirely Arab. The Gulf states are, after all, countries on the Arabian Peninsula with Arabic as their official language and ruled by Arab leaders. Public figures and most corporate CEOs are, of course, local Arabs. The local Arab community is squarely in control of political affairs and key strategic industries, controlling all the public sector assets, comprising most of the government workforce, and holding the lion's share of private wealth. From many perspectives, the locals are the region's core constituency.

A closer look at the GCC's demographics, however, reveals figures that may surprise the outside observer. As illustrated in Figure 2.6, half the GCC countries have more expatriates than locals—and one-third of the region's total population is foreign.

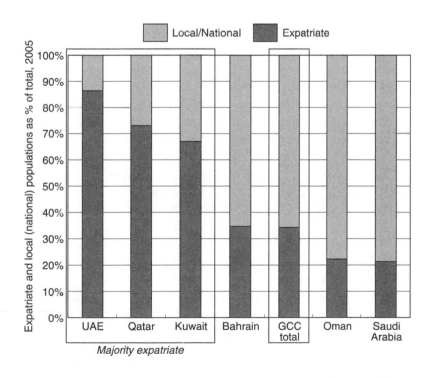

Figure 2.6 Half the GCC states are majority expatriate (Source: GCC government data and *CIA World Factbook, 2006*)

Expatriate populations across the region consist of Arabic-speaking and non–Arabic speaking nationalities. Arabs from Egypt, Lebanon, Yemen, and elsewhere come to work in the GCC for its higher standard of living and its opportunities. Asian communities from the Indian Subcontinent, the Philippines, and elsewhere also comprise a large component of the expatriate population throughout the region. Managerial and professional expatriates from Europe, Australia, and the United States are increasingly common—especially in cosmopolitan and attractive Dubai. One interesting and fast-growing expatriate sector is made up of EU and US nationals of Middle Eastern descent choosing to work in the GCC due to the scale of opportunities there and their cultural and linguistic affinity with the region.[23]

One result of the GCC's diversity is that English is used as the primary language in most private-sector institutions. Even government documents such as driver's licenses and visas—as well as street signs—are typically in both Arabic and English. While Arabic is the official language, English is the lingua franca in many of the more cosmopolitan areas and especially in the UAE, where expatriates are the majority. In fact, UAE police officers are required to learn English, and one sometimes finds Arabs who speak formal English more fluently than formal Arabic!

While expatriate populations are large, they may not always be the most attractive customer segments. As already noted, locals control the bulk of the resources and the private wealth. Many expatriates are workers with low skills with minimal disposable income. It is also crucial to note that much expatriate wealth is deposited outside the GCC (often in the "home country") in the form of remittances or investments. The prosperity visible in the GCC, therefore, is largely a reflection of local wealth. Expatriates may comprise a third of the GCC population, but their purchasing power is less than a third of the regional total.

Nonetheless, multinationals that enter the GCC market cannot afford to underestimate the importance of expatriates to the local economies. For one thing, expatriates from a firm's home country are a natural affinity group to target as the firm explores the GCC. In addition to comprising a large consumer base with attractive, professional subsegments, expatriates are an immensely important pool of talent. Hiring expatriates already in the market is an efficient way to find professionals who combine experience in global institutions with local knowledge of the GCC region. The GCC may be comprised of Arab countries, but the expatriate community plays a central role in its commercial life.

KEY LESSONS

- Sound strategies rely on sound assumptions. Multinational companies must actively seek to *remove the five "deadly" misconceptions* about the GCC that could cause them to misjudge the region's opportunities and risks.
- Beyond energy, the GCC offers *promising opportunities across a broad range of sectors*, most notably: infrastructure and real estate, industry and manufacturing, tourism, retailing, and services.
- Not all GCC consumers are rich: *midmarket propositions* comprise a large opportunity.
- *GCC buyers embrace global brands* when the products meet their needs and the brands are responsibly managed.
- *Women play a central role* in the GCC's economic life, making purchase decisions, comprising an appealing, educated consumer segment, and increasingly taking positions of leadership.
- *Expatriates are crucial* to GCC economies and make up one-third of the region's total population.

CHAPTER 3

Here to Stay: GCC Market Attractiveness and Risks

INTRODUCTION

Not long ago, no Hollywood studio was complete without a set it could use as a ghost town for western movies. "Wild West" movies were often set in largely abandoned towns located in rough terrain, and these movies were full of cowboys, bandits, and rugged lawmen. Ghost towns were great settings for movies because of their faded glory: they were towns that had seen boom times during the nineteenth-century gold rushes but later lost their luster as the mines shut down and local economies lost their steam. As a result, tumbleweed rolled through Main Streets once bustling with economic activity.

The GCC today has, in some respects, the feel of a gold rush town: there is rapid growth and economic transformation, the level of wealth is unprecedented, and outsiders are pouring in as never before. GCC markets are attractive to growth-seeking global companies that would have overlooked them before. Sophisticated business-people read headlines about GCC investments in marquee global assets like the Four Seasons Hotels or Aston Martin and about Western companies paying ever-more attention to the region: Halliburton has even announced plans to move its headquarters to Dubai. No one denies that the GCC is glittering. The question, though, is whether the glitter is merely a flash in the pan or whether the GCC will remain an economic powerhouse in the years ahead. Might the Gulf capitals, rapidly expanding today and competing to create the sleekest offices and most attractions, become ghost towns with the bursting of an economic bubble?

Our analysis suggests otherwise. A fundamental assessment of the GCC economies indicates that they will remain strong and important into the foreseeable future. The reasons for the region's economic attractiveness are rooted in basic economic trends: sustained prosperity and growth, attractive demographic shifts, and ongoing regulatory reform. These three fundamental factors give the region lasting appeal to multinational companies. In addition to its inherent appeal, the GCC is attractive for the linkages it enjoys with the Far East, South Asia, and the broader Middle East—all of which are expected to be engines of growth for the global economy for decades to come.

The GCC, however, does possess significant risks and drawbacks. Chief among these risks is overdependence on oil, without which the Gulf economies would collapse. Despite the current stability of the regimes of the GCC countries, the region is exposed to geopolitical risk related to conflict in the broader Middle East (especially Iran). Regimes in the GCC states must also continue to curb religious extremism and terrorist threats—threats that become more dangerous if unemployment and the frustration associated with joblessness grow. And even though the Gulf is quite comfortable, social issues such as the continuing restrictions on social freedoms (for women and men), a dearth of political discourse, and the prevalence of racism are real drawbacks. By no means is life in the GCC countries perfect.

Overall, however, the GCC represents a meaningful business opportunity rooted in solid economic fundamentals. Savvy leaders of multinational corporations will recognize the region's opportunities while acknowledging the material risks and drawbacks associated with doing business there. Our view is that the GCC's economic importance will endure: global leaders should recognize this and craft strategies that capture growth while judiciously navigating the risks.

THE GCC'S OPPORTUNITY FORMULA

The GCC has become—and, we believe, will remain—a highly attractive place to do business. What makes the place so appealing for business is a combination of factors that have converged to create economic dynamism and opportunity. Three core elements, when put together, form the "Opportunity Formula" behind the GCC's ongoing success story (see Figure 3.1).

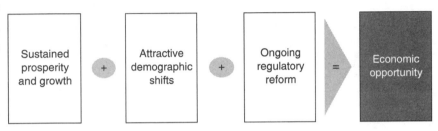

Figure 3.1 The GCC's Opportunity Formula

Sustained prosperity and growth, attractive demographic shifts, and ongoing regulatory reform are the pillars that have made—and continue to make—the GCC an attractive place to do business.

Sustained Prosperity and Growth

The GCC is a prosperous place—especially by emerging-market standards. In 2006, the region's GDP per capita in PPP (purchasing power parity) terms was around $20,000. This figure compares favorably with other hot markets—roughly three times that of China ($7,600) and more than five times that of India ($3,700).[1] This prosperity gives the average consumer in a GCC country a much higher level of disposable income than his or her counterpart in other markets. And while the GCC has a much smaller consumer base than China and India—about 40 million people—its combined population is about two-thirds that of the UK. Moreover, the GCC's consumer base is heavily concentrated in 8 to 10 key urban centers. It is therefore not surprising that the GCC has increasingly become a target market for luxury goods such as perfumes, designer fashions and accessories, and high-end automobiles. Services for the wealthy such as private banking and asset management are also areas of focus for domestic and international companies seeking to benefit from the region's prosperity.

As important as the GCC's absolute wealth is the remarkable economic growth it is experiencing. In the five-year period between 2001 and 2006, the GCC's combined real GDP has grown at an annualized rate of 6.5 percent—almost three times the rate of the most developed OECD (Organization for Economic Cooperation and Development) markets. Figure 3.2 compares growth rates across regions.

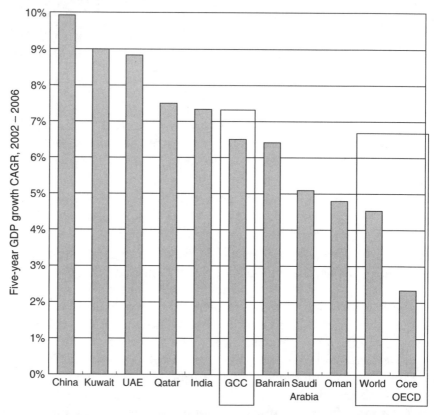

Figure 3.2 GCC economies have grown much faster than world and core OECD averages (Source: EIU, *CIA World Factbook, 2006*; "Core OECD" excludes Czech Republic, Hungary, Mexico, Poland, Slovakia, and Turkey.)

While China's nearly 10 percent growth rate surpasses that of any GCC economy, Kuwait, Qatar, and the UAE have all been growing faster than India while enjoying a GDP per capita many times higher. Only Oman, with 4.8 percent growth, is below 5 percent. During the same period, global GDP grew at 4.5 percent yearly and the core OECD (most developed) economies grew at 2.3 percent. The GCC is therefore growing almost three times faster than the world's most mature markets.

The GCC's prosperity has enabled the region to accumulate impressive surpluses. According to 2006 estimates, the combined GCC current account surplus in 2006 was $193 billion—about $5,000 per person.[2] This aggregate figure is slightly higher than China's—$179 billion, according to the *Economist*—a surplus that many have seen as an ominous sign of China's economic rise and dominance as a trade partner.

While impossible to measure precisely, there is no doubt that the GCC's global savings are tremendous. One recent estimate of GCC private wealth—the vast majority of which is invested abroad—was between $1.3 and 1.5 trillion.[3] The region's institutional wealth adds to this figure enormously. While extremely guarded about its figures, the Abu Dhabi Investment Authority (ADIA) is believed to be one of the world's largest institutional investors, with assets well over $500 billion.[4] Kuwait and several other GCC states likewise have investment funds worth tens and hundreds of billions of dollars. A global economist at UBS Investment Bank recently estimated that petrodollars are funding up to 45 percent of the current US account deficit.[5] Perhaps most promising from a macroeconomic perspective is the remarkable savings rate of certain GCC countries—for example, around 40 percent of GDP in the UAE and Kuwait.[6] On a per capita basis, the GCC's public and private savings pool is not far behind legendary Japanese levels.

There is no shortage of evidence of the GCC's increased prosperity. Perhaps most famous are the marquee global investments made by GCC institutions and individuals, including the Fairmont Hotels and other luxury properties, a 5 percent stake in Ferrari, the largest stake in Daimler AG (until recently DaimlerChrysler), one of the largest stakes in Deutsche Bank, a piece of Aston Martin, a significant stake in J Sainsbury's (the British supermarket chain), and a whole host of other assets. Emirates Airlines has ordered $37 billion worth of new aircraft, including the largest order for the new Airbus A380 double-decker plane.[7] In turn, the largest customer for the wide-body Airbus A350 is Qatar Airways, with 80 aircraft on order for a list price of $16 billion.[8] Between 2004 and 2005, GE reported an 80 percent increase in orders from the region, to $8 billion, citing big-ticket items for the health care, power, and aircraft industries.[9] In fact, GE recently sold its plastics unit—where Jack Welch began his career—for $11 billion to Saudi Arabia's largest public company.[10] The controversial acquisition of P&O by Dubai Ports World was an illustration of a GCC acquisition made not as a passive investment but by a port operator with world-class capabilities looking for international growth.

Consumer prosperity and spending are at an all-time high in the GCC. In a 2006 survey of consumer confidence, the UAE ranked ahead of the UK, France, Germany, and Italy. Today, Dubai has four times the per capita shopping area of the United States, and retail space is expected to quadruple in Dubai from 2006 to 2010.[11] Part of this expansion is the massive Mall of Arabia project—a mall that, in the course of two phases, expects to reach 10 million square feet of retail space and over 1,000 retail outlets. This is more than twice the size of the Mall of America (4.2 million square feet total, of which 2.8 million is leasable space),[12] which is itself in the midst of an expansion. The world's largest mall today, in terms of gross leasable area, is the South China Mall near Hong Kong with 7.1 million square feet. The Mall of Arabia has already booked tenants from all over the world for 80 percent of its retail space; these tenants include the Virgin Megastore, which will have its largest outlet anywhere in this new mall.[13]

Conspicuous consumer spending in the GCC countries is evident in the growing presence of luxury cars, designer jewelry, high-fashion clothing, and other signs of wealth. Consumerism has, however, also introduced among many locals the bad habit of acquiring excessive personal debt. As already mentioned, not everyone in the GCC is rich— in fact, many are unemployed or subsist on modest salaries. In Bahrain, for example, a third of the native Bahraini (not expatriate) workforce earns less than $600 per month.[14] Banks (both international and local) and consumer finance companies have been quick to tap into the region's growing consumerism in order to build credit card and personal loan businesses. According to a study by McKinsey & Co., loans to individuals in the GCC surpassed $100 billion in 2005 (37 percent of total lending), but this market still has a large potential to grow as consumer loans (including mortgages) represent only 17 percent of GDP in Saudi Arabia, compared with upward of 70 percent for major Western nations.[15]

A concern of leading bankers today is that the "credit culture" may have gone too far in the GCC, as borrowers are known to be spending lavishly or sometimes even investing borrowed cash in highly volatile stock markets. As consumer lending and credit cards are fairly new to the GCC market, many borrowers are inexperienced with borrowing and quickly find themselves in over their heads. Companies naturally offer high-end goods to middle-class GCC consumers as "aspiration" products—consumers, for their part, need to know their limits and exercise discretion. If interest rates were to rise, we would likely see an unprecedented level of personal bankruptcy and even foreclosures on homes. One billboard on a busy road in Dubai encourages consumers to "own the home of your dreams" with 100 percent financing. Like their counterparts in the United States and elsewhere, these homeowners risk waking up to a nightmare if they are unable to sustain the monthly payments.

Attractive Demographic Shifts

The second element in the GCC's Opportunity Formula is the attractive demographic shifts taking place in these markets. The GCC countries are experiencing population growth, increased literacy and quality of life, and an expanding middle class—all of which are helping make these markets more attractive to multinational companies.

Figure 3.3 provides an outlook on population growth in the GCC. The vertical axis indicates the total expected population growth from 2006 to 2050; the horizontal axis indicates the current average number of live births per woman.

The first observation to be made about population growth is that the UAE, Kuwait, Qatar, and Saudi Arabia are expected to nearly double in population between now and 2050. A high number of births, extended life expectancy, and significant migration can all be expected to continue into the foreseeable future. Population growth in GCC countries is particularly striking when compared with the forecast of 40 percent growth in the United States for the same period—less than half the amount of the four GCC countries named above.

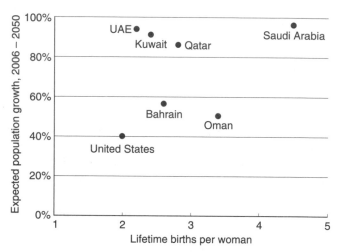

Figure 3.3 GCC countries have high birthrates and high expected population growth (Source: Population Reference Bureau)

Equally striking is the number of births per woman: all GCC countries have a higher fertility rate than the United States has. The figure for Saudi Arabia—an astonishing 4.5 births per woman—is more than twice that of the United States (2.0) and UAE (2.2). The high Saudi birthrate is quite troubling when one considers the country's high unemployment and daunting social challenges. The forecast of a 96 percent increase in the Saudi population by 2050 highlights the urgent need to create jobs—a need that the government is keenly aware of.

The population of the GCC countries is, on average, quite young. Roughly half of the GCC citizens are under 16 years old.[16] GCC citizens, the region's most sought-after market, tend to have significantly more children per family than expatriates. Parents in the region tend to spend heavily on their children: according to a 2006 study, parents spend an average of $327 per year on toys and video games—twice as much as their counterparts in Europe and

America.[17] Retailers are therefore intensely targeting GCC-region parents and the market for children's goods is booming.

Because of the large numbers of foreign laborers—who generally are unable to bring families to the Gulf—the region's overall gender balance is skewed toward males. This is likely to change over time as the workforce becomes more "nationalized" and expatriate workers become less common. Another key trend is the increase in the proportion of the population that is over 65 years old. The boom in this segment is understandable, as the quality of health care and standard of living have improved tremendously in the Gulf since the oil boom of the 1970s.

One important sign of healthy demographics is the percentage of the population who are in their productive or working years. As illustrated in Figure 3.4, most GCC countries are expected to have more than two-thirds of their populations in the age range 15–64 for the foreseeable future.

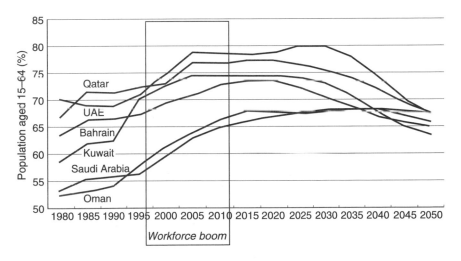

Figure 3.4 GCC countries have growing workforces (Source: UN, medium variant)

This is a good sign, as it suggests that for every person who is either too young or too old to be employed, there will be at least two people in the active workforce driving the economy forward. Even if oil income and government surpluses become more modest, the underlying demographics of the region suggest that there will be a reasonably large number of economically productive people to support the needs of the unemployable. This demographic picture is much more favorable than that of some developed nations, in which baby boom generations are aging and being replaced by a smaller number of working people with taxable incomes to fund social benefits to retirees.

The rise of a middle class in the GCC states, while difficult to measure precisely, is apparent in the marketplace. One sign already mentioned is the increase in consumer credit—often a near necessity for middle-class consumers. Another sign is the rise of moderately priced "lifestyle" retailers such as IKEA and H&M—both of which are enjoying remarkable success in the region. These companies offer average consumers a taste of elegance and flair at more modest prices than those of high-end designers. Their appeal has been to both expatriates and locals who, based on their income, could be categorized as belonging to the middle class. This growing middle class has, in fact, recently become the subject of more detailed examination by outside observers—and the outlook is positive. James Zogby, for example, in conjunction with McKinsey & Co., in 2007 published an initial study on middle-class attitudes in the Gulf in which most respondents reported a sense of job security and a feeling that life had improved in recent years.[18] Improvements in the Gulf's education system, media availability, and connectivity with the broader world have made consumers from GCC countries more sophisticated and more demanding. In the technology sector, for example, savvy media users are aware of the latest innovations and expect them to be made available in the local market. Fashions from around the world are visible through satellite channels, the entertainment media, and online. This trend of increasing sophistication can be useful to savvy multinational firms who can leverage best practices and insights from other markets and apply them intelligently to the GCC. The businesses that may suffer most as a result of increased consumer savvy are local firms that once enjoyed less competitive, relatively closed economic regimes and now are subject to more intense market pressures.

At the high end of the market, the number of wealthy individuals is increasing. According to Cap Gemini and Merrill Lynch, the number of "very rich" people (owning over $1 million in financial assets) in the Middle East has been growing significantly and is expected to grow sixfold between 2005 and 2010, to almost 2 million individuals.[19] While this segment has long been the target of private banking and other financial services, it is now also the target of a growing array of "elite" products and services across a wide range of sectors. Ultraluxury hotels, like the $1.1 billion Emirates Palace Hotel in Abu Dhabi, have suites costing thousands of dollars each night largely to appeal to intra-GCC elite travelers.

Ongoing Regulatory Reform

To many outsiders, GCC markets appear opaque and shrouded in mystery. These perceptions are likely the result of a dose of exoticism fueled by the entertainment and news media. GCC markets do have a long way to go before they are fully liberalized, but even today they are quite open by emerging-market standards. GCC leaders have committed (at least in principle) to continuing the economic reform process, recognizing that opening up their markets is a critical factor in their economies' long-term success. This deregulation process—which includes encouraging international trade, privatizing state-owned enterprises, expanding property rights for foreigners, among other reforms—is the crucial third element in the Opportunity Formula.

The Heritage Foundation, a US think tank, publishes an "Index of Economic Freedom" each year, scoring countries around the world and assigning a "Freedom Percentage." The results of its 2007 Index, some of which are listed in Table 3.1, may be surprising.[20]

TABLE 3.1

Freedom % for Selected Countries around the World

Country	Freedom %
United States	82.0
Bahrain	68.4
Oman	63.9
Kuwait	63.7
GCC average[21]	62.7
Brazil	60.9
Qatar	60.7

Continued

TABLE 3.1

Freedom % for Selected Countries around the World—cont'd

Country	Freedom %
UAE	60.4
Saudi Arabia	59.1
India	55.6
China	54.0
Russia	54.0

The average rating for the GCC countries was higher than for any of the celebrated BRIC (Brazil, Russia, India, and China) emerging markets. Half the GCC states—Bahrain, Oman, and Kuwait—scored better than Italy's 63.4. While multinationals rush to build their franchises in India and China, few executives realize that these markets are actually less free from a business perspective than those of the GCC states.

International Trade

The pride of the GCC countries' economies is their long history of international trade. Indeed, their circumstances have demanded such a role. The harsh terrain of the region, with very limited agricultural resources, has compelled the people of the Gulf to trade fish, pearls, dates, and other goods in order to procure the broader range of goods available in the outside world. Being situated at the crossroads of Africa and the Levant (with waterways leading to South Asia) enabled the traders of the Gulf to create value as middlemen, brokers, and transporters of goods from one region to another. Even the Qur'an makes reference to the caravans of the winter and summer trading seasons—including caravans carrying goods to Yemen and to the Levant. Two powerful trading civilizations of the Gulf in times past were Yemen and Oman, and both have a deep sense of this cultural heritage. Today, however, Yemen is a marginalized economy, left behind due to a relative lack of natural resources and a modern history of political division as the GCC member states have propelled themselves forward.

The very creation of the GCC was an important step in the liberalization of Gulf markets. While the countries of the Gulf share common cultural practices and often ethnic and historical origins (the ruling family of Qatar, for example, is from the region that is now central Saudi Arabia), the countries have distinct identities and histories, often including long-standing disputes and feuds. Trade has been a cause both of greater collaboration and of occasional conflict. The gradual creation of a common GCC market has been—somewhat like the creation of the European Community and later the European Union—a breakthrough that often required putting aside centuries-old feuds for the sake of common progress. Forming the GCC was a crucial first step in the opening of the region's economies.

From a global perspective, the GCC's most important step has been its entry into the World Trade Organization (WTO), which meant adopting a number of international trade reforms in order to be accepted into this powerful and prestigious world economic community. As illustrated in Table 3.2, all six GCC countries are now WTO members.

TABLE 3.2

Accession of GCC Countries to WTO

Year of WTO Membership	Country
1995	Bahrain
	Kuwait
1996	Qatar
	UAE
2000	Oman
2005	Saudi Arabia

It is not surprising that Bahrain, Kuwait, Qatar, and the UAE—all countries with small native populations and relatively nimble regulatory systems—were quickest to join. Oman, with its additional domestic challenges and more modest national wealth, joined next. Saudi Arabia's accession has been the most complex and challenging given the scale of the economy, trade flows, and domestic hurdles to clear.

In principle, WTO accession should radically open the GCC economies. The requirements for membership in the WTO, which include agreeing to treaties on goods (GATT), services (GATS), and intellectual property (TRIPS), are sweeping.[22] For example:

- WTO members must provide "most favored nation" (MFN) status to other members, providing access to all and not choosing among them.
- WTO members must give "national treatment" to foreign companies—not treating them differently than they treat domestic firms.[23]

In the old GCC, where economies have long been closed and local companies and business families have acted as gatekeepers and agents for foreign firms, these changes would have been nothing short of revolutionary. In recent years, however, economic realities have prevailed and the GCC states have negotiated significant exemptions and graduated timelines in order to ease the transition to WTO compliance. Each country's provisions are complex and need careful study by corporate legal teams when considering a multinational firm's prospects in Gulf countries. By way of illustration, however, it's worth noting a few of the exceptions in place.

A few of Saudi Arabia's negotiated terms were as follows:

- In the services sectors open to foreign investment such as telecommunications, foreign equity was limited to 49 percent, to be increased to 51 percent by the end of 2006 and to 60 percent by the end of 2008. Moreover, the foreign investment had to be in the form of a joint stock company.
- The provisions covering the retail sector were more liberal: 51 percent equity ownership was allowed on accession, and the figure would increase to 75 percent after three years.
- However, retailers were subject to minimum investment amounts, minimum outlet sizes, and the requirement that 15 percent of their employees trained each year be Saudis.[24]

These terms ensure that Saudi business owners will continue to play a central role in the evolving economy. Local owners cannot be completely cut off from the business; locals will always have sizable equity in key sectors. By reserving the right to define minimum outlet sizes, the Saudi authorities can protect small retailers such as neighborhood stores and convenience outlets. These protections may prove crucial for helping the Saudi middle class absorb the shock of economic transformation.

Oman's exceptions also reflect the need to protect key local industries. The local agriculture sector in particular is well protected—duties on dates and bananas are 100 percent of the original price; importing fruits that compete with Oman-grown crops have 80 percent duties when in season. Many service sectors are protected: at least 51 percent of ownership of restaurants must be by locals. The financial services industry, however, is remarkably open: foreign banks can fully own branches. One regulation that is particularly onerous to international firms is the one creating a maximum of foreign staff within foreign companies—fixed at a mere 20 percent. To make matters worse, foreign staff visas, which last two years, are renewable only for a maximum of four years. [25] Inclusion in the WTO marks a fundamental leap forward for the GCC countries in opening their markets—tariffs are reduced and eliminated in some cases, foreign investment is made more welcome, and the GCC nations submit themselves to the WTO's mechanisms for resolving trade disputes. At the same time, however, companies must study the details of each country's agreements and regulations, as the exceptions and timelines negotiated impact market openness tremendously. Although change is in the air, the fine print must be read.

In addition to WTO accession, several GCC countries have negotiated bilateral agreements with major economic powers. Both Bahrain and Oman have agreements with the United States, ratified in 2006. The UAE was engaged in similar negotiations with the United States but talks were put on hold in the wake of the Dubai Ports World controversy. Few business leaders appreciated the adverse impact of that controversy on US economic ties with one of the world's most dynamic economies. While President George W. Bush has announced a vision for a US–Middle East Free Trade Area by 2013,[26] US foreign policy in the region presents a major roadblock to building deeper economic ties.

Meanwhile, bilateral negotiations between the GCC (as a collective) and the EU were at an advanced stage at the time of this writing. These talks have been ongoing for decades—they initially began in 1990. The EU is the GCC's top trade partner and the GCC is the sixth-largest trade partner for the EU.[27] That the negotiations are taking place at the level of the GCC secretary-general and not of the individual countries is a sign of things to come and reflects the increased maturity of the GCC as a common economic bloc.

Other trade agreements in the works include GCC-India, GCC-China, and GCC-Japan, all of which can have major consequences in aligning the region more closely with Asia. GCC-Singapore talks are also under way: one interesting fact is that much of Saudi Arabia's crude oil passes through Singapore on its way to East Asia, creating some interdependence between the economies.[28] Ties with Australia and New Zealand are being deepened by both the GCC and the UAE, and negotiations of agreements are reportedly under way.

Privatization

Another area in which regulatory changes are creating significant opportunity is privatization. Throughout the GCC states, governments are rapidly privatizing firms across a wide range of sectors. Privatization is expected to bring greater efficiency and higher performance to previously state-owned enterprises and will also have the effect of increasing the scope in which international companies can operate. Privatization has also been seen by governments—and by rulers personally—as a way of sharing the country's wealth with private business families and individual shareholders. At the height of the recent GCC stock market boom, I was a consultant to a private-sector investment firm in one of the GCC countries that saw as one of its key roles to invest in privatizations in order to bring wealth into the hands of the common citizens who composed its shareholder base.

Investment firms such as the Dubai-based Abraaj Capital expect between $300 billion and $400 billion worth of assets to be transferred from governments to the private sector in the coming few years.[29] In Saudi Arabia alone, no fewer than 20 state-owned enterprises are in the process of privatization according to a WTO report. In fact, 30 percent of the lucrative utility Saudi Telecom has already been sold to private shareholders. Private contractors have been engaged to rehabilitate and operate airports and seaports. An astonishing 100 private firms were established to handle postal services. Studies are under way regarding privatization of some roads and railways. And the strategically crucial health care sector, in which rapid change and expansion are expected, has been privatized to some extent through management contracts with private firms. Management contracts are also being explored in the education sector.[30] As the private sector is, by nature, more open to global firms than is the public sector, expanding the private sector means growing the set of opportunities for multinational firms. The companies that win mandates to run formerly state-owned enterprises will seek to learn from the best practices of global firms: hospital operators, for example, will actively pursue the latest technology, methods, expertise, and personnel. Multinational firms that identify this trend can develop relationships with such clients and play a pivotal role in enhancing both their own business and the performance of the privatized companies. Privatization may also be seen as a crucial first step toward greater openness in the economy: a time may come, for example, when management contracts for some formerly public assets are awarded to international firms. Already being on the ground and having local relationships will be important for winning this type of business.

Other Forms of Regulatory Reform

Deregulation in the GCC economies has by no means been limited to international trade and privatization. Changes in regulation are taking place in a wide range of areas, as governments are recognizing the benefits of liberalization in stimulating the economy. One area of extensive deregulation has been capital markets, in which guidelines are evolving rapidly. Since 1999, non-Saudis have been able to invest in the Saudi stock market through Saudi mutual funds. In 2006, a further relaxation of ownership rules allowed non-national residents of Saudi Arabia to directly own individual stocks.[31] In the UAE, deregulation seeks to create more flexibility while enhancing shareholder protection. When the IPO boom was getting out of hand in recent years authorities introduced a law requiring companies to have a three-year track record before listing—thereby protecting individual investors from fly-by-night institutions listing to make a quick buck. The UAE's minister of economy stated in a recent interview that new IPO guidelines—yet to be implemented—will allow families to list only 30 percent stakes in private businesses (as opposed to the previous minimum of 55 percent). This change will give them more flexibility in raising capital while permitting them to retain control of their enterprises.[32] Reform in the transportation sector is under way as well: several GCC states are implementing "open skies" agreements to enable foreign carriers to operate more freely. Dubai already follows an open skies policy, which has been one factor in its airport's phenomenal growth.

Two of the most crucial areas of regulatory reform are those of property rights and labor laws. The creation of "free zones" in which foreigners can own businesses has—as we will discuss at length later—catalyzed entrepreneurship and made foreign businesses much more comfortable entering GCC markets. The UAE's breakthrough Freehold Property Law allows foreigners to purchase freehold properties in designated developments: including the most desirable areas such as the Palm Islands and Jumeirah Beach Residence. Owners of freehold properties can receive resident visas in Dubai, and therefore enter the country freely. The Freehold Property Law has helped solidify the UAE's role as the most favored destination in the region for expatriate talent, as it makes outsiders feel much more rooted and secure. Labor law reforms have been delicate due to political concerns and the need to create jobs for young locals. Bahrain, however, has recently introduced a "levy" system by which employers who seek to hire foreigners must pay a fee that will be channeled to a "labor fund." This fund will be directed toward developing the skills of the Bahraini-national labor pool. This innovative, market-based mechanism is a more savvy approach than the classic quota system for foreign workers and may spread to other GCC countries as well.[33]

As the governments of the GCC states engage in ongoing regulatory reform, one source of positive feedback for them is the strong ratings they receive for creating transparency and for curbing corruption. According to Transparency International's 2005 index, GCC countries are more transparent than most emerging markets and far more transparent than China, India, and Russia.

The average rating for the GCC states was broadly in line with those for the economies of many EU members.[34] The strength of their reputations should be a factor further enabling the deregulation (and especially the privatization) of the GCC states, as transparency signals trust and general confidence in the public sector's integrity.

TRENDSETTER FOR THE BROADER MIDDLE EAST

Beyond the Opportunity Formula of prosperity, demographics, and regulatory reform, the GCC is a very attractive place to do business due to its role as a trendsetter for the broader Middle East region. In many respects, the GCC nations are the most admired of the Middle East and North Africa (MENA) states. The commercial, professional, political, and cultural linkages between the GCC and other Middle Eastern economies are an important factor in the GCC's appeal to global firms.

Although the Arab population of the GCC countries represents a small minority of the entire Arab world, its purchasing power and economic clout make the GCC consumer base the most sought-after Arabic-speaking customers. While the population of Arab North Africa (including Egypt), for example, is roughly five times that of the GCC states, its GDP per capita is less than a third of the average for those states. The Levant region (Syria, Lebanon, Israel and the Palestinian Territories, Jordan, and Iraq) is also more populous than the GCC yet far less prosperous and stable. Companies in other Arab countries, therefore, actively target GCC consumers for their goods and services, leveraging their common language (despite differences in dialect) and cultural values to gain access to these buyers more effectively.

Tourism is one sector in which GCC-MENA links are especially strong. Lebanon, with its milder climate, beaches, and nightlife, has long been a popular destination for tourists from GCC countries. Political developments in recent years have had a significant impact on Lebanon's role as a getaway destination for Gulf travelers. Many observers note that since September 11, 2001, and the subsequent War on Terror, travel to the United States (and, to a lesser extent, Europe) has become much more of a hassle for Arabs and GCC nationals. Added security measures, involving additional scrutiny, long delays, and the risk of denied entry (for which no reason need be given), have made GCC nationals less interested in coming to the United States except when absolutely necessary. The economic impact of this phenomenon is not small—in 2002, for example, a leading hospital in the northeastern United States contacted me to request my help in reversing a severe decline in its private patient population due to decreased willingness by patients and their families from GCC countries to bother with flying to America. Lebanon, however, has remained open and welcoming and is therefore attracting tourists who otherwise might vacation in Florida or London. Lebanese and international investors are pouring capital into the tourism sector and building more luxury hotels and resorts to accommodate demand. While the 2006 war between Israel and Hezbollah brought tourism to a standstill, the longer-term trend is toward increased travel between the Gulf and Lebanon.

Egypt is another key MENA destination for GCC travelers. Summer travelers pack Cairo's streets and markets—especially at night. During one stretch, while I was working with a multinational client in Egypt in the summer of 2005, it took us much longer to walk or drive across the Nile bridge to our hotel at 11 p.m. or midnight than it did at 8 in the morning—the city was bustling and visitors were out and about. By 4 a.m., Cairo was quiet again. Cairene shopkeepers report that sales in July and August can be equivalent to the rest of the year's revenues combined,[35] due largely to spending by Gulf visitors with high disposable incomes and upscale tastes who are escaping their home countries' summer heat. Observers also note that Gulf travelers often stay in Cairo more than European tourists do; the latter tend to frequent Red Sea resorts.

Professional linkages between the GCC and MENA regions are related largely to the Gulf's need for outside talent. The GCC countries have become, without question, the most attractive place to work for Arab talent—in both professional and working-class roles. Ferries crossing the Red Sea, for example, every day transport tens of thousands of Egyptian laborers who work in Saudi Arabia or in other GCC states.[36] Much like Mexican migrant workers in the United States, these Arab workers leave less-developed home markets and work for higher wages in the Gulf region. They travel without their families and send remittances home: the World Bank estimates that Arab expatriates (both professionals and working-class) send about $25 billion home each year from the Gulf. After the United States, Saudi Arabia is the world's largest source of remittances.[37] Professionals from Lebanon, Egypt, Jordan, and other Arab nations comprise the bulk of middle management and administrative support in offices in GCC countries: middle managers, accountants, office managers, salespeople, and the like. More fortunate expatriates are able to bring their families to their GCC country and lead more settled lives. Without the vital MENA talent pool, GCC economies would come to a standstill.

MENA expatriates find the GCC states compatible with their backgrounds due largely to language, religion, culture, and access. The Arabic language, while shared in its most classical and official form (called *al-fusha* in Arabic), varies significantly from country to country. The Egyptian dialect, used commonly in films, music, and television, pronounces certain letters (including as the *j* and *q*) differently and uses words (especially in everyday conversation) that are not from classical or formal Arabic. The Levantine dialect also has its distinct characteristics, especially in certain everyday words. The Gulf dialects are closer to classical Arabic but certainly not identical—Kuwaitis, for example, will ask each other *"Ish lawnak?"*—literally, "What is your color?"—rather than the classical *"Kayfa haluk"* for "How are you?" Many Saudis, especially those with Yemeni roots, will pronounce the *q* as a *g*. Nonetheless, the key point is that Arabic speakers can converse and understand one another despite their differing backgrounds, and this capability is a huge asset for MENA expatriates in the Gulf. The MENA and Gulf regions also share a common religion: Islam. While there are some differences in the practice of Islam across schools of thought (even within the Sunni schools, as well as between Sunnis and Shiites), the basics are common, and there is great compatibility among Muslims. Geographic proximity also makes it easier for MENA talent to reach the GCC countries and travel home frequently, and the rise of low-cost airlines is making the two regions ever more accessible to one another.

While MENA talent looks to the GCC for opportunities, savvy GCC institutions understand the importance of attracting and developing the best Arab minds and business leaders. One stated objective of Qatar's Education City, for example, is to "act as a 'brain magnet' to retain talent by combating brain drain from Qatar and the Arab world."[38] Part of this rationale is long-term and strategic, as human capital is essential to these economies' competitiveness. Another part is more immediate: the educational and training facilities developed in smaller Gulf states need to attract students beyond their own nationals in order to reach the size to which they aspire.

Political collaboration between the GCC nations and the broader MENA region has also increased with the growing economic and political clout of the Gulf. Although the role of secretary-general of the Arab League (the association of Arab states) has almost always been held by an Egyptian, the Gulf states are the largest financial contributors to the League. According to the most recent public figures available, Saudi Arabia and Kuwait each contributed over 10 percent of the League's budget.[39] Saudi Arabia is also the home of the Organization of the Islamic Conference (OIC), a group of over 50 Muslim countries worldwide. The Saudi city of Jeddah is home to the OIC's Permanent Secretariat, as well as the Islamic Fiqh (jurisprudence) Academy and the Islamic Development Bank (IDB). The IDB, which is the world's largest Sharia-compliant financial institution, was created with a mandate similar to those of the World Bank and IMF to foster economic development and financial stability. The GCC is also, naturally, the center of gravity for OPEC (the Organization of Petroleum Exporting Countries)—the global oil exporters' coalition that includes several Arab states.[40] Saudi Arabia, with its massive reserves, is always the central power at OPEC meetings; Kuwait and the UAE usually align with their GCC neighbor. Together, this bloc can dominate the organization.

Further, the GCC provides substantial humanitarian aid to the MENA world. After the 2006 war in Lebanon, the Saudi government committed $1.1 billion in grants and aid, and the Islamic Development Bank pitched in $250 million.[41] Humanitarian assistance to the Palestinians is also large: the UAE, for example, gave over $800 million between 2000 and 2005, including a project to build housing over the ruins of evacuated Israeli settlements.[42] Private-sector charity, sometimes raised through television or other mass-market appeals, is also substantial. The GCC's charitable contributions to the broader MENA region both reflect and strengthen the sense of affiliation between the two areas.

The entertainment media and other cultural outlets are another aspect of connectivity that cannot be overlooked. Egyptian films, television, music, and literature flow into the GCC countries and are a bedrock of Arabic-language culture. Lebanon is another key source of music and television programming. Arab celebrities enjoy recognition throughout the MENA world—including the GCC states. Take, for example, Nancy Arjam. Arjam is a highly popular Lebanese singer who endorses Coca-Cola as well as the UAE-based but rapidly expanding Damas jewelry chain throughout the region. "Arab" restaurants in the GCC countries and elsewhere largely serve cuisine from Lebanon (e.g., hummus and shawarma) and Morocco (couscous and tahini), as traditional Gulf dishes are few and fairly simple.

LINKAGES WITH ASIA AND BEYOND

Another factor that adds to the GCC countries' market attractiveness is the markets' linkages with Asia (especially South Asia) and beyond. These linkages make the commercial footprint of the GCC far larger than the domestic markets of its constituent countries.

South Asia: "Dubai–Mumbai Express"

South Asian workers—especially those in working-class roles—make up about half of the GCC nations' expatriates. In the UAE, the figure may be as high as 60 percent.[43] A portion of these expatriates come from families that have been based in the GCC countries for multiple generations but retain their expatriate status. Expatriate South Asians, even more than expatriates from the MENA world, are tied strongly to their countries of origin. This is partly because they face more barriers to "being at home" in the GCC countries; language is a large hurdle for most South Asians, and religion is another separating factor for non-Muslim Indians. Muslim Indians sometimes feel a greater affinity with the region than do their Hindu, Sikh, and Christian counterparts.

There are institutional mechanisms in place that keep expatriate workers linked to their homeland: the immigration process for such workers makes it virtually impossible for them to attain citizenship in any GCC country; residence status is almost always linked to employment; employment arrangements are generally short-term (renewable) contracts; and professional job packages typically include airline tickets "back home" each year. Because low-level workers are unable to bring their families to the Gulf, their hearts remain focused on their homeland. Expatriate workers also tend to support relatives in their home country: nearly $10 billion of remittances flowed from the UAE in 2004, of which 45 percent went to South or East Asia. Paradoxically, the workers who earn the least tend to remit the greatest proportion of their income: the 65 percent of expatriate workers in contracting and construction, as well as housemaids, send an astounding 70 percent of their income to their home countries.[44] Clearly, the financial focus of these workers is on supporting relatives abroad, accumulating savings, and returning home one day.

Many educated South Asians, like their counterparts in the MENA region, see the GCC region as a land of opportunity. The UAE—especially Dubai—is seen as a place where South Asians can work for higher wages and enjoy a higher standard of living while retaining the cultural feel of being in India, Pakistan, or Bangladesh. Hindi and Urdu are spoken commonly in Dubai shops, especially in more Asian neighborhoods, and traditional South Asian clothing is visible almost everywhere. Bollywood stars come to Dubai frequently for shows and now even for filming movies. The ARY broadcasting network, an Urdu-language channel serving Pakistanis worldwide, is based not in Pakistan but in Dubai. Wealthy South Asians are snapping up freehold properties in the UAE for its quality of life, infrastructure, and health care. The Gulf thus captures the attention of many of the billion-plus South Asians of all social classes, and activities in the GCC are followed closely by South Asians with friends and relatives there or with aspirations to migrate.

Investment ties between the GCC and South Asia are also increasing rapidly. In 2007, Indian investments in the UAE are expected to reach $5 billion—more than 60 percent higher than the year before. There are over 3,000 Indian companies registered in the

UAE, and nonoil trade between the UAE and India is over $14 billion per year. India's massive infrastructure needs (more than $300 billion over the next five years) are expected to be significantly funded by GCC investors.[45] Etisalat, the UAE telecommunications provider, acquired 26 percent and management control of Pakistan Telecommunications Company Ltd. in Pakistan's largest privatization deal. The UAE-based Emaar is undertaking a massive joint venture with a Pakistani agency to develop a 12,000-acre zone near Karachi into a modern city; the Abu Dhabi Group is working on a joint venture in Lahore to create a 55-story Shaikh Zayed Centre. One UAE enterprise is also exploring the development of a $5 billion oil refinery in South Asia. These projects are rooted in fundamental economic realities: the GCC has capital to export and needs large-scale, genuine businesses to fund while South Asia represents a huge consumer market in need of a vast array of businesses and infrastructure upgrades.

Capital of the Muslim World

The greater Muslim world is deeply connected with the GCC states—and especially with Saudi Arabia—due to a common belief in Islam. Of the over 2 million pilgrims who travel to Makkah each year, about 1.5 million are foreigners. Even among the domestic pilgrims, a majority are expatriates taking advantage of their time in Saudi Arabia to visit the holy sites.[46] A hefty $31 billion in spending (12 percent of the Saudi GDP) is linked to pilgrims and their needs: transportation, lodging, food, shopping, and other activities.[47] Pilgrims typically purchase gifts for loved ones, further stimulating the economies of the holy cities of Makkah and Madinah.

Multinational firms and local real estate developers have long appreciated the economic opportunity provided by religious visitors. Arguably the most conveniently located hotel in Makkah, just yards from the main entrance to the Grand Mosque, is the Makkah Hilton. Not far away is Le Meridien, another five-star hotel. Among the food outlets near the mosque is a prominent KFC. In December 2006, the massive Abraj Al Bait Mall was opened; it includes an array of international retailers such as Starbucks, Cartier, and H&M. The mall even contains an amusement park. And this is only the first step in a larger Abraj Al Bait project, which is envisioned to include housing, hotels, hospitals, and the world's seventh-tallest building.[48] While the core of these holy cities remains the religious sites, the surrounding business activity is accelerating at a remarkable pace.

Trade among Organization of the Islamic Conference (OIC) markets is steadily increasing as ties among Muslim countries grow. GCC investments in Turkey, for example, are on the rise: the Saudi firm Oger won out a hotly contested bid for the privatization of Turk Telekom in 2005[49] in which a UAE joint venture was also considered.[50] Kuwait Finance House, a Sharia-compliant bank, is pursuing an aggressive growth strategy in Malaysia. Al Rajhi Bank, a Saudi institution, has secured banking licenses in Malaysia and Indonesia. Dubai Islamic Bank is expanding rapidly in Pakistan. A resurgence of Muslim identity and Islamic cultural values worldwide is furthering the impetus to link OIC markets more closely, as is the basic need of GCC firms to expand abroad into markets where they can build viable and enduring franchises.

Links to Europe: Play and Stay

GCC countries, and especially the UAE, have built strong ties with Europe as a trade partner, tourist destination, and—increasingly—as a sunny place to work. The Gulf has become a tourist hot spot for British, German, French, and other visitors: London–Dubai is the fastest-growing long-haul air route in the world, and there are an amazing 62 flights per week between Dubai and London on Emirates Airlines alone. European tourists are well served in Gulf hotels and resorts, which offer sun, sand, and world-class customer service year-round. Europeans also enjoy working in the GCC countries because of the favorable conditions, which include no income taxes, English-speaking workplaces, generous compensation packages, and a high quality of life.

Of all Western countries, the UK has the deepest ties with the GCC and the UAE. There are about 120,000 UK nationals living in the UAE alone,[51] and another 30,000 in Saudi Arabia.[52] For perspective: there are more British citizens in the UAE than there are people living in Cambridge, and the number of UK residents in the UAE and Saudi Arabia combined is about the same as the population of Oxford.[53] More than 100,000 Britons have purchased homes in Dubai as primary or secondary residences since 2002.[54] British retailers have quickly realized that a presence in Dubai is crucial for tapping the expatriate market and providing them with familiar products in their second home. British Commonwealth nations such as South Africa, Australia, and New Zealand are also deeply connected to the UAE, through tourism, trade, and expatriate workers. Some 45,000 South Africans now reside in the UAE, attracted largely by the country's quality of life.[55]

Dubai has also become an appealing playground for wealthy Russians and other Eastern Europeans. There are an estimated 30,000 Russians living in Dubai,[56] and significant property holdings are believed to be controlled by Russian investors. About half a million Russians stayed in Dubai hotels in 2005 alone.[57] Dubai offers wealthy Russians a secure environment, loads of sun, and a degree of anonymity that is often welcome. The oil industry provides another set of reasons for linkages between Russia and the GCC countries, including their being ideal places in which to hold conferences and the opportunities for finding deals and establishing advisory relationships there.

China: Fast Friends

Trade between the Middle East and Asia more than doubled between 2000 and 2005, when it reached $240 billion. Trade between the GCC and China constitutes a large chunk of this activity, and investment flows between the two are growing at unprecedented levels. Leading global bankers estimate that GCC buyers may in 2007 alone make up to $30 billion in Asian investments, a large portion of which will head to China. Prince Alwaleed Bin Talal of Saudi Arabia has become one of the largest GCC investors in newly listed Chinese companies, particularly in its massive banks.[58]

China's voracious thirst for petroleum makes it a natural partner for the GCC states, and its need for investments complements the Gulf's excess capital. There are also political overtones to the relationship: China is widely seen as the greatest hope for restoring a balance of power between the United States and the rest of the world. As ties with the United States become awkward due to the war in Iraq and the global War on Terror, building bridges with China is a way to strengthen the Gulf region's geopolitical standing.

In April 2006, President Hu Jintao of China was accorded an uncommon level of hospitality by Saudi Arabia. He was invited to address the country's Shura Council and was escorted around the country by members of the royal family.[59] China could conceivably become one of Saudi Arabia's most important customers as Chinese prosperity rises and automobiles become more common. As BMWs increasingly share the roads with Beijing's famous bicycles, Saudi petroleum will find a highly lucrative market.

RISKS AND DRAWBACKS: THE ROSE HAS THORNS

Despite the overall attractiveness of the GCC countries as places to do business, doing so certainly has its risks and drawbacks. These risks and drawbacks—economic, political, and social—must be understood carefully by multinational firms as they craft their regional strategies.

Overdependence on Oil

In Chapter 2, I argued that the GCC economies are not all about oil—in fact, multinationals can grow their businesses in a much broader range of sectors. While this is certainly true from the perspective of business opportunities, the underlying driver of wealth creation in the region overwhelmingly remains oil and gas. All governments of GCC states derive the bulk of their income from hydrocarbons alone—due largely to the fact that taxes, service fees, and duty revenues on other goods are often negligible. Despite the Gulf-wide initiative to rapidly diversify economies, only the UAE and Bahrain have less than 60 percent of their total exports coming from the nonoil sector.[60] Even in these two nations, oil revenues account for three-quarters of government revenue. The hard reality of the matter is that a collapse in oil prices would severely curtail the wealth generation of the GCC, reducing the ability of the public and private sectors to invest and spend in the local economies. Firms must understand that betting on the GCC's sustained prosperity is largely a bet on oil prices not collapsing in the years ahead.

Fundamental indicators, however, suggest that oil prices are likely to remain above $40 per barrel in the medium and long term.

Figure 3.5 represents the forecast oil price, as seen by the US government's Energy Information Administration (EIA), and presents three scenarios—reference, high, and low.[61]

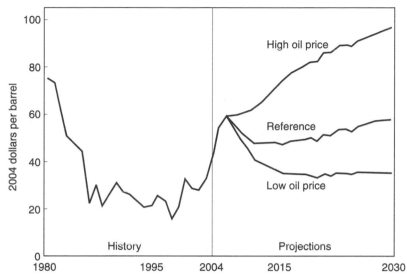

Figure 3.5 Oil prices under three scenarios, 1980–2030 (Sources: **History:** Energy Information Administration [EIA], *Annual Energy Review 2004*, DOE/EIA-0384[2004] [Washington, DC, August 2005], Web site, www.eia.doe.gov/emeu/aer **Projections:** EIA, *Annual Energy Outlook 2006*, DOE/EIA-0383[2006] [Washington, DC, February 2006])

The "reference" scenario is what the EIA believes to be most likely. The EIA expects a short-term dip in oil prices following their 2006 highs of $60 a barrel, but does not see prices dipping below $40 in real terms in the foreseeable future.[62] While $40 per barrel is a meaningful dip from the high prices of 2006, it is at the mid-2004 level: a boom period for the GCC. Even in a low-price scenario, the GCC is far better positioned than other oil exporters because its oil can be produced at a cost of $1 to $2 per barrel.[63] GCC oil can flow no matter how low the global market price goes.

The core reason why oil prices are expected to remain high is that the global demand for oil is growing. The EIA expects global demand for oil in 2030 to be at 118 million barrels per day—a 48 percent increase from the 2003 level of 80 million barrels per day.[64] An increasing share of this demand will come from

Asia—whose consumption of oil is expected to more than double between 2003 and 2030. China and India will be the main markets driving this rise in consumption as their massive populations continue to enjoy greater prosperity and more industrialized standards of living.[65] (See Figure 3.6.)

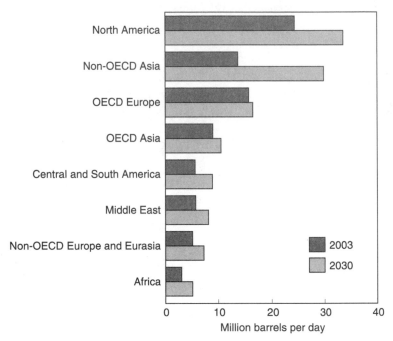

Figure 3.6 Oil consumption by region, 2003 and 2030 (Source: **2003:** Energy Information Administration [EIA], *International Energy Annual 2003* [May–July 2005], Web site, www.eia.doe.gov/iea/. **2030:** EIA. System for the Analysis of Global Energy Markets [2006])

Yes, a bet on the GCC is a bet on sustained oil prices. This seems like a fairly reasonable wager, however, as fundamental indicators suggest that $40-plus oil is here to stay. And under a "high" price scenario, oil prices could be 30 percent higher than they have ever been by 2030, and GCC wealth would be far greater than it is today.

Short-Term Corrections: Will the Bubble Burst?

With the high values currently placed on GCC assets, there is a definite risk of short-term market corrections in certain sectors.

One such sector is real estate: after a sustained boom, there is a real risk that the market is overpriced and will need to adjust. In Dubai, as of mid 2007, there were already signs of such a market correction. Another GCC sector that may be privatized is that of infrastructure and utility firms, which are overvalued today far above their peers in other emerging markets.

Such a burst in key sectors is likely to occur, in the same way that a correction in the GCC stock markets was needed in 2006 to make valuations more reasonable. Unlike that stock market correction, however, it is unlikely that the value of real assets will plummet 60 to 80 percent the way many listed securities did then. The fundamental drivers of real asset values—economic growth, business activity, and consumer demand—all seem to be in place. One can therefore expect some short-term decrease in value but long-term appreciation as the underlying economies develop.

Dangerous Neighbors: Political Risk

Although the GCC states have been remarkably stable, there is no doubt that they have some dangerous neighbors. One of them is Iraq, whose invasion of Kuwait sparked the first Gulf War in 1991 and whose ongoing occupation and reconstruction brings significant instability to the Middle East. Another troubling neighbor, which shares the very Gulf from which the GCC takes its name, is Iran.

Should war break out in Iran, mixed effects can be expected in the GCC. Oil prices would again go up, bringing increased short-term wealth (assuming that the oil could be safely transported out during the conflict). The multiple US bases in the GCC countries would likely be sprung into action, the political impact of which would depend on whether Iran was seen as a threat to the Gulf world or as merely a target of Western aggression. If Iran was seen as a threat to Arab states, supporting an American or Western attack would be considered more reasonable. If not, GCC regimes would be in the delicate position of being seen as a party to outside aggression in the region. The GCC states would likely try to dissuade the West from an attack on Iran, but if war broke out they would have extreme difficulty siding against the United States or the West.

While the Gulf states are well fortified, there is some risk of their being targeted for attack if they are seen as US or Western allies.

Under a worst-case scenario, the GCC states might need to hunker down and defend themselves, at the expense of their posture of openness and booming economic growth.

Avoiding the Unspeakable: Extremist Violence and Terrorism

Extremism and radical ideologies, though actively suppressed by the regimes of the GCC states, are a real threat to the region's sustained growth. Terror attacks in Saudi Arabia (not to mention the Saudi affiliation of many of the 9/11 terrorists) have had a palpable impact on the business environment and quality of life in the country and especially in Riyadh, the capital. Terror incidents elsewhere in the GCC states have hitherto been negligible or nonexistent. A terror attack could, however, cause great damage to GCC economies that are today noted for their openness and peaceful environment—especially the UAE. Dubai, seen by some as too permissive, could potentially be a target.

Extremist movements find followers when there is unemployment, dissatisfaction with the government, and poor education of the masses. The GCC states are increasingly concerned with creating jobs for young people and spreading prosperity not only as the right things to do but also as the best way to prevent extremism. Educational systems are being reviewed to ensure that there is intervention against extremist messages before young people have had a chance to hear or be influenced by them. Foreigners who are identified as terror threats are unwelcome and can swiftly be removed. The risk of extremist violence is present, but is being actively managed by regimes across the Gulf.

"Huddled Masses . . . "

The low standards of living and mistreatment of many foreign workers is a major issue for the GCC. According to observers such as Human Rights Watch, Dubai's low-paid construction workers toil for 12 hours or more each day, six days a week, for $150 per month. Companies provide housing, but in cramped and dreary quarters.[66] Instances of workers not being paid on time or not at all have become common: one Dubai resident told me about a person who was hired as a watchman for the construction site of a private home but was not paid for months. After living off the gifts of neighbors and well-wishers he finally made a complaint to a third party, embarrassing his employer. As a result, he was promptly shipped home. Other tales are told of overburdened workers who die from heat-related conditions and whose bodies are sent back with token payments to the relatives of the deceased.

While labor laws in the UAE and other GCC states are written to protect basic rights, the enforcement of these laws has historically been uneven. Although recent laws have allowed workers to form associations, most laborers feel powerless and unable to voice their concerns for fear of losing their jobs. Besides the basic ethical concerns raised by the mistreatment of workers, such cases of gross injustice are bad for business and for society in general, as they breed more deprivation, leading to resentment and then hostility between social classes—all of which threaten stability.

"... Yearning to Breathe Free"

Political rights—especially for expatriates—are extremely limited in the GCC states. Even as steps toward democratization are taken (e.g., elections for local councils and national assemblies) in various GCC countries, there are few political parties, and open discourse is very limited. Rarely in the GCC countries will you hear residents openly criticize their rulers. Satellite channels such as Al Jazeera provide a more balanced and critical view of government policy than ever before, but public expressions of discontent are few and far between.

Expatriates are, of course, excluded from voting because of their foreign nationality. Unlike the United States or many EU nations, however, there is hardly any path to citizenship: nonnational residents remain foreigners forever. The bargain with foreign workers is therefore clear: they are in a GCC country to work and to earn, but never will this be their country. This alienation from the political process is a real drawback for some expatriates—especially those from countries in which political participation is more widespread. Multinationals, when sending staff to the GCC, are well advised to ensure that their employees understand these dynamics and are willing to live with them.

Restrictive conditions of property ownership for expatriates—while improving greatly through the creation of free zones—are still another cause of alienation. The inability to own a business or a home (except in a free zone or in certain residential developments) acts to curtail one's sense of belonging and thus limits foreigners' feelings of allegiance to the countries in which they are living.

Still an Insider's Game

In all markets, connections matter. This is especially true in the GCC, where business communities are small and tight-knit and business success in great part relies on understanding the next moves the government will make and how they will create commercial opportunities. For multinational companies, this poses a challenge—but not unlike the challenges posed by China, India, and other foreign markets.

Savvy multinational firms build long-term relationships with local business leaders, actively cultivate those leaders' personal networks, and hire locals for key positions. These efforts require an investment of time, but can pay off handsomely. Commentators have noted, for example, that Swiss bankers' orientation toward long-term relationships with clients has often made them more successful than their American competitors in the GCC.[67] As GCC economies privatize, decision-making rights will become more widely distributed. While on the one hand this implies more "typical" and open market dynamics, it also speaks to the importance of a wide network of business relationships that can provide access to a broader set of opportunities. And in the GCC—more than elsewhere—the "insiders" need outside help to run their businesses and take them to the next level.

Race Matters

Racism in the GCC countries is a real issue, especially for nonwhite expatriates. While locals are often seen by outsiders as being beyond reproach, the locals themselves typically value white Europeans and Americans more highly than expatriate Arabs, Asians, and Africans. Nor is it uncommon, for example, for expatriate security guards to turn a blind eye to misbehaving local children whereas they would take action if the children were those of expatriates.

White customers may receive preferential treatment and be viewed as more important, wealthy, or deserving. A former colleague once reported astonishment at how local clients would look to a junior, white member of his team for the answers to tough questions when in fact a nonwhite manager was the team leader.

One area in which racism is often institutionalized is in pay scales. For the same job, locals will often receive higher pay, followed by Western expatriates, followed by Arab expatriates, with other Asians and Africans occupying the lowest end. I once worked with a client—himself an expatriate—who wanted us to assign different salaries when budgeting for new roles in the organization depending on the nationality of who was hired. For example, he wanted us to say that the salary for job X would be A if filled by a local, B if filled by a European, and so on. In line with our personal ethics and global standards, we refused. The board of the company, in a positive sign of changing times and a new mentality, later agreed with our stance.

KEY LESSONS

- The GCC states are a *highly attractive place to do business*, but are not without their risks and drawbacks.
- The GCC's market attractiveness is rooted in its *Opportunity Formula:* sustained prosperity and growth, attractive demographic shifts, and ongoing regulatory reform.
- The GCC *economies have been growing* at a rate of 6.5 percent—almost three times the rate of the world's most developed economies, with a GDP per capita many times higher than that of China and India.
- *A population boom and an emerging middle class* create new pockets of opportunity in the GCC countries.
- All GCC countries are *members of the WTO*, but read the fine print to see how open they really are.
- The Gulf's *linkages with the broader Middle East, Asia, and Europe* add to its market attractiveness.
- There are real *risks and drawbacks* to doing business in the GCC countries, including economic, political, and social factors.

Silicon from Sand: Essential Background on the GCC

INTRODUCTION

At the height of the oil crisis of the 1970s, Henry Kissinger, the renowned US secretary of state, paid a visit to King Faisal of Saudi Arabia. Saudi Arabia, through its charismatic oil minister Zaki Yamani, was at the forefront of an oil "embargo" that was having a huge and painful impact on the global economy. Insiders report that Secretary Kissinger's objective was to threaten the king by telling him that the embargo must be lifted or force might be used by the United States against Saudi Arabia. As the Saudi military was no match for US forces, Kissinger expected the threat would alarm King Faisal. The king's response was telling: "We come from the desert, and we have been living on camel milk and dates . . . and we can easily go back and live in the desert again."[1]

Saudi Arabia was not intimidated, and it continued to navigate oil markets through the crisis. King Faisal was later named *Time* magazine's Man of the Year for 1974.

At first glance, one might mistake the GCC states as a place with little history. Drive through the major cities of the region and you will find skyscrapers; new cars; state-of-the-art roads, infrastructure, and shopping malls; the pervasive use of mobile phones; and many other symbols of modernity. The running joke in Dubai is that the national bird has become the crane—not the animal, but the construction vehicle. Unlike London or New York, in Dubai you will see hardly any buildings more than 30 years old. Historical monuments are few and far between—arguably they are just being built today.

Don't let the overwhelming newness of the GCC countries mislead you. The region has a long history and values many of its traditions. Its public-sector and business leaders remember when times were very different, wealth was scarce, and commercial attention from the outside world was far less. Deeply connecting with GCC markets requires awareness of the region's history; social, political and economic dynamics; and evolving business environment. Multinational business leaders who understand the region's background can build deeper relationships with decision makers from all segments of the population—merchants and big-business leaders, consumers, public officials, and others. As with many emerging markets, efforts made to learn about the past and background of present conditions will often result in a better future for those who take the trouble to do so. Such research will surely produce a more rooted and strategically sound view of the current markets.

This chapter will provide you with the essential background you need—the must-have information about GCC markets. The goal is not to present an exhaustive history lesson, but rather, to convey the essence of each market through highlights of its past and present experiences. You will find that each GCC market has its own unique characteristics—like a distinct organic entity—shaped by its natural resources, geography, leadership, demographics, development strategies, and a host of other features.

Silicon is made from sand, and in the GCC this metaphor is particularly relevant. In the following pages we will distill the essentials of each market and how it has reached its current state. After reading this chapter, you will be able to approach each GCC country— and the entire region—with a more informed understanding.

THE UNITED ARAB EMIRATES: "THE TRAILBLAZER"

Over the past decade, the United Arab Emirates (UAE) has emerged as the GCC's trailblazer and center of innovation. The UAE—most notably Dubai—is the country that captures the most international attention because of its open business environment, fast-paced development, media savvy, and assertive global ambitions. Dubai has quickly become the region's economic hub, but it is not stopping there—it is also rapidly becoming a leading business player on the global stage. This is certainly an impressive feat for the UAE, a nation whose total population is a little more than 4 million—just half that of New York City. The UAE's progress is even more remarkable when one reflects on its origins: like the rest of the GCC, the UAE has humble roots.

The UAE consists of seven emirates, or states, federally united to form a sovereign entity, with each emirate remaining somewhat autonomous when it comes to local decisions. Abu Dhabi, the wealthiest and largest emirate, and the location of most of the country's oil, is the UAE's capital. Dubai, the next most powerful emirate, is a commercial center with global prominence. The remaining emirates are Sharjah (next door to Dubai), Ras al-Khaimah, Ajman, Fujairah, and Umm al-Qaiwain. The seven emirates were brought together in 1971, before which the term "UAE" did not exist.

For centuries, the coast of the Arabian Gulf consisted of small chiefdoms who were perpetually engaged in dynastic feuds and territorial disputes. The tribes of the region had common cultural traits but were not organized as a united political entity. In the mid-nineteenth century, the rulers of the states that currently compose the UAE entered into a landmark agreement with the UK in order to resolve a number of long-standing maritime disputes. In 1892, another agreement with Britain was made, under which local rulers agreed to two conditions: (1) not to enter into agreements with any foreign powers without UK approval, and (2) not to cede territory to anyone but the UK. In return, the Trucial States— as they came to be known after this truce—would receive protection from the British. The Trucial States, while never colonized, did accept a large measure of British influence over their international affairs in exchange for protection. The UK and its Commonwealth nations have, as a result, had greater connectivity with the UAE than have other Western nations.

As colonialism faded in the postwar period and smaller nations began to assert their sovereignty, it was inevitable that the Trucial States' agreement with the UK would be ended.

One proposal for the States' future disposition was to create a federation that would include all the Trucial States plus Bahrain and Qatar. Terms could not be agreed on, however, with the latter two states, and therefore the remaining states formed the United Arab Emirates in December 1971.[2] Abu Dhabi was chosen as the capital, and its ruler, Sheikh Zayed bin Sultan Al Nahyan, became president of the UAE.

According the UAE's constitution, the presidential term is to last five years. One vision for the federation was that the office would rotate among the rulers (emirs) of the constituent states, who collectively form the country's Supreme Council of the Union (SCU). In practice, however, the presidency has remained with Abu Dhabi since 1971, which is a reflection of Abu Dhabi's economic dominance: Abu Dhabi controls 94 percent of the UAE's oil reserves and contributes the largest share of its GDP. Sheikh Zayed ruled the UAE from its formation until his death in 2004, after which his son Sheikh Khalifa bin Zayed Al Nahyan was made ruler of Abu Dhabi and president of the UAE. The Supreme Council of the Union plays a central role in setting federal policy, combining legislative and executive powers. The SCU is empowered to legislate on all matters of state, and it ratifies federal decrees.

As the presidency of the UAE has de facto become Abu Dhabi's role, the role of vice president and prime minister belongs to Dubai. As head of the government, the prime minister leads the Council of Ministers (the cabinet) and shapes the executive policy of the country. The current prime minister is Sheikh Mohammed bin Rashid Al Maktoum, the ruler—some say CEO—of Dubai and the figure credited with driving much of Dubai's development over the past decade. Since Sheikh Mohammed assumed the role after the death of his older brother, Sheikh Maktoum bin Rashid, in 2006, many observers have been looking forward to an increased spirit of dynamism and openness at the federal level in line with Sheikh Mohammed's track record in Dubai.

The closest equivalent to a parliament in the UAE is the Federal National Council (FNC), which consists of 40 members and plays only a consultative role and does not make laws. Abu Dhabi and Dubai are allocated the most seats in the FNC, followed by Ras al-Khaimah and Sharjah and then the other emirates. There are no formal political parties in the FNC or elsewhere in the UAE political system.

ECONOMIC TRANSFORMATION

Historically, the UAE's core economic activities have been modest, consisting mainly of pearl diving, fishing, and commodity trading along its coasts, small-scale agriculture in the oases, and animal herding in the vast deserts. Facilitating trade between the Arab world and South Asia allowed many local merchants to accumulate wealth as brokers. As related to us by a senior Emirati[3] business leader, "seeing foreign faces [in the market] was a good sign"—it meant business was strong. In the 1950s and 1960s, imports grew more than tenfold, and Dubai became an increasingly important—though regionally focused—trade center.[4]

The UAE economy has changed radically, of course, since it began exporting oil in 1962. The country possesses over 8 percent of the world's proven oil reserves,[5] almost all of which are controlled by Abu Dhabi. In 2005, Dubai and Sharjah collectively exported only 6 percent of the UAE's oil. Total UAE oil exports were close to $50 billion in 2005.

Oil income has affected the emirates differently. Abu Dhabi, which controls nearly all the oil, became more firmly established as the dominant emirate in the federation. The leadership of Abu Dhabi is now—at least openly—beyond question. Abu Dhabi has also become a huge exporter of capital, largely through the Abu Dhabi Investment Authority (ADIA). ADIA guards its secrets carefully, but expert observers have estimated its assets under management to be at least $250 billion. According to the Oxford Business Group, only one institutional investor—the Bank of Japan, the nation's central bank—has more assets. Although ADIA's investment philosophy is quite conservative, its portfolio continues to grow at a healthy pace, and the institution is strong due largely to the expertise of the world-class management team it has assembled through global recruiting. Investment managers from around the world come to ADIA with their proposals, seeking funding from this blue-chip institution. In a recent article, a senior executive from a leading global bank confessed that ADIA was one of very few institutions that the bank's CEO would visit at the drop of a hat.[6] Without a doubt, ADIA is one of the most important investors in the world.

Dubai's prosperity, however, is linked less directly to oil. In fact, oil revenues contribute less than 10 percent of the emirate's

GDP—and that figure is declining, due to both the emirate's active diversification strategy and a relative scarcity of oil resources. Insiders report that Sheikh Rashid bin Saeed, the ruler of Dubai from 1958 to 1990 and father of Dubai's current ruler, when congratulated by geologists who had discovered that Dubai's oil reserves were larger than originally thought, urged his advisors to plan as if oil were to run out sooner. This was consistent with Dubai's long-standing attitude of caution and skepticism toward its oil reserves. Thus, for decades, in addition to nurturing its oil business, Dubai has also focused on developing itself as a center of trade and commerce. As early as the time of Sheikh Maktoum bin Hasher, who ruled Dubai from 1894 to 1906, Dubai abolished commercial taxes so as to attract traders and develop its regional profile.[7]

Oil resources have, nonetheless, brought huge capital flows into Dubai from Abu Dhabi and the broader GCC. This phenomenon has been especially noticeable in recent years, which have witnessed a sustained boom in Dubai's real estate market and other key sectors. Wealth from the broader region has poured into Dubai in the form of both investment and consumption: Dubai hotels, for example, are full of visitors from Saudi Arabia and other GCC states who come to Dubai for weekend getaways. Dubai is the destination of choice for training seminars and management retreats, not to mention for family holidays.

Prosperity in the UAE has also benefited the other, smaller emirates despite their limited oil reserves. Sharjah, for example, has come to play a central role as a "suburb" of Dubai and a source of housing for Dubai's booming workforce. Traffic between Sharjah and Dubai has become a chronic problem in recent years, with many commuters spending hours in bumper-to-bumper traffic every day. Sharjah's more conservative social environment is sometimes seen as more family friendly than the glamorous, more cosmopolitan Dubai. Ras al-Khaimah is also becoming an increasingly important business hub, partly because it is less crowded and more affordable than Dubai.

OPEN FOR BUSINESS

Perhaps the single most important element in the UAE's success story is the country's remarkable effectiveness in creating a business-friendly environment. While being open for business is in some ways a long-standing attitude in the UAE—and especially in Dubai—measures taken in recent years have had a tremendous impact in transforming the country's business environment.

As illustrated in Figure 4.1, four main strategies have been actively managed in order to drive the open-for-business environment that marks the UAE and especially Dubai.

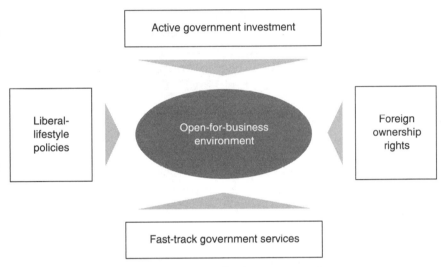

Figure 4.1 Creating the UAE's open-for-business environment

Active Government Investment

The first—and arguably the most critical—strategy has been active government investment in the local economy. While the GCC's oil states have overall been net exporters of capital, Dubai has invested its relatively modest oil income in development of its business infrastructure and environment. This long-term strategy, sustained through the administrations of Sheikhs Rashid (1958–90), Maktoum (1990–2006), and now Mohammed (2006–present), has consisted of an investment scope that begins with infrastructure but expands ambitiously to a broad set of other industries.

Although far less glamorous than later investments by the government of Dubai, bread-and-butter infrastructure spending has been essential to the emirate's success. The government's investment in Port Rashid and in developing the Dubai Creek (an important waterway snaking through the city) during the 1970s set a trend of sustained focus on transportation infrastructure. In 1980, the massive Jebel Ali Port—costing $3 billion to build[8]—propelled the emirate's shipping capabilities to a new level. Jebel Ali was able to receive and re-export goods from the Far East, South Asia, Europe, and Africa in unprecedented volumes, and could accommodate the increasingly massive container ships favored by the shipping industry. Dubai's global leadership in ports management and its prominent Dubai Ports World company can trace their roots to these investments. Jebel Ali created real trade flows, distinct from oil, which laid the groundwork for onshore economic development. Many insiders therefore credit Jebel Ali—the massive, boring zone of shipping containers—for driving Dubai's long-term development more than sleek and glitzy assets like the world-famous, "seven-star" Burj al-Arab hotel.

Equally important, UAE governments have extended their investment scope beyond their core infrastructure sectors such as transportation, power, and telecommunications in order to include those sectors, such as media and health care, that are becoming ever more essential in the twenty-first century. Dubai has led the way with its Internet and Media Cities, Health Care City, Knowledge Village, and a host of other similar ventures. In addition, the massive Dubailand project, planned to be twice the size of Disney World, aims to spur the booming tourism industry even further. Abu Dhabi is developing a major free zone on its Saadiyat Island, whose goal is to span a broad range of industry and service sectors including manufacturing, hotels, financial services, and even agriculture. Sharjah has its own Hamriya Free Zone, Ajman has the Ajman Free Zone, and Fujairah has a Free Trade Zone (FTZ). Ras al-Khaimah's equivalent—the RAK FTZ—is growing rapidly and positioning itself as a "stress-free zone,"[9] subtly contrasting itself with its increasingly crowded and expensive counterparts in Dubai.

Abu Dhabi, which has long focused its investment activity outside the region, has recently undertaken significantly more local endeavors through various vehicles. Mubadala, a major investment platform for the emirate, has invested in shipping and ship terminals, as well as the local IT sector, training and education, and health care. One noteworthy local investment is a project to create a

Cleveland Clinic Abu Dhabi—combining the expertise of the renowned Cleveland Clinic in Ohio, often ranked America's top hospital for heart disease, with Mubadala's capital—catering to the health care needs of a wealthy and growing region.

Active government investment, while crucial in jump-starting the UAE economy, does carry the risk of "crowding out" the private sector. The various emirates are managing this balance by increasingly focusing their investments on early-stage and strategic projects for which the private sector may lack the expertise or appetite and by building zones for the private sector rather than building businesses. Another important step is that government investment agencies are funding companies that later list on stock exchanges and thereby transfer to the private sector. Tabreed (a cooling company) and Aldar Properties (Abu Dhabi's leading real estate company) are two of Mubadala's listed investments.

Foreign Ownership Rights

Despite their remarkable prosperity, the GCC nations remain largely closed economies. Deregulation is occurring rapidly, but rules requiring majority ownership by local citizens remain the norm[10] throughout the Gulf and also in UAE. For example, operating companies require 51 percent ownership by UAE nationals. As implied in their names, however, the "free zones" are business parks in which foreign individuals and firms are able to fully own their businesses.

By providing foreign ownership rights, free zones have been able to attract a diverse set of businesses and entrepreneurs. Major multinational firms such as CNN, Microsoft, and Oracle have set up offices in Dubai's Media and Internet cities in order to take advantage of both the commercial opportunity of the broader region and the entrepreneurial freedom of full ownership rights. Major banking institutions such as Deutsche Bank and Goldman Sachs feel comfortable entering the Dubai International Financial Centre, where they can fully control their own businesses. Giving majority control to local partners, as required outside a free zone, would almost certainly not be acceptable to these companies.

Far greater in number than these large multinationals, however, is the pool of entrepreneurs from the Arab world, South Asia, and the West who set up shop in the UAE to benefit from its opportunities and quality of life. In 1999, for example, the Dubai Airport Free Zone (DAFZ) reported that 82 percent of companies operating there were European or American.[11] Media City attracts a large number of Arab journalists and aspiring media moguls, and Internet City attracts a substantial pool of South Asian IT entrepreneurs and companies. Free zones are playing a crucial role in fostering a culture of entrepreneurship in the UAE, in addition to their role in attracting multinational firms and the economic boost they bring.

Foreign ownership of "freehold" residential properties both attracts international real estate investors and makes expatriates more comfortable living in the UAE. Foreign freehold is restricted to certain development areas and projects, but includes high-profile ventures such as the Palm Island complex. A series of man-made islands that form a palm-tree shape, the project is the self-declared Eighth Wonder of the World. Dubai has also announced another residential project, known as the World Islands, which will include 300 small, private islands in the shape of various nations and states, with prices beginning at around $7 million each. Among the first purchasers of World Island properties is Sir Richard Branson of Virgin, who bought the island representing Great Britain.

Fast-Track Government Services

The economies of the GCC countries are all highly regulated, and regulation inevitably brings with it bureaucracy. Bureaucracy especially affects expatriates, who, in addition to the universally required documents such as driver's licenses and birth certificates, need to obtain further documentation permitting them to remain in the country, to work, to maintain a bank account, and to engage in a host of other activities that would be routine in their home countries. To cancel a resident visa and return home, for example, foreigners need to dispose of local property, close out their leases, and even close bank accounts linked to resident status.

Within this environment of bureaucracy, the UAE has significantly differentiated itself from its neighbors by creating a network of remarkably efficient government services. These services, especially in Dubai, generally operate on a "fast track"—or at least are fast compared with the time required to render the same services by similarly regulated countries. These fast-track capabilities contribute significantly to the country's open-for-business environment.

On flights into the UAE, you will not see any flight attendant walking through the cabin handing out landing cards. The reason is simple—landing cards are not required by the UAE. GCC nationals just show their passports and enter. Citizens of the United States, the EU, and several other nations simply have their passports stamped by an immigration officer on arrival and come into the country without hassle. Citizens of countries requiring visas can have visas arranged for by their hotels or hosts, and they can pick up those visas at desks located in the airport. For a fee, travelers can arrange for premium service (called "Marhaba" in Dubai) and have an airport worker whisk them through the process. Residents of Dubai and very frequent travelers can have electronic passcards made, which enable them to complete the entire entry process with just a swipe of the card.

For perspective, contrast this process with that required to enter the United States. Well before flights land, instructional videos are shown demonstrating how to fill out various forms. There is a white form for some, a green form for others, and a blue form for all. Visitors get their pictures and fingerprints taken at immigration. Consider this: American citizens have to fill out more paperwork to enter the United States than they do to enter the UAE!

Dubai "eGovernment" is another example of fast-track government services at work. The suite of electronic tools includes an "ePay" service through which residents—called "customers"—can pay fees, fines, and other charges with credit cards and by other electronic means. There is an "AskDubai" service, which allows customers to communicate at any time with all relevant Dubai government agencies via phone, fax, e-mail, and online chat. There is even an "mDubai" service connecting customers to government agencies through cell phone messaging, or SMS.

Liberal-Lifestyle Policies

Dubai is renowned worldwide for its live-and-let-live attitude toward personal lifestyles. Unlike its stricter neighbors, Dubai has bars and nightclubs in its hotels, which are active with tourists and expatriates. Personal attire is not strictly regulated, and you will often see tourist and expatriate women in tube tops and miniskirts in the same hotel lobby as Emirati women dressed in traditional robes and head scarves. A female American colleague of ours who visited Dubai on business packed a suitcase full of long skirts and tops only to spend a week in disbelief at how scantily clad other foreign women were in malls, restaurants, and bars.

While the international media often sensationalizes the lifestyle freedoms of Dubai (the emirate is often called the Las Vegas of the Middle East), Dubai is not a binary society composed of puritanical traditionalists on the one hand and ultramodern hedonists on the other. The emirate's policies were designed to make the place hospitable to all—including the European business traveler or expatriate who likes a glass of wine with his or her dinner. Dubai's permissive environment, however, is in stark contrast with that of some of its neighbors, and this has made the emirate more visitor friendly for many.

Abu Dhabi has a much more conservative social environment than Dubai. Abu Dhabi has the feel of an Arab city, with Arabic spoken more frequently than in Dubai. People dress more conservatively—not by law, but as a matter of custom. Alcohol is served in hotels, and bars, and nightclubs are emerging, but not nearly as rapidly as in Dubai. Abu Dhabi's form of relaxed lifestyle is more like that of a traditional Middle Eastern city in which conservative norms are preserved but strict rules of dress and social behavior are not enforced.

(USUALLY) HEALTHY COMPETITION

While certainly united as a federation, the emirates of the UAE retain their distinct identities and do engage in subtle rivalry and competition. Abu Dhabi executives will, for example, privately express how important—"unlike Dubai"—it is to them to preserve their traditional culture and social environment. Dubai's movers and shakers, at the same time, often consider themselves the real drivers of change in the country despite officially being the second-fiddle emirate that can never control the federal government. The other emirates carve out their niches as well, eager not to be left behind as the UAE advances onto the global stage.

For the most part, competition among the emirates has been good for business, as each one has tried to outdo the others to attract firms, tourists, and staff. The creation of free zones in smaller emirates is one example of how competition is creating more opportunities for business. Competition is also raising service standards in the public sector: Ras al-Khaimah's RAK FTZ, for example, has announced an on-site Naturalization and Immigration Office dedicated exclusively to serving the more than 2,400 companies in the free zone.[12]

Rivalry among the emirates, may, however, at times lead to the inefficient allocation of capital. Air travel is a prime example of this phenomenon. Until 2003, the UAE's official carrier was Gulf Air: a joint venture enterprise including Bahrain and Oman. Dubai launched Emirates Airlines in 1985—in one sense, breaking away from the national carrier—and rapidly made it an international success. Despite Emirates Airlines' being fully owned by UAE investors and having a record of excellent performance and a growing international reputation, Abu Dhabi decided to retain the Gulf Air joint venture as the UAE's national carrier. Abu Dhabi then founded Etihad Airways in 2003, made it the UAE's national carrier, and invested heavily in it to ensure world-class service. The result is that the UAE now has two state-of-the-art, and very expensive, international airlines with hubs about 90 minutes apart by road and 20 minutes by air—and the UAE's total population is less than half that of New York City!

SAUDI ARABIA: THE CORE MARKET

To many outsiders, the Kingdom of Saudi Arabia (abbreviated as KSA) raises more questions than answers. Saudi Arabia is a complex place with a long history, plays an important role in world affairs, and has deep social issues that need to be addressed. Many outsiders see the KSA as mysterious, opaque, and even scary. Commercially, however, one fact is clear: Saudi Arabia is the core market of the GCC, and understanding it is critical to building a large-scale franchise in the Gulf.

Here are some hard facts about the Kingdom:

- The Saudi population is 25 million—two-thirds of the GCC total.[13]

- The Saudi GDP is around $400 billion—half the total for the GCC countries.[14]
- Saudi Arabia has the world's largest oil reserves—22 percent of the world's total and more than those of Kuwait and the UAE combined.[15]

The modern state of Saudi Arabia traces its roots to an alliance in the middle of the eighteenth century, and in the center of the Arabian Peninsula, between a local ruler named Muhammad bin Saud and a religious leader named Muhammad Abd al-Wahhab. Abd al-Wahhab was a reformer, seeking to return the peninsula to an austere form of Islam that he believed to be more authentic and free of superstition and of other modern innovations. The Al Saud family fought for over 150 years with other local rulers, the Ottoman Empire, and even Egypt in its efforts to solidify control of the Arabian Peninsula. Abdul Aziz Al Saud, the founder of the modern kingdom, captured the city of Riyadh in 1902 and went on to take control of most of the rest of the peninsula in the coming decades. In 1932, the country now known as Saudi Arabia—named after the ruling family—was unified.

Saudi Arabia is made up of three main regions, each with a very different character. Toward the coast of the Red Sea (the western area) is the region known as the Hijaz. Islam's holiest cities, Makkah and Madinah, are located here, and this is also the birthplace of the Prophet Muhammad. Through centuries of hosting pilgrims and trading via land and sea, the Hijaz became the most cosmopolitan, diverse, and international part of the Arabian Peninsula. Saudis of the Hijaz trace their roots back to many regions and cultures, including Africa, Muslim Asia, and Iran. The holy cities of Makkah and Madinah shape the ethos of the Hijaz, while the port city of Jeddah is the commercial center.

At the center of the peninsula is the region known as the Najd. This desert region is home to Riyadh—the Saudi capital—and the area from which the Al Saud family traces its roots. The Eastern Provinces have, since the discovery of oil, become centers of oil production and industrial activity. The most important commercial center there is Al Khobar. Saudis from different regions will adhere to somewhat different cultural attitudes and practices, with the people of the Najd often known for toughness and strict religious beliefs, while the people of the Hijaz are better known for their hospitality and warmth.

To understand the complexities of Saudi Arabia, it is crucial to grasp the roles of the country's three central sociopolitical groups, whose interactions and interdependencies shape the KSA's political and economic life. The three legs of the Kingdom's "delicate tripod," are the monarchy, the religious establishment, and the private business sector, as depicted in Figure 4.2.

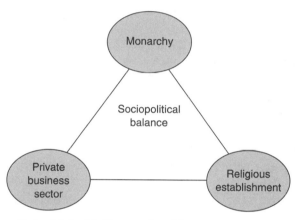

Figure 4.2 Saudi Arabia's "delicate tripod"

The Monarchy

Since King Abdul Aziz's death in 1953, the monarchy has rotated within a single generation: from one to another of the sons of Abdul Aziz. His first successor, Saud, reigned for 11 years but was then replaced during his lifetime by his half brother Faisal. Faisal, supported by the royal family and the religious authorities, was seen as more capable of handling state affairs and brought a more institutional approach to the government. Prior to the accession of King Faisal, for example, government salaries were paid directly from the king's personal accounts instead of from the state treasury.

King Faisal, who ruled from 1964 to 1975, steered the Kingdom through the first oil boom and was seen as down-to-earth, upright, and firm. He was assassinated by a relative (who was executed after an investigation) and then succeeded peacefully by his half brother

Khalid. Khalid was succeeded by King Fahd, whose rule—1982 to 2005—was the longest since that of King Abdul Aziz. During the last 10 years of his reign, however, Fahd was in deteriorating health, and day-to-day affairs were increasingly managed by his successor King Abdullah. Abdullah is considered a strong and capable leader, better able to assert himself and Saudi interests than was his predecessor.

The Saudi monarchy has had a long and fruitful relationship with the United States. King Abdul Aziz met directly with President Franklin Roosevelt and Great Britain's Prime Minister Winston Churchill and was famously photographed in his traditional garb on the deck of a ship with the two. Even from the early days, the core elements of the implicit pact were evident: Saudi Arabia was to provide a steady, cheap supply of oil in exchange for full support of the monarch, including whatever technical support was required, and—if needed—military protection. During the first Gulf War of 1990–91, the pact was honored, when, after Iraq's invasion of Kuwait, the United States mobilized an international coalition to protect Saudi Arabia and repel Saddam Hussein's forces from Kuwait. Saudi Arabia was made to foot much of the bill for the military support, which had a deep and lasting impact on the Kingdom's fiscal health, and the United States and its allies were ensured a stable supply of oil.

On the economic front, the vehicle of Saudi-US cooperation has been the all-important national oil company now known as Saudi Aramco. Throughout the 1930s and 1940s Saudi Arabia signed a number of concessions with a group of US oil companies, and in 1944 the operating umbrella company was named the Arabian American Oil Company (Aramco). The terms of agreement between the Saudis and Aramco have continued to evolve over time. As more oil was discovered, Aramco's mandate was extended in return for greater fees going to the Saudis. The original rental fee (before oil was discovered) was a mere 5,000 British pounds plus a loan to the Saudi government and a modest royalty payment on the sale of any discovered oil. By 1950, a 50-50 profit sharing agreement between Aramco and the government had been reached.[16]

As Saudi Arabia became more sophisticated, it increasingly demanded a greater role in Aramco. Oil Minister Zaki Yamani first publicly called for a Saudi stake in Aramco in 1968, and five years later Saudi Arabia took a 25 percent stake in the company. Ownership reached 60 percent in 1974, and by 1988 the company—renamed Saudi Aramco—was fully owned by the Saudis. Aramco's first Saudi president—Ali Al Naimi—took the reins in 1984 and today is the Kingdom's oil minister. Al Naimi began working with Aramco at the age of 11, and his rise embodies the phased manner in which Saudi Arabia and its nationals have taken control of their oil industry.

While full control of the oil revenue grants the monarchy formidable power, and its foreign alliances give it international protection, to be secure the Crown needs another crucial element: the perception of religious legitimacy. It's very telling that the monarch's official title is not King of Saudi Arabia, but instead the much more faith-based Custodian of the Two Holy Mosques, referring to the sanctuaries of Makkah and Madinah. He controls the country's natural resources, and in return maintains the public services and religious sites without directly taxing people's incomes. But in a country so deeply defined by Islam, the monarch also needs to justify his role in religious terms before his people by enforcing Islamic law and upholding religious practices.

The Religious Establishment

Islam is at the core of Saudi Arabia's identity. The country's flag is Islam's declaration of faith: "There is no god but God and Muhammad is the Messenger of God." The country's constitution, according to its official documents, is the Qur'an. The legal system, at least officially, must be entirely consistent with Islamic law.

In this environment, institutions that represent Islamic authority will naturally be influential. While Islam has no formal system of clergy or ordination, it does have religious scholars—called *ulema*—who are trained to interpret Islamic law. A judge in an Islamic court is called a *qadi*, and a *qadi* must be trained by scholars. In Saudi Arabia, government courts are fully Islamic and presided over by *qadi*s, as the judicial system is Islamic law. The arbitration of commercial disputes, however, can occur through nonreligious institutions with ultimate recourse to the state-run Islamic courts.

Besides their role in the Islamic courts, the *ulema* also wield significant influence in the government and society. Several government agencies, such as the Ministry of Endowments (which oversees the mosques) and the unique Authority for Enjoining Good and Forbidding Evil, are inherently religious institutions. Additionally, religious scholars hold significant popular sway over the Saudi people through their lectures and lessons in mosques and elsewhere. While the media has become a great deal more liberal, giving Saudi readers and viewers a much broader set of perspectives with which to view the world, religious scholars, who have generally remained conservative and traditional, continue to speak with authoritative voices on the public and satellite airwaves.

Religious extremism is a serious problem in Saudi Arabia. In addition to several Saudi nationals having been involved in the 9/11 attacks in New York City and Washington, DC, and to Osama bin Laden being a renegade Saudi, domestic terrorism has become a major issue. Contrary to the perception of many outsiders, the extremists' core target is not foreigners; it's locals who are seen to be compromising their values and the national interest. The Saudi government, which itself is a major target of terrorist activity, has every incentive to crack down on extremists and is doing so. The religious establishment is also intent on confronting Islamic extremism, as it misrepresents Islam, discredits religious education, and puts legitimate religious scholars at risk.

In recent trips to Saudi Arabia, I have personally noticed the effect terrorism is having on public life and the public discourse. Parking lots of many five-star hotels have been closed for fear of bombings. Metal detectors stand at the doors of hotels. The front pages of newspapers show photographs of terror suspects being hunted, and one particularly graphic cover showed a series of photographs with "X"s over the photos of suspects who had been apprehended. Editorials in the Arabic press discuss the need to understand the "true Islam" and to denounce the violence. On evening television, I saw a religious scholar discussing how "our brothers from Afghanistan" who were resorting to terrorism had misunderstood the religion and needed to be guided. Privately, an insider confided to me how surprising and painful it had been for Saudis to see their youth—"and they are from us" he explained— taking extremist views. He interpreted this as an embarrassing failure of elders and educators.

The Private Business Sector

The role of the private business sector in Saudi Arabia has been increasing steadily. This trend is natural when one considers the underlying forces shaping the economy. First, population growth has created enormous pressures to create jobs—unemployment was at 13 percent in 2006, and excess employment in the public sector masks the true scale of the problem.[17] As everywhere, Saudi Arabia turns toward the private sector to create jobs. In return, the private sector calls for greater privatization and economic reform.

A second force propelling the private sector is the transfer of control of major business conglomerates from their founders to cadres of professional managers working alongside the children of founders. This second generation of private-sector leadership tends to be highly educated (often in America), well trained in global business practices, and eager to drive their businesses and the broader economy forward. This trend is not specific to Saudi Arabia but is apparent throughout the GCC countries.

The private sector is driving reform to spur economic growth and make the Kingdom more business friendly. One segment in which this is clearly visible is the media, with the growing prevalence of satellite TV. Another segment in which rapid growth is occurring is that of financial services, for which an unprecedented number of banking and insurance licenses were issued in 2006. More fundamental is the role that private business leaders are playing in reshaping the country's business regulations to conform with global standards: Saudi Arabia's WTO accession in 2005 would not have been possible without the involvement of private-sector leaders in framing the reforms. As the Kingdom shifts toward a more open posture, private business leaders are at the forefront.

QATAR: THE UPSTART

Qatar is a tiny state with huge ambitions. The upstart of the GCC, Qatar is pursuing a development strategy that draws on lessons learned from its neighbors and actively seeks to avoid pitfalls that have caught other GCC economies. Although the number of Qatari citizens is less than the number of people in a single US congressional district, the state has become a serious actor in the global economy due principally to its abundant natural gas reserves.

Like other GCC states, Qatar entered into an agreement with the UK in the early twentieth century according to which it would not enter any other foreign partnerships and would not dispose of territories except to the UK. Sheikh Abdullah bin Jassim Al Thani, recognized as the ruler, was from a family that had been in Qatar for centuries and that traced its ancestry to the Najd area of the Arabian Peninsula. Through a series of agreements, Qatar deepened its military and political ties to the UK. Oil was discovered in Qatar in 1940, but due to World War II Qatar did not begin exporting it until 1949.

Qatar was, for a brief period, one of the nine Trucial States negotiating to become a new political entity after the end of the era of British protection in 1971. Qatar and Bahrain, however, did not agree to the terms that the seven emirates that formed the UAE did, and therefore Qatar became an independent state.

Since independence, the role of ruler has changed hands only twice—and both times, through bloodless coups within the royal family. The first time in 1972, when Khalifa bin Hamad took over from Emir Ahmad. The second transfer of power occurred in 1995, when Sheikh Hamad bin Khalifa deposed his father. Sheikh Hamad, still Qatar's leader, has declared his vision for a more democratic Qatar, with municipal and eventually parliamentary elections. The trend toward elections at municipal and parliamentary levels is common in the GCC countries, and a blend of monarchy and elected local officials represents what could be dubbed Gulf-style democracy. In the political realm, Qatar, like other GCC states, is a strong ally of the United States and served as the staging ground for American operations in the 2003 invasion of Iraq. It remains the regional base for the US Central Command.

Qatar's rise to prosperity has been rapid, and its level of wealth is expected to increase substantially. Until 1973, when oil production and prices rose sharply, Qatar's economic status was very modest. Today, Qatar's GDP per capita is among the highest in the world. The reason is simple: Qatar has the third-largest natural gas reserves on earth and is expected, by 2010, to be the world's largest exporter of liquefied natural gas (LNG). According to some forecasts, Qatar could supply one-third of the planet's LNG needs.[18] Yet it has a population of under 1 million; native Qataris number only a couple hundred thousand. As a result, some have speculated that Qatar's GDP per capita could become the highest in the entire world.

Intense public-sector investment is a theme of the Qatari economy that is likely to continue for the foreseeable future. According to press reports, the Qatari government has committed to a $100 billion investment program that includes $75 billion for oil and gas, $15 billion for infrastructure, and $10 billion for tourism and cultural projects.[19] Multinational companies are hotly pursuing the lucrative contracts associated with these massive projects and are eager to demonstrate their commitment to Qatar. GE, for example, has established a research center in the state as a sign of the long-term partnership it wishes to foster. The economic activity associated with natural gas is expected to extend far beyond the energy sector into areas such as health care, construction, real estate, retail sales, telecommunications, and a host of population-linked industries.

Qatar, taking lessons learned from its GCC neighbors to heart, has wisely focused on diversifying its economy as rapidly as possible. One prominent nonenergy asset is the media outlet Al-Jazeera, which has rapidly become a key source of Arab and Muslim outlooks on world affairs. Al-Jazeera has maintained the independence of its voice and opinions, criticizing Arab states (and even Qatar) and ensuring that it not be seen as a mouthpiece for government propaganda. This, along with an extensive network of correspondents worldwide, has allowed Al-Jazeera to differentiate itself from local news stations in the region that are seen as not as free from government influence. Experts see Al-Jazeera as a breakthrough for free speech in the Arab world and have viewed its phases of sensationalism and increased restraint with much interest. Another example of diversification is in the financial services sector: the new Qatar Financial Centre (QFC) represents the state's commitment to developing a world-class banking and investment sector.

To quickly migrate toward a knowledge-based economy, Qatar has made a remarkable level of investment in its educational system. Qatar has partnered with leading US universities to create its Education City complex and has attracted several marquee institutions. Cornell University, for example, has established a degree-granting medical college in the country with a high level of connection with Cornell's medical school in New York. US-based faculty members travel frequently between the two campuses and transfer best practices to Qatar-based colleagues in an ongoing manner. Other universities, including Texas A&M and Carnegie Mellon, have also created Qatar campuses.

Qatar's balanced investment in both hard (e.g., gas pipelines and water plants) and soft (education and health care) infrastructure bodes well for the country's future. Qatar's leaders are keen to apply significant capital from their current prosperity to making the state even more competitive in the longer term. Qatar is thus an upstart whose vision is to ensure that its success is truly lasting.

BAHRAIN: WALL STREET OF THE GULF

Bahrain, a small island-state off the coast of Saudi Arabia, has played a central role as the Wall Street of the Gulf. Bahrain's economic history is one of transition—from being mainly a supplier of energy to being involved in a range of other sectors, the most important of which is financial services. Bahrain has been the GCC's banking hub since the 1970s and is aggressively striving to maintain that role as financial centers in Dubai, Doha, and elsewhere threaten its leadership in the sector.

Bahrain, like Qatar, chose not to join the Trucial States in forming a common state and instead became fully independent in 1971. Also like Qatar, Bahrain has fewer than a million people, although its population includes a smaller percentage of expatriates (less than one-third) than does Qatar's. And again like Qatar, Bahrain is home to a major US military installation—in Bahrain's case, the US Navy's Fifth Fleet. The Al Khalifa family, which has ruled Bahrain for centuries, remains in power today. While the ruling family—like all rulers of the GCC states—is Sunni, the majority of Bahrain's population is Shiite. This phenomenon has created a unique dynamic in Bahrain and has made the increased democratization of the country particularly consequential.

Sheikh Hamad bin Isa, who succeeded his father as ruler in 1999, came to office with an agenda of widespread political reform. His vision was to make Bahrain a constitutional monarchy, with a balance of power between the ruler and a parliament. The king appoints the upper chamber of parliament, and the people elect the lower chamber. Although several Shiite parties (called societies) boycotted the first elections in 2002, overall turnout was strong.

Some might be surprised to learn that the majority of voters—52 percent—in municipal elections were women.[20]

Bahrain was the first GCC country to export oil, building its first refinery in 1935. The island continues to refine oil from both domestic and imported sources (principally Saudi Arabia, whose offshore oil wells are very close). Bahrain's own oil reserves, however, are rapidly diminishing and may run out in the next 10 to 15 years.[21] While Bahrain's diversification efforts include the massive Aluminum Bahrain (which has the world's largest smelter outside Eastern Europe) and major tourism initiatives, such as the only Formula One racetrack in the GCC states, the most important sector in the country is clearly financial services.

When the oil boom of the 1970s brought unprecedented wealth to the GCC, Bahrain was well positioned to be the region's banking hub. The country's human capital pool was strong—Bahrain has had a public education system since 1932—and the Bahraini dinar had been introduced in 1965 and was becoming internationally relevant. In addition, the regulatory environment was favorable to building banking institutions—14 commercial banks were operating in Bahrain by 1974.[22] In 1975, the Bahrain Monetary Agency made the environment more attractive by introducing Offshore Banking Unit (OBU) licenses that allowed foreign banks to manage international deposits in a very flexible and tax-efficient manner. Twenty-six OBUs were established in the first year alone. The banking sector was fueled by the regional oil boom, a strong regulatory framework, and the migration of regional banking headquarters from Beirut as Lebanon slid into civil war in 1975.

By 2006, the number of offshore banks and representative offices in Bahrain had reached 370. International banks consider a presence in Bahrain essential to maintaining themselves as truly global institutions. Bahrain has also established itself as the leading center for Islamic (Sharia-compliant) finance—hosting organizations concerned with meeting industry standards, especially in the areas of accounting and governance—as well as for over 30 Islamic financial services firms. Perhaps the greatest sign of the success of Bahrain's financial services industry is that it has become the largest sector of the national economy, contributing an astonishing 28 percent of GDP, the same share as in Luxembourg.[23]

As its neighbors develop "international financial centers" and offshore havens, Bahrain's role as the GCC's banking hub has increasingly become threatened. Dubai, with its Dubai International Financial Centre, is perhaps the most serious threat: the lifestyle of the UAE combined with attractive, more liberal regulations creates an appealing environment for many international bankers. "Selling" Bahrain to an expatriate banker can be much harder than selling Dubai. One compelling factor in favor of Dubai, Doha, and even Saudi Arabia's King Abdullah Economic City, is the recent increase in local investment and infrastructure projects. As being "close to the client" is generally helpful in financial services, these other cities—closer to many large projects— become more attractive homes for financial services institutions.

Bahrain is investing heavily in its Bahrain Financial Harbor and other projects in an effort to retain its leadership as the region's banking hub. Just as New York's Wall Street needs to work actively to retain its luster relative to London, Bahrain must continually upgrade to maintain its pivotal role.

KUWAIT: COMFORT AND VULNERABILITY

Kuwait, the small and oil-rich state, has enjoyed remarkable prosperity for decades. This prosperity has made the country a perennial exporter of capital to global and (increasingly) regional markets. Kuwait's prosperity has also made it a target of aggression by Iraq, whose 1990–91 invasion and occupation of the country was a defining event in the Kuwait's recent history.

Kuwait awarded its first oil concession in 1934, to a joint British-American venture. By 1976, however, Kuwait had nationalized its oil company in order to control its resources more directly. Kuwait has the world's fourth-largest oil reserves, controlling more than 8 percent of the world's oil.[24] Like other oil producers, the country experienced an upturn in prosperity during the oil boom of the 1970s. As Kuwait's population has always been small relative to its oil resources, the state has been able to channel wealth into domestic services and international investments at a remarkable level.

About half of Kuwait's 2.5 million residents are Kuwaiti citizens. These citizens enjoy a wide range of social benefits including free, high-quality education, free medical services, housing loans, and retirement income. There is even a marriage bonus for Kuwaitis who marry, providing an incentive for (and greater means) to marry. Unemployment is minimal—barely 2 percent.[25] Many Kuwaitis study abroad on government scholarships. Overall, Kuwaitis enjoy a remarkably high standard of living.

Kuwait has developed sophisticated investment channels for the large budget surpluses it achieves each year. The government has created a Fund for Future Generations, in addition to its General Reserve Fund, as an endowment whose purpose is to sustain Kuwaiti society in the future. Kuwait is also a substantial donor nation, through the Kuwait Fund for Arab Economic Development. This fund has now broadened its mandate and provides assistance to non-Arab nations as well. Kuwait's banking sector and investment management firms are well developed: investment managers have long been making international investments for both the public and private sectors. One leading investment firm, Global Investment House, was founded by Maha Al-Ghunaim in 1998. In 2006, Al-Ghunaim was listed number 91 in Forbes's global ranking of Most Powerful Women.[26] Kuwaiti banks have long maintained foreign offices in order to serve traveling or expatriate Kuwaitis, and the banks now increasingly look abroad for new customers. Kuwait Finance House, the country's leading Sharia-compliant bank, is aggressively pursuing a growth strategy in Malaysia.

Tiny Kuwait is sandwiched between two much larger states: Saudi Arabia and Iraq. Kuwait's conflict with Iraq stems from a long history of territorial disputes. For decades, Iraq has claimed that Kuwait is rightfully part of Iraq. The matter was so serious that it appeared before the UN in the early 1960s (at Kuwait's request) after Iraq became increasingly belligerent. When Saddam Hussein invaded Kuwait in 1990, Kuwait was unable to resist on its own and required a US-led and UN-sanctioned international coalition to reclaim its territory. All GCC countries sided with Kuwait, as did most Arab and Muslim nations. The Kuwaiti ruler and leadership remained operational from Saudi Arabia, the UK, and elsewhere during the crisis and dug into Kuwait's substantial reserves to fund the government while oil revenue was unavailable. Since Kuwait was reclaimed and the government reinstalled, Kuwait's foreign policy has largely been shaped by its interest in showing loyalty to its defenders and deterring any future aggression. Kuwait has, for example, strongly supported America's Operation Iraqi Freedom and in October 2003 pledged $1.5 billion in aid for Iraqi reconstruction.[27]

Another important trend in Kuwait—also shaped by the experience of the first Gulf War—is increasing democratization. Like several other GCC states, Kuwait is an emirate, and its ruler (the emir) has been a member of the Al Sabah family for hundreds of years. Kuwait has had a national assembly on and off throughout its history, but since its liberation in 1991 the elected national assembly has played an increasingly important role. The national assembly can initiate legislation, question cabinet ministers, and even influence the succession of emirs by approving the ruler's choice of crown prince. The crown prince must, however, be from the Al Sabah family. Women were not allowed to vote until 2005— a sign of how nascent Kuwait's partial democracy actually is.

OMAN: A "REAL" ECONOMY

Come to Oman and it does not take long to realize that you are in a place quite different from its GCC neighbors. Some differences strike you right away: men here, for example, wear colorfully embroidered turbans rather than the white or red-checked headdress (called a *ghutra*) found elsewhere in the GCC. Look out into the horizon and you will find an unmatched diversity of terrain—a mix of mountains, beaches, desert, and oases that sets it apart from all other GCC countries. Explore Oman's religious practices and you will see that the majority adhere to the Ibadhi school of Islam—a school that is found almost nowhere else in the world. Hop in a taxi and your driver is likely to be Omani—as is the young person working the checkout counter at the supermarket or the cashier at a restaurant. A nation of 3 million, Oman feels much more like a "real" economy than do the other GCC states, and the reasons for this become apparent as one explores the country's background more deeply.

The Sultanate of Oman has been independent throughout its history. Rather than succumb to colonial influence, Oman built an empire itself, taking control of areas in East Africa and along the Makran coast (a region now part of Pakistan). Oman was the most powerful state on the Arabian Peninsula by the early nineteenth century.[28] Although Oman did sign treaties of friendship with the UK, the Al Said family has independently controlled the Sultanate for about 250 years. The current ruler, Sultan Qaboos bin Said, has been at the helm since 1970, when he deposed his father. Sultan Qaboos has therefore led the Sultanate's modernization efforts across the full range of sectors: economic, social, and political.

Oman has been an oil-producing state since 1967; its operations in this enterprise are conducted through the government-controlled Oman Petroleum Development company, which operates as a joint venture with Royal Dutch Shell. Oman is not, however, a member of OPEC like most of its GCC neighbors. Oman's oil capacity and reserves are modest: at current rates of production, the country's reserves will last only about another 20 years.[29]

One consequence of having modest oil production capabilities is that Oman's economy is significantly more diversified than that the economies of other GCC states. As illustrated in Figure 4.3, nearly 60 percent of Oman's GDP is derived from the services sector.[30]

While much of the services sector is directly linked to the oil industry (e.g., construction of housing for oil workers), Oman's economic diversification is noteworthy. Throughout the Sultanate major infrastructure, industrial, and commercial projects—such as port construction, copper mining and refining facilities, and other

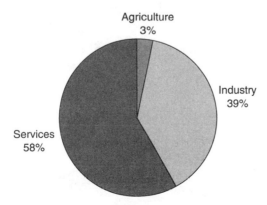

Figure 4.3 Oman's GDP by sector (Source: *CIA World Factbook, 2007*)

efforts are under way. One creatively named project in the tourism sector is called "Omagine"—a beachfront complex designed to mix cultural, tourist, commercial, educational, and residential elements. Stimulating the economy is a crucial priority: unemployment is 15 percent[31] and demographic pressures threaten to drive the figure even higher if Oman cannot create more jobs for locals.

Tourism is a high-potential sector for Oman due largely to the quality and diversity of the country's tourist attractions. Oman has the benefit of having a long history, and it has wisely preserved many historic sites. Along the Batinah coast, one finds towns in which ancient forts are still standing. Muscat itself has Qasr al-Hosn—the fort from its ancient days as a walled city. In Salalah, another port town that is quickly being developed as a tourist destination, there are ancient ruins and a tomb said to house the Prophet Job. The city of Sohar boasts its own ancient castle. Oman's terrain offers mountains, dunes, beaches, coral reefs, and wadi oases that attract visitors from around the world.

While Oman's relatively modest wealth puts it somewhat on the periphery of the GCC states, the Sultanate does have features that its neighbors might do well to emulate. Oman has built a fairly diversified—albeit by necessity—economy, and it has a substantial middle class of Omani citizens. Oman has also preserved its heritage and historical sites in a manner that gives the place a sense of authenticity sometimes missing from the sleek, modernist environs of its neighbors.

KEY LESSONS

- Don't let the newness of sleek cities of the GCC states fool you: *the Gulf is a place with a long history and that values its traditions*. Knowing the background of each country is important.
- Within the GCC, *the UAE is the trailblazer*, quickly establishing itself as the region's commercial hub largely through its open-for-business environment.
- *Saudi Arabia is the core market*, representing 70 percent of the region's population and some 50 percent of the total GDP.

- *Qatar is the upstart*, applying the wealth from its natural gas boom to build a diversified, knowledge-based economy.
- *Bahrain is the Wall Street of the Gulf*—the region's banking hub since the 1970s. It now faces fierce competition to remain the financial services capital.
- *Kuwait is marked by comfort and vulnerability*. The tiny, oil-rich state is a massive global investor with strong alliances in place for its protection.
- *Oman is a "real" economy*, with greater diversification, a local middle class, preserved historical sites, and a range of terrain.

PART 2

Developing Corporate Strategies

CHAPTER 5

A Piece of the Action: Strategies for Entering the GCC Market

INTRODUCTION

Toyota's Saudi Arabian franchise is one of its most successful in the world. It is so successful, in fact, that in 2004 the Saudi franchisee was invited to open a showroom in Japan and in 2005 a senior delegation came from Japan to Jeddah to celebrate 50 years of successful partnership. From the results of this partnership, one might have thought Toyota's Saudi Arabia strategy was deliberately crafted from Japan, drawn in painstaking detail, and executed as a high-priority project by the global head office.

History, however, shows otherwise. According to both official corporate histories and popular legend, Abdul Latif Jamil— Toyota's Saudi agent—was an entrepreneur with a modest auto business who began his career as a customs clerk in Jeddah. He opened his business with about $2,000 in 1938, started selling spare parts, and eventually built the business to the point that he owned a gas station by 1952. Legend has it that in the mid-1950s, Toyota executives came to Saudi Arabia looking for an agent and stumbled across Jamil. True to his reputation, he took a chance on Toyota and agreed to import a Land Cruiser. Jamil's first Toyota customer was

Prince Khalid bin Abdul Aziz, who would later become king of Saudi Arabia. Toyota vehicles—durable and well equipped for rugged Saudi terrain—quickly grew in popularity and Jamil's business has thrived for half a century.[1]

Not every company can count on Toyota's good fortune. In earlier chapters we discussed the factors that make the Gulf a highly attractive place in which to do business today. The states of the GCC are prosperous, growing fast, and evolving in ways that make their markets very appealing to multinational businesses. There is no shortage of reasons for companies to enter the GCC as one of their main strategies, which should serve as an engine of profitable growth far into the future. By now, we can see why the Gulf should not be ignored by global firms seeking to expand their worldwide presence. The question facing senior managers is not *whether* to enter the GCC, but *how* to enter the market most effectively.

There are three basic ways of entering a market. The first is through simple distribution: a multinational firm desiring to enter the market licenses a local firm to act as a surrogate and sell its goods. This approach limits the multinational's risk but also limits its reward. The second approach is through a joint venture: a multinational pools capital and expertise with a local partner and they manage the business together. This approach increases the multinational's potential reward but involves significant effort and attention. The third approach is to enter the market directly: the multinational either sets up shop itself or acquires a local business that becomes its own. This, of course, is usually the most challenging and risky method, but allows the global firm to fully control its local operations and fully enjoy the fruits of its labor.

Most major multinationals have approached the GCC through simple distribution agreements. As the GCC market has become more attractive, however, joint ventures with strong local partners are increasing. Direct market entry has generally been limited due to regulatory barriers and senior managers' limited appetite for Middle Eastern risk, but this approach is now becoming more common. In this chapter we will discuss how deeper engagement with the GCC—which often means migrating from simple distribution to joint ventures or direct market entry—can enable multinational firms to access more fully the substantial business opportunities that the Gulf has to offer. Deeper engagement carries with it new challenges and risks, but the rewards will often outweigh the risks, and such enterprises can often yield large profits. Below we highlight some of the key benefits and challenges of the more serious forms of market entry in the GCC.

THE ENGAGEMENT SPECTRUM

Multinational firms, in their perpetual quest for growth, must nonetheless be selective about which markets they engage and how they approach these markets. Not all markets are equally promising, and not all are worth the effort required to seriously enter them. Many of the world's leading companies—especially those that are consumer-facing—have mastered the techniques of market assessment and of gradual commitment and exposure to growth markets. Firms like Procter & Gamble and Coca-Cola, despite their nearly universal market reach, simply cannot invest equal attention and resources in all markets. Their "engagement," as we will call it, with various potential markets differs significantly based on the business case for each market.

The Gulf has historically not been seen by most leading nationals as possessing enough high-priority markets to make it worth their while to explore deeply. As discussed in previous chapters, the region has only recently become wealthy. Sustained prosperity, together with demographic changes and regulatory reforms—one such reform was the very creation of the GCC—has made the Gulf much more attractive to potential entrants. Another important factor is that the growth agenda of multinationals has previously been focused on more developed markets rather on those of places like the GCC countries. American firms, for example, have typically looked first for growth opportunities at home in US markets, next in Europe, and then in the richer parts of Asia, such as Japan. European firms have typically had a more international perspective, but have naturally preferred large markets or countries in which colonial-era linkages might facilitate access and credibility. Due to the relatively small size of its markets and the substantial challenges associated with entering them, the Gulf has been far down on the multinationals' list of priorities.

Today, however, the game has changed. The Gulf is much more attractive than ever before The investor community, guided largely by savvy research analysts and global strategists, is always on the lookout for opportunities that promise fast growth in prosperous emerging markets—seen as a sign of a firm's long-term expansion prospects. Emerging market revenues often capture, in fact, a premium over mature market revenues when analysts value global firms. China and India, therefore, have established roles for themselves near the top of most multinationals' agendas. And now the time seems right to turn to the GCC and to capture the abundant opportunity.

Figure 5.1 shows the three different levels of engagement at which international firms typically enter a new market. Each of these levels contains its own set of market-entry strategies to be employed once the level of engagement is decided on. Taken together, these three levels of market engagement can be called the "Engagement Spectrum."

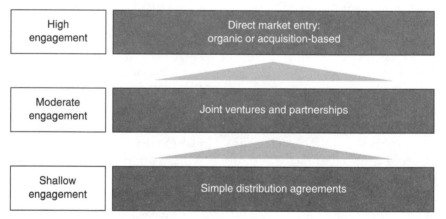

Figure 5.1 The Engagement Spectrum of market-entry strategies

"Shallow engagement" strategies are typically for the most minimal form of engagement, involving simple distribution agreements by which a local firm sells goods that are manufactured, branded, and provided by the multinational. The local firm is typically granted exclusivity—the sole right to distribute goods within a particular market on behalf of the multinational. In return, the multinational is paid for the goods it provides and may also insist on a revenue-sharing agreement beyond the direct fee for products and services. The multinational will also insist on certain quality standards and marketing guidelines, though local marketing, sales, and follow-up services (within the guidelines provided by the global head office) will be the responsibility of the distributor.

Classic franchise agreements fit into this model of shallow engagement. The local franchisee pays a fee for the right to open an outlet (say, a fast-food restaurant) and also pays a percentage of revenues to the global head office. Further, the local franchisee buys goods and raw materials (in this case, kitchen equipment, appliances, furniture, food ingredients, etc.) from the multinational, thereby providing another revenue stream. The local franchisee operates the business within global guidelines issuing from the multinational's headquarters. He or she then enjoys the profits earned after operating and franchise costs are covered.

"Moderate engagement" typically involves joint ventures (JVs) or partnerships. Under such arrangements, the multinational identifies a local firm to work with (just as it does in the case of a simple distributorship) but takes the relationship further by actively building the business with the local partner. A new entity is formed, in which ownership is shared by the multinational and the local partner or set of local partners. Management responsibility can either be shared or be contracted to one of the parties to undertake solely. In the case of the GCC, for example, management responsibility is often given to the multinational, as it brings its breadth of experience, global systems, and global talent pool. Management is supervised by the board of directors of the JV entity, which is composed of representatives from both the global and local firms that created the joint venture.

JVs and partnerships can either be privately held by the companies and investors who created them or "spun off" for sale to third parties or listed on public stock exchanges. The Saudi banking industry, for example, has many examples of joint ventures in which ownership is shard by international banks and Saudi investors. The international bank provides management expertise and world-class systems; the locals provide capital, governance, and regulatory status. The banks are listed on the Saudi stock exchange, and the share price generally moves with little relation to the overall share price of the global bank.

"High-engagement" strategies involve direct ownership by the multinational firm, in both the literal and figurative senses of ownership. One form of a high-engagement strategy is to enter a market directly, by purchasing or leasing a store, putting up your shingle, and beginning to sell your goods; this form is commonly referred to as organic entry. Much of globalization has occurred this way, and the phenomenon is much more common in highly deregulated markets. Globally owned Starbucks and Gap outlets in Europe, for example, represent direct market entry. In the GCC context, an example would be Microsoft's establishment of an office in Dubai Media City. Strategy is first set at the global level and then transferred to the in-market organization. Authorization to invest start-up funding comes from the global headquarters, and the initial staff is typically brought in from other markets. The local team is expected to perform at global standards. The foreign outlet may be based in a different country, but it is very much part of the "family" of the global firm.

A second form of high-engagement market entry is through the acquisition of a local business that is then (partially or fully) integrated into the global parent company. Ford's 1999 acquisition of Volvo is an example: Ford's purchase of Volvo gave it a strong presence in the Swedish and European markets, as well as a strong product to distribute in the United States and elsewhere. In recent years, companies founded in emerging markets have increasingly reversed the typical acquisition flow and have begun acquiring companies in the OECD. Mittal Steel's (India) acquisitions in Europe (including Arcelor) and the United States, Lenovo's (China) purchase of IBM's personal computer business, and indeed Dubai Ports World's (UAE) acquisition of P&O are recent high-profile examples of this kind of high-engagement market entries. While integrating the acquired entity into the structure and systems of the global parent is usually helpful from an efficiency and savings perspective, the brand and local feel of the acquired firm are often preserved to help retain customers and fuel in-market growth. While regulations in the GCC have hitherto made acquisitions impossible, changes in the regulatory environment may make Gulf acquisitions a real possibility for multinational firms.

The landscape of the GCC markets today includes examples of all three levels (shallow, moderate, and high) of engagement outlined in the Engagement Spectrum (see Figure 5.1). Each level contains its own strategies, which have their own benefits and drawbacks, and there is no "right" answer to the question of how multinationals can best enter the GCC market. In the rest of this chapter, we will explore some of the paths that leading global firms have taken in their journeys into these new markets to see what lessons we may draw from their experiences.

SHALLOW ENGAGEMENT HAS BEEN THE NORM

The bulk of multinational firms that have a presence in the GCC countries have approached the market through shallow-engagement strategies. The most common approach has been straightforward distribution agreements by which a local firm markets and sells the multinational's products while paying for the goods and (potentially) sharing in overall revenues. Distributorships are the norm across a wide range of sectors—especially those of wholesale and retail consumer goods, restaurants, and other consumer-facing services. One reason for choosing the strategy of distributorships has been the restrictive regulatory regimes (to be discussed below at greater length) existing in the GCC states until only recently, which have made higher-engagement strategies less attractive or impossible. As well as the regulatory constraints, however, there are some solid business reasons for choosing a shallow-engagement approach to the GCC markets.

First, shallow-engagement strategies can make sense because they minimize the multinational's exposure to risk. In the case of goods manufacturers, for example, the only financial risk they might incur is that they might lose some inventory given on consignment or with deferred payment terms. In the case of service firms, there may be more oversight and standards enforcement required by the head office, but their financial exposure is minimal. Although there is a small amount of risk, the multinational receives the benefit of having its brand and reputation spread across a new region—increasing its global presence and demonstrating, to whatever degree, its ability to compete with the comparable local offerings. The distributor bears the local market risk while the international firm sees its profile rise and may even decide at some point (even if after a long-term contract ends) to enter the market directly if doing so subsequently becomes attractive. At the same time, the global firm enjoys steady income streams from goods sold in the region. There can also be additional income in the form of franchise fees, training fees, and revenue-sharing arrangements. One can easily see the attraction of the shallow-engagement model from a multinational's perspective.

Many of the leading business families in GCC countries have, not surprisingly, built a large part of their fortunes acting as distributors for multinational firms. The Al-Hokair Group[2] of Saudi Arabia, is the creation of one such family; it is the distributor for some 50 international brands having both mass-market and luxury-market appeal. In Saudi Arabia, Al-Hokair distributes Ann Harvey, Zara, Monsoon, Massimo Dutti, Nine West, and a host of other prominent brands.[3] Though it began only around 1990, the Group has enjoyed phenomenal growth by pursuing a strategy of "offering a world-class doorway through which [international brands] can take advantage of [Saudi Arabia's] retail opportunity." Al-Hokair has succeeded by convincing international brands that its platform is the most effective one for tapping into the Saudi market, and the booming Saudi economy of recent years has undoubtedly helped bolster Al-Hokair's standing. Al-Hokair positions itself as grasping the Saudi consumer's buy-now-wear-now lifestyle attitude better than its competitors do and, therefore, is a superior distribution agent for global firms seeking to benefit from Saudi consumerism. As of spring 2006, the Al-Hokair Group was operating 617 stores in Saudi Arabia, with plans to open 90 more.[4] It is easy to see why multinational firms, after learning of the Group's strong market presence in the country, its deep market experience, and its strong track record of representing other global firms, might choose Al-Hokair as their distributor.[5]

The UAE's Al Tayer Group has likewise built a substantial portfolio as a distributor for international brands, with a concentration on luxury goods. The Group represents, among others, Gucci, Giorgio Armani, Dolce & Gabbana, and Yves Saint Laurent. Al-Tayer has also opened the largest Harvey Nichols (UK luxury retailer) store outside Britain. The Group's leadership of the luxury sector extends well beyond fashion: it distributes Ferrari, Maserati, Jaguar, Land Rover, and other high-end automobiles; it even represents exclusive perfumes and cosmetics.[6]

In 2006, Al Tayer secured a landmark agreement with Gap to open 35 Gap and Banana Republic stores by 2010. The terms of the deal are both remarkable and instructive. Unlike other distributorship and franchisee agreements, this one involves multiple countries: five of the six GCC states (the exception being Saudi Arabia). Further, Gap has retained control of marketing, advertising images, and product design—preserving the brand positioning worldwide that the firm has always sought. Al Tayer is responsible for store operations, finding real estate for store locations, and hiring staff. This agreement is a noteworthy departure from Gap's long-cherished strategy of company-owned stores. Even Gap's stores in the UK, France, and Japan are company owned and not franchised—a policy choice that some observers have seen as inefficient.[7] That Gap chose to adopt a shallow-engagement approach for its stores in the GCC, which policy deviated from its global norm, was most likely the result of the Gulf opportunity being just too attractive to pass up. Regulations would not allow Gap to own these stores, but the global firm saw it as nevertheless worthwhile to engage a local franchisee.

Carrefour, the French hypermarket, has similarly, in order to accommodate the GCC, made exceptions to its general practice of having only company-owned stores. Of the nine countries in which Carrefour operates exclusively through franchisees or partners, four are in the GCC—in Saudi Arabia, the UAE, Qatar, and Oman.[8] Carrefour's hypermarkets are very popular in the Gulf states, where family units are large and grocery shopping can be an important family event. Carrefour is an anchor tenant of Dubai's City Centre shopping mall, and its Muscat location is viewed by many as the most useful place to shop in the entire city. It is noteworthy that Carrefour—Europe's largest retailer and the second largest in the world, behind Wal-Mart—would take a keen enough interest in the Gulf to fundamentally modify its business model to enable market entry.

One factor that undoubtedly gives Carrefour comfort as it pursues its aggressive market-entry strategy in the Gulf countries is the strength of its franchisee, the Al-Futtaim Group of the UAE. Al-Futtaim is Carrefour's franchisee in the UAE, Qatar, and Oman and a joint franchisee with the Al-Olayan Group for the Saudi Arabian business. Al-Futtaim is, without a doubt, one of the strongest family enterprises in all of the GCC states and one of the most effective local agents any multinational could find. Besides representing an impressive—and comprehensive—list of multinational firms such as IKEA, Toys "R" Us, Hertz, and Honda, Al-Futtaim has been at the forefront of retail property development through its portfolio of shopping malls (known as MAF Shopping Malls for Majid Al-Futtaim). Its City Centre shopping mall in Dubai—the city's most popular destination and a must-see for visitors—has been a convenient venue for locating and promoting Al-Futtaim businesses such as the Carrefour store and Toyota-Lexus showroom. Al-Futtaim has expanded its shopping mall development capabilities well beyond Dubai, undertaking projects elsewhere in the UAE and the other GCC countries. Muscat City Centre in Oman, for example, is an MAF Shopping Malls property. Al-Futtaim's powerful real estate capabilities give multinationals confidence that, if they partner with the Group, their outlets will be in prime locations with significant shopper traffic.

As an illustration of how broad and influential a local franchisee or distributor can be, it is worth taking a closer look at the business portfolio of the Al-Futtaim Group. Table 5.1, though far from comprehensive, presents some highlights of the Group's activities.

TABLE 5.1

The Al-Futtaim Group at a Glance[9]

Attribute	Description
Origins	It was founded in the 1930s as a trading enterprise and grew into a conglomerate through the 1940s and 1950s.
Number of Companies	Over 40 companies bear the Al-Futtaim name, not to mention all the international brands the Group represents through distribution and franchise agreements.
Geographic Presence	While the UAE is its home market, Al-Futtaim has operations in Bahrain, Kuwait, Qatar, Oman, and Egypt.

TABLE 5.1

The Al-Futtaim Group at a Glance—cont'd

Attribute	Description
Operating Divisions	Automotive Electronics Retail Services Overseas (International) Insurance Industries Real Estate
Key Retail Brands	IKEA, Carrefour, Toys "R" Us, Marks & Spencer, Seiko, Raymond Weil
Key Auto Brands	Toyota/Lexus, Honda, Chrysler/Jeep/Dodge, Volvo, Hertz
Key Electronics Brands	Panasonic, Sanyo, Toshiba, Alcatel

Al-Futtaim has managed to build formidable businesses across a range of industries and has entered into distribution agreements with leading US (e.g., Chrysler), EU (e.g., Carrefour), and Asian (e.g., Toyota) firms alike. The breadth and depth of their expertise, along with their capital base, make firms like Al-Futtaim highly attractive as distributors and franchisees for the multinationals. In fact, one important reason why straightforward distribution agreements have thus far been the norm is that there are such compelling local distributors available, as IKEA's experience with Al-Futtaim demonstrates.

IKEA and Al-Futtaim: A Match Made in Sweden

European retail brands have long found a home in the GCC, but few have attained more success than the flat-pack, home furnishings manufacturer IKEA. The company describes its Swedish traditions of modernism, functionalism, and social equality as follows: "The IKEA Concept is based on offering a wide range of well designed, functional home furnishing products at prices so low that as many people as possible will be able to afford them."[10] IKEA outlets tend to be massive—the largest covers over 10 football fields—and, because of their scale, few. Southern California, with 20 million consumers, has just five IKEA stores.

In line with the IKEA concept, franchise agreements serve as the practical incarnation of the Swedish giant's global growth strategy. Only organizations capable of capturing a large share of the home furnishings market and maintaining competitive pricing receive franchises. According to IKEA, such organizations have these advantages: (1) retail experience with extensive local market knowledge; (2) an outstanding understanding of, and a strong commitment to, the IKEA concept; (3) considerable financial strength; and (4) identified, well-located sites for retail activity.[11] For their part, franchisees receive the necessary support to execute the IKEA concept, though all start-up expenses are borne by the franchisee.

In the GCC countries, IKEA's stringent franchisee requirements immediately eliminated most of the smaller players in the retail market. Of the larger, well-capitalized companies, the Al-Futtaim Group—with its diversified, international-brand portfolio and extensive retail experience—stood out as the ideal business partner. Run by Emirati billionaire Abdulla al-Futtaim, the Group's financial strength complements IKEA's low-cost strategy.[12] One major advantage of working with Al-Futtaim is its large and growing real estate business, which provides retailers access to prime locations. Additionally, the Emirates-based conglomerate enjoys an extremely positive brand image in the region, thanks to projects like the Dubai City Centre, and controls retail real estate across the GCC states. As a business in Al-Futtaim's portfolio, which includes IBM and Toyota, IKEA benefits from positive brand association and overall retail strength. Furthermore, IKEA is able to piggyback on Al-Futtaim's regional expansion plans to fuel its own growth. Al-Futtaim intends to double its $270 million retail operations in the next three years through $70 million in investments for new IKEA outlets in Qatar, Oman, the UAE, and Egypt.[13]

The IKEA–Al-Futtaim partnership highlights the key benefits that multinationals can capture by working with established GCC conglomerates. First, these conglomerates have a higher risk tolerance for local projects than do multinationals, making otherwise unfeasible projects possible. In addition, homegrown firms have a more complete understanding of the needs and preferences of the local population. Finally, local conglomerates, because of their different business lines and familiarity with markets in the region, already have extensive distribution networks set up, enabling the foreign firm to reach GCC consumers soon after an agreement is arrived at. As IKEA's experience with Al-Futtaim illustrates, the established operational capabilities provided by the local conglomerate can be a key source of competitive advantage.

Sometimes, a multinational will enter a distributorship agreement not merely because of regulatory barriers or to limit risk exposure, but because its business model is inappropriate for the GCC markets it seeks to enter. Dell, the e-commerce giant that operates in the Middle East through authorized sellers and service agents, provides an example.

Dell in the GCC: Adapting the Business Model

When Michael Dell started building personal computers in his dorm room at the University of Texas at Austin in 1984, he believed that by selling customized computers directly to buyers, he could better cater to their needs. Two decades later, he still continues to realize his vision of selling directly to consumers, this time as the head of the Fortune 500 behemoth Dell Computer. Efficient supply chain management, robust electronic commerce Web sites, and a religious dedication to passing on cost savings to customers form the heart of Dell's sell-direct strategy in North America and Europe. In the GCC states, however, where technological and social barriers have slowed e-commerce development, Dell has been forced to adapt its business model.

Relative to North America and Europe, the GCC is at an early stage of its development of electronic commerce. A lack of widespread credit card use, a mistrust of e-commerce stemming from the many stories of online fraud, less convenient postal services, and social preferences for shopping at brick-and-mortar stores have slowed the transition to online purchasing. Not surprisingly, few retailers and distribution companies in the GCC have transformed their business models to accommodate the demands of e-commerce, contributing to the slow transition from the supply side.

To work around this obstacle until the online retailing model evolves into a viable option in the GCC economies, Dell has entered into product distribution and service agreements with local partners in the region. Specifically, these "Dell Partners" sell personal computers, and can provide warranty support and other after-sales services as well as round-the-clock enterprise service support after they pass Dell's certification programs.[14] Each GCC nation has at least one Dell Partner; the larger ones have several. In essence, these partners serve as extensions of Dell Inc. in the GCC, even though they are not owned directly by the multinational. To the consumer, dealing with a Dell Partner is no different from dealing with the American computer giant itself.[15]

Dell's relationship with its GCC partners demonstrates the power and flexibility provided by partnership agreements. From Dell's perspective, qualified local partners provide speedy, low-cost access to the GCC market, and potentially just as quick an exit if operations do not succeed. Instead of taking on the burdens of constructing sales outlets (which would be a major departure from Dell's sell-direct model), hiring qualified professionals, dealing with regulatory reform as the GCC integrates more completely into the WTO, and worrying about minimizing losses if it became necessary to close up shop, Dell uses these partnership agreements as a hedge against expansion risk and a speedy path to market.

DRAWBACKS OF SHALLOW ENGAGEMENT

The shallow-engagement level of the Engagement Spectrum does, however, have significant limitations. The first of these is straightforward business economics: multinationals who rely on local firms to bear the risk must forgo a significant portion of the rewards that come from being in the market. Multinationals who engage in simple distribution and revenue-sharing agreements gain a stable income stream but have no equity stake in the underlying business they enable. Although the firm's business in the region may grow in value, ownership of that business resides entirely with the local distributor or franchisee. Local firms are often able to use the foreign brand, retain control of the market, and expand their organizational capacity (not to mention their capital base) while the multinational firm gets a check in the mail from a business it may not fully understand. Many savvy executives—especially when they view a business as a strategic priority—seek to capture both annual income and long-term capital growth through owning equity in their businesses and therefore seek to migrate beyond shallow engagement.

A second, and related, drawback of straightforward distribution agreements is that such agreements inherently limit the multinationals' control of daily business operations. The local distributor generally decides where the product is stocked and, in the case of service businesses, who serves which client. Multinationals have, of course, developed control systems that help mitigate this risk: they have clauses in their agreements about quality control, marketing, branding, and other core processes that have the potential to put their global franchise at risk. Some firms can go further and align on business practice guidelines and operating procedures. As important and helpful as these measures are, long-distance control mechanisms are not the same as running a business oneself. Even when the local distributor does everything by the book and fully complies with global standards and guidelines, the multinational has no way of knowing if the business *could* be doing better if managed directly.[16] Distribution agreements are a good way to minimize one's direct operating risk, but the downsides of relying on a partner are not insignificant.

A final, subtle drawback of distribution relationships is that they can lead to conflicts of interest. Major local conglomerates will often act as distributors or franchisees for multiple firms in the same sector—firms that may even be in fierce competition with one another globally. I once advised a multinational client who had business interests in Saudi Arabia; its local agent (a highly prominent family enterprise) was also the agent of several key competitors. By representing several leading multinationals in the same industry, the distributor had built deep relationships with all key local shops that carried goods in its category. The distributor also could exercise significant market power in collecting receivables, managing cash flow, and even in lobbying for favorable regulations. The challenge, though, was to get the distributor to promote my client's products more vigorously than it promoted the competing products.[17] Though different in many ways, the situation is not unlike selling a home through a real estate broker in the United States: you may have wished that she was representing only your home, but in fact she represents many and may show them all to the same potential buyers and your challenge is to make your house stand out. Once you have many properties to sell or are more serious about controlling the process, you will seek an agent who is exclusively yours, or you will simply sell the home yourself.

Shallow-engagement market-entry strategies are often the best choice when firms wish to test a new region and at the same time minimize their risk and investment. These strategies also make good sense when high-performing local distributors with good track records are available. Protective regulatory regimes also encourage such low-risk strategies. For multinational firms testing the waters in GCC economies, the conditions described above, and others, have pushed them toward the lower end of the Engagement Spectrum of market-entry strategies. Recently, however, the situation has been changing.

MODERATE-ENGAGEMENT STRATEGIES FIT BETTER AS YOUR GCC BUSINESS GROWS IN STRATEGIC IMPORTANCE

The goals of shallow-engagement strategies are modest: market exposure at minimum risk. As the GCC becomes a more integral part of a firm's global strategy, however, senior executives will seek to ensure maximum return on investment and to encourage more aggressive growth in the region. In essence, they will seek more control. Without a stronger measure of control, senior management at the global level will struggle to make the GCC a genuine priority in the business: How can we grow a market or create effective strategies if we don't actually run our business there?

There are three core goals of moderate-engagement strategies:

- More direct management of the business
- A reward of equity value created in the venture
- The benefit of knowledge and expertise provided by the local partner

All of these goals reflect a multinational's desire to take its Gulf business to the next level and make the GCC countries areas of greater focus overall. The typical mechanisms for moderate-engagement strategies are joint ventures (JVs) and partnership agreements by which both the multinational and the local partner(s) invest capital and share ownership. Often the multinational firm will also be granted a management contract under the terms of which it is responsible for operating the business, in line with its global standards, on a day-to-day basis. Oversight and strategic direction are provided by a board of directors composed of representatives of both the multinational and the local partner(s).

In addition to the three core goals listed above, participation in JVs places multinationals in a stronger strategic position as markets deregulate. As full foreign ownership becomes more broadly feasible in the GCC, global companies that have experienced the market directly through joint ventures will enjoy a real advantage over competitors that have not. Firms without JVs or partnerships may well have their brands in the market and some customer goodwill built up, but they will lack the in-depth understanding enjoyed by companies that are already established. As deregulation plans are laid and begin to be implemented, multinationals that have participated in joint ventures are well positioned to renegotiate terms with local partners in order to capture more value. Indeed, as the regulatory environment shifts, more negotiation leverage accrues to the multinationals. Partners that fail to add adequate value to their international affiliates face the risk of being marginalized, having their profit share renegotiated, or—as the laws evolve—being bought out entirely. Multinationals that enter JVs today have the wind at their backs and can expect more favorable regulations going forward.

One sector in which JVs have long been prevalent is that of financial services. A close look at the Saudi banking market will reveal how changes in market attractiveness and in regulatory regimes have driven the sector toward a joint-venture model.

Joint Ventures in Action: The Saudi Banking Market

The Saudi banking sector today consists of two types of institutions: domestic banks and international joint-venture banks. The prevalence of JV banks is striking, and the JV banks play a crucial role in meeting the needs of institutions and individuals with global assets and sophisticated product needs. These JV banks have local names but international management. Saudi Hollandi Bank (literally, the "Saudi Dutch Bank") is a JV with ABN Amro. The Saudi British Bank (now branded as "SABB") is a JV with HSBC; Banque Saudi Fransi ("Saudi French Bank") is a JV with Calyon Crédit Agricole. The international banks view the Saudi entity as "affiliate" institutions or partly owned subsidiaries. The Saudi American Bank (now branded as "Samba") was previously a joint venture with Citigroup, but Citi subsequently divested.

Table 5.2 shows the leading banks in Saudi Arabia and, where relevant, the associated international bank.[18]

TABLE 5.2

Leading Banks in Saudi Arabia

Rank	Name	International Partner
1	National Commercial Bank (NCB)	
2	Samba (formerly the Saudi American Bank)	Citigroup (since divested)
3	Al Rajhi Bank	
4	Bank Al Riyad	
5	Banque Saudi Fransi	Crédit Agricole
6	Arab National Bank	
7	SABB (formerly the Saudi British Bank)	HSBC
8	Saudi Hollandi Bank	ABN Amro
9	Bank Al Jazira	
10	Bank Al Bilad	

While 7 of the top 10 retail banks are purely local, the international JVs control significant market share and influence.

How the JV Model Evolved

For much of its history, the Saudi banking market was dominated by international banks. The first foreign bank was Algemene Bank Nederland (ABN)—a forerunner of ABN Amro. Established in Saudi Arabia in 1926, ABN enjoyed a virtual monopoly until a handful of foreign banks—Banque de l'Indochine (now part of Crédit Agricole), Arab Bank Limited, the British Bank of the Middle East (forerunner of SABB), and the National Bank of Pakistan—entered between 1947 and 1950. World War II had ended, and although Saudi Arabia was not yet a very wealthy place, oil was being exported and capital was flowing in.

In 1952, the Saudi Arabian Monetary Agency (SAMA) was established to regulate the fast-expanding banking market. Several banks—including the First National City Bank of New York, the forerunner of Citigroup—entered the market in the 1950s.[19] Domestic banks such as National Commercial Bank (NCB) and Riyad Bank sprang up during this period of modernization and growth. Banks played a role in financing the Kingdom's increased commercial activity, and provided retail customers the basic financial products they needed. The sector included a mix of foreign and local banking institutions.

The oil boom of the 1970s changed the game fundamentally. As wealth flowed in at an unprecedented rate, the Saudi banking market became much more attractive. The level of cash in the economy called for new products, deeper branch networks, and larger banking institutions. At the same time, the politics of the oil crises of the 1970s created some strain between Saudi Arabia and the West. In 1976, the Saudi government decreed that all banks in the country would need to be owned by a majority of Saudi nationals. Foreign banks could participate, but as minority shareholders in Saudi-owned institutions. One explanation given for this new policy was that foreign banks were not investing enough and were underserving the market. A more plausible explanation is that the banking sector became too attractive, profitable, and strategically important for the Saudi establishment to leave in the control of foreigners. To multinational banks, the dramatic change was a shock.

The change also created a dilemma for the foreign banks: should they stay in the market as minority shareholders, or exit entirely? Ownership of the business had slipped away, but the fundamental attractiveness of the banking market was higher than ever. Also, while Saudi investors and institutions had a regulatory edge, they generally lacked the organizational capabilities to take over management of the institutions. A natural bargain was struck: international banks would remain as minority shareholders, but be awarded management agreements that gave them day-to-day control of bank operations. Saudi investors would have control of the boards of directors, but would not interfere in operational matters. Another implicit part of the deal was that the JV banks would actively work to develop Saudi talent and groom them for positions of leadership. And as a reward to all parties, the JVs would be listed on the Saudi stock exchange, creating equity value and liquidity for both the international banks and the local investors. The international bank might own less of the total venture, but its share of the venture could be worth more than the equity value of their previously fully owned business.

Since the 1970s, the JV banks have struck a delicate balance by which they use both their "local" status and their global affiliation to stand out in a competitive marketplace. The Saudi American Bank changed its brand to "Samba," presumably to reflect its embedded status and local authenticity. The Saudi British Bank changed to "SABB." Nonetheless, SABB still proudly displays the HSBC hexagon as part of its logo, just as Saudi Hollandi uses the ABN Amro logo. These emblems signal global presence and world-class standards—helping the banks attract some of Saudi Arabia's most sophisticated and lucrative clients.

What Next for the JV Banks?

The sustained oil boom of the 2000s has again made the Saudi banking sector a hot market to be in. Unlike the 1970s, however, the regulatory trend is toward openness: Saudi Arabia is a member of the WTO and is liberalizing its economic policies. There is a vision for the future that would allow foreign banks to hold controlling stakes in JV banks (not to exceed a 60 percent interest, however).[20] The Saudi regulators, even as they allow international banks to increase their investment and have majority control, seem determined to protect the equity privileges of the local investors. World-class expertise will also be needed more than ever as competition in the sector mounts. In late 2006, for example, the Saudi cabinet granted a remarkable 12 new insurance licenses in a single session—making the sector more competitive than ever. In fact, foreign banks have become more active in the riskier parts of the banking business, such as the investment banking, asset management, and brokerage operations. The international banks' negotiating position relative to local investors is improving markedly, signaling the possibility of another meaningful shift in the industry landscape. When the dust settles, where will foreign banks stand? Time will tell.

Joint ventures can be a promising vehicle for multinationals to pursue more intently opportunities in GCC countries, but they are by no means easy to execute. Several factors must converge—from market attractiveness to a supportive regulatory environment and beyond—to enable a multinational to move up the Engagement Spectrum. Figure 5.2 illustrates some of the key requirements.

Fundamental Market Attractiveness

The first factor that multinationals must assess is whether there are aspects of the GCC market that are attractive *to them*—and, if so,

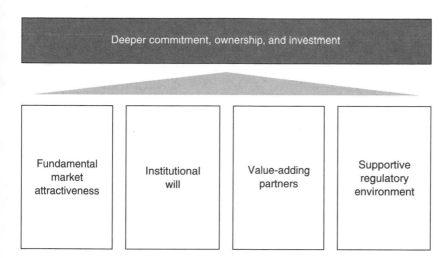

Figure 5.2 Moving up the Engagement Spectrum

which market opportunities make most sense to pursue. It's not enough to say that the Gulf is becoming appealing overall, as we have argued earlier in this book; individual companies must take the crucial next step and examine whether their offerings and capabilities are a good match with the GCC market. Will our company's products and services resonate with the needs of customers in the GCC countries? Will customization be required—and, if so, how much and will it be worth the effort? In other words, will we be able—either ourselves or with others—to effectively serve the market?

Few sectors, I would argue, are fundamental misfits for the GCC market. Some, such as ski gear and heavy winter clothing, will obviously have limited appeal.[21] The needs of the GCC nations are broad and span nearly the full range of industries that exist in the Western world. Even the oil and gas sector, long the domain of nationalized energy companies, is being opened up to foreign participation to some degree. However, companies must understand their own positioning and core competencies to see if the GCC market is right for them. If they're not sure, then simple distribution agreements are a good way to test the waters.

Institutional Will
Moving along the Engagement Spectrum requires investment: it calls for capital, human resources, and the attention of senior management.

These are all scarce commodities and are deployed only when a solid business case is made to a receptive and open audience. Writing the proposal for such a business case is not easy, but it is within the control of the business leader seeking to champion the GCC project. Finding a receptive audience within a corporation can sometimes be a real challenge.

Corporate strategists seeking to make a GCC effort should expect a struggle when attempting to build institutional will at the main office. As with any new project, there are tough questions to be answered about the business case. Historically, even finding accurate data on Gulf markets has been a struggle—though the situation has improved markedly in the past few years. Beyond the hard facts of the business case, there will be questions about the political environment, quality of life, and a whole set of "softer" concerns such as how the brand will be received. Some of these will be rooted in genuine issues and realities; others will likely be based on misconceptions. In any case, these concerns will need to be addressed to overcome institutional resistance and build toward consensus.

As more and more leading global firms increase their commitment to the GCC market, it becomes easier to muster the institutional will required to mobilize the needed resources. By the same token, waiting for others to enter can reduce a firm's competitive advantage once it finally wakes up to the business opportunity. Firms must do their homework, undertake the analysis, and test the business case. Once confident that an opportunity exists, they need to move forward boldly to capture the prize before others do.

Value-Adding Partners

In the case of joint ventures, finding the right partner is absolutely essential. A "value-adding" partner is more than just a financial investor; that partner helps shape the overall strategy, identifies opportunities, and gives the multinational an edge beyond any it would have on its own. But meeting the regulatory requirements is not enough: in today's competitive environment, local partners must bring vision, capabilities, and resources to the table. How, then, should multinationals select their potential partners?

The first screens to undertake are those that look to the basics: ability to commit the required capital, control of (or access to) the other resources required by the venture, relevant operational expertise, reputation and track record for transparency and fair dealings, and a solid management team able to execute and oversee the venture's anticipated projects. As mentioned previously, conflicts of interest can be a serious issue, and policies aimed at avoiding or managing them need to be agreed upon from the very start. One of the worst impediments to a JV to endure is the partner's commitments (contractual or otherwise) to other parties that could detract from coleading the JV adequately.

Beyond these basic elements, there are more intangible ones, such as corporate cultural fit. Will your international staff "gel" with your prospective partners? Will board members focus on the key issues, or will they be distracted by side issues of lesser consequence? Will managers from both sides be able to address the tough issues head-on? Is there any chance that either party will feel exploited, or that they are receiving the worse end of the bargain? If so, these issues need to be addressed forthrightly before entering into a JV.

The good news is that the more savvy local firms, such as the UAE's Al-Futtaim Group and Saudi Arabia's ALJ Group, have a great deal of expertise in dealing with multinationals. They understand multinationals' concerns, meet or exceed their quality standards, and are often good cultural fits. Global firms need not worry that there are no value-adding potential partners in the GCC; there certainly are many there that can add value. The challenge is finding one that "fits" from the perspective of capabilities, lack of conflicts of interest, commitment, and cultural compatibility.

Supportive Regulatory Environment

As is the case when entering any new market, multinationals need to feel comfortable that the regulatory environment is favorable. The most basic issues concerning this, such as those involving the rule of law and property rights, are not problems in the GCC countries. On the contrary, all of the GCC states included in the World Bank's most recent "Ease of Doing Business" rankings—Saudi Arabia, Kuwait, Oman, and the UAE—were ranked significantly higher than both China and India. China (excluding Hong Kong and Taiwan) ranks 93rd from the top; India ranks 134th. The four GCC states included range from 38th to 77th in terms of the ease of doing business.[22] While not spectacular, these rankings are certainly respectable relative to other emerging markets.

Regulatory due diligence is required for more strategic issues such as the likelihood of ongoing reform and the long-term regulatory benefits and drawbacks of various market-entry strategies. A multinational's internal legal and corporate affairs teams, along with outside advisors and in-market counsel, need to assess in detail the pertinent regulations that would govern them and to understand all of the implications. Without feeling comfortable about the regulatory issues, for a company to move along the Engagement Spectrum is a risky and potentially unwise venture.

HIGH-ENGAGEMENT STRATEGIES ARE BECOMING MORE RELEVANT

Historically, the high-engagement strategies presented earlier in this chapter—organic market entry and acquisition-based entry—have not been possible in the GCC states. Since the boom days of the 1970s, the governments of these countries have seen it as vital to protect local firms (and promote the creation of new ones) by keeping foreign entities from owning businesses in their homelands. Behind closed doors, however, GCC leaders will readily admit that policy of keeping their economies closed has had its costs. The rationale for such a policy, they argue, is that local GCC companies were simply not ready to compete with foreign firms at the time prosperity suddenly came to the region. Oil wealth made the Gulf a lucrative place to do business and therefore a magnet for the attention of multinational firms, yet the local firms lacked the capability to outperform these multinationals on a level playing field. Whereas more advanced economies had achieved their level of prosperity over a period of centuries, involving industrialization, growing research and development capabilities, ever-improving educational and training facilities, cultural changes including greater consumer awareness and sophistication, and other key outgrowths of affluence, wealth in the GCC came—literally—out of the ground and all at once, in a geyserlike rush. It was out of a sense of responsibility toward a local community, which they believed needed protection, that the rulers of the GCC states adopted their restrictive policies. The restrictions on foreign ownership is one reason why, according to industry statistics, mergers and acquisitions in the entire region of the Middle East and Africa make up less than 1.5 percent of the world's total.[23]

Today, deregulation is occurring rapidly. As we discussed in Chapter 3, deregulation is one of the core elements of the Opportunity Formula that has made the GCC countries such an attractive place to do business. All six GCC states are now members of the WTO. Privatization is on the rise, and barriers to entry are either falling or set to fall across a wide range of industries. As each GCC state has negotiated its own WTO accession terms, including the exceptions to deregulation, it is crucial to read the fine print in order to understand the nuances of government policies.

In the case of Saudi Arabia—the region's largest market—ownership rights are governed by the country's Foreign Investment Act, with oversight by the Saudi Arabian General Investment Authority. While the act permits the notion of businesses being wholly owned by foreign entities, it also contains a list of excluded or protected industries, (even though the act enjoys full WTO support). Here are a few highlights of the act:[24]

- Foreign investment in manufacturing is generally permitted, except for oil exploration, military equipment, and a few other categories.
- The broad "services" sector is partly protected, with areas such as real estate brokerage and security and detective services either fully or largely protected.
- Retail and distribution firms are artfully protected, with maximum equity ownership caps persisting even into the long-term future under Saudi Arabia's WTO agreement, albeit at a high level of 75 percent. Minimum capital and outlet size requirements will bar foreign ownership of small retail businesses and distributorships, and there are stipulations for training of Saudi employees.[25]
- These restrictions aside, Saudi Arabia is committed under the WTO to significant opening of its economy. In many cases, the opening was to occur immediately, without any grace period. In addition to a general lowering of many tariffs and simplification of nontariff barriers, key sectors such as mobile telephony, health care, big-box retailing, and financial services are open to foreign investment—with, of course, certain rules and exceptions in the fine

print. Protection of intellectual property rights is also to be strengthened.

As deregulation takes root, international firms will be able to enter the GCC markets more directly than ever before. One potential effect could be that multinationals that thus far have been averse to joint ventures due to a global practice of company-owned outlets will now enter these markets. Wal-Mart, Target, and the Home Depot, for example, might consider the GCC nations viable markets once they are able to have majority control of their stores in the region and can implement their sophisticated distribution and inventory-control systems. Global firms could also start making acquisitions of local firms in order to access the market more quickly and aggressively. As many family-owned conglomerates will be looking to sell businesses that are underperforming or outside their core competency, multinationals are apt to find attractive acquisition targets if they look for them carefully. Increased attention to the region by global investment banks will help multinationals identify acquisition opportunities more easily.

Another and potentially farther-reaching implication of deregulation could be its impact on the relationships between multinational firms and their local distributors or agents. Being able (at least in theory) to enter the market themselves allows multinationals to push their distributors and agents to perform better. Simply providing market access through one's regulatory status will have no value, and local firms will need to position themselves as truly value-adding partners. This change, while possibly making some local firms uncomfortable, will likely raise everyone's level of performance and ultimately benefit GCC consumers.

The creation of free zones—pioneered by Dubai and the UAE and now present in other GCC countries—has had a deep impact on the viability of high-engagement market-entry strategies. In free zones, international firms are able to fully own their businesses and can repatriate all profits to the home office, often tax-free (though profits may ultimately be taxed in the home country). Besides the benefit of full equity ownership, free zones typically provide a full suite of support services, including office space, telecom infrastructure, meeting areas, and even on-site support for visas and other government paperwork. Free zones have made it easier for multinationals to enter certain GCC markets than one might have thought possible only 10 years ago. Especially as GCC states compete for international presence, free zones will need to demonstrate even greater appeal to multinationals in order to draw them in. One prime example of competition among free zones is that between the Dubai International Financial Centre (DIFC) and the Qatar Financial Centre (QFC). Both offer state-of-the art infrastructure and support services, and both boast impressive lists of multinational firms doing business there.[26]

While free zones provide global firms an easy way to establish a presence, market access is not always complete. First of all, free zones are not available in every country and are specialized by sector (e.g., technology, health care, education, etc.). Further, being registered in a free zone does not give the firm the same status and privileges as those enjoyed by "onshore" (local) firms. Institutions registered at the DIFC, for example, are prohibited from taking deposits, offering credit, or offering direct insurance in the UAE (although reinsurance and insurance brokerage and management are allowed, perhaps because of the risk involved).[27] They therefore act more as "offshore" entities or headquarters offices for the region. While Dubai Internet City has attracted leading firms such as Microsoft, HP, and Oracle, the offices there are not consumer facing. Upcoming free zones such as the Dubai Flower Centre Free Zone and the Dubai Carpet Free Zone promise to be more retail in nature, possibly with access to the general UAE market. Indeed, WTO requirements for greater foreign access to domestic markets may slowly erode the advantages of free zones.

As multinational firms migrate across the Engagement Spectrum in the GCC markets, direct market entry and acquisitions will become more feasible. The ongoing attractiveness of the region, along with multinationals' need for increased involvement in emerging markets, will fuel this growing strategic focus. For the short- and medium-term future, however, shallow-engagement and moderate-engagement strategies, when executed well, can help global firms tap the significant opportunity of the GCC while limiting risk and allowing an unschooled foreign firm to learn from highly sophisticated local partners.

KEY LESSONS

- In entering a GCC market, multinational firms can choose from a set of strategies within a *three-tier "Engagement Spectrum."*
- "Shallow-engagement" strategies such as straightforward *distribution agreements have been the norm but have their limitations* in terms of control and return.
- *As businesses grow in strategic importance, "moderate-engagement" strategies* such as joint ventures and partnerships *are key* to steering the business and capturing value.
- Effectively *migrating up to "high engagement" requires companies to assess fundamental market attractiveness*, foster institutional will, identify value-adding partners, and find a supportive regulatory environment.
- While acquisitions and direct market entry have historically been impossible, *regulatory reform and the rise of free zones* are making high-engagement strategies more feasible.

CHAPTER 6

Making Your Pitch: Marketing to GCC Buyers

INTRODUCTION

You return to your hotel room after a day of business meetings in Dubai (or another major Gulf city) and turn on the TV set while you unwind. As you flip through the satellite channels, much of what you see is familiar: Hollywood movies, European television channels, and other signs of Western culture. As you surf the cable channels, you come across a commercial that reminds you of so many that you've seen before—it features young, attractive, hip people enjoying themselves while music plays in the background. You see a familiar logo—Doritos chips—and will soon hear the classic Doritos *crunch*. Only after you turn up the volume do you realize that the music is from the Middle East and the language being spoken is Arabic. Not until then do you remember you're in Dubai, not Dallas.

A major advertising CEO has noted that "the challenge [of global marketing] is to take the best of an international brand and localize it."[1] So far in this book, we've discussed how the GCC countries present an increasingly attractive market, full of opportunity for multinational companies that approach it strategically.

We've discussed the backgrounds of each Gulf market and how, despite their similarities, each has its unique dynamics. We've also covered a range of market-entry strategies that span from simple distribution arrangements to joint ventures and organic market entry. By now you probably know you want to be in the market and you have a sense of how you might enter it.

The question now is how will you make your pitch: what should you do to attract GCC buyers?

There is, of course, no single answer to this question. Developing your marketing strategy for the region requires you to understand your target audience, their needs and aspirations, and how best to address those needs and aspirations in a fashion that resonates. If you are like many leading global companies, you will work with the local offices of another global firm—a marketing and advertising company that has been operating in the region for a while—to study the environment and hone your messaging. Also, regional marketing may be the responsibility of your local distributor or partner and, therefore, not at the top of your priority list. However, as your Gulf-region business becomes increasingly central to your global strategy, it is more important than ever that you understand the marketing challenges directly. A solid strategy relies on solid customer insights and a value proposition—a set of benefits to the customer—that is enduring and differentiated. Your only option is to build a marketing strategy that is region-specific.

While a region-specific marketing approach is crucial, the extent to which you customize your proposition for the Gulf is a complex issue. In many cases, customization helps—in others, it doesn't. In general, there are four levels of customization of marketing strategies that companies in the region typically employ. We call these the "Four Degrees of Adaptation," and they range from no customization at all to developing market-specific products and services exclusively for the GCC countries. The right degree for your business will depend on a host of factors: our research of the market, however, suggests that all four can be valuable depending on the circumstances.

If you choose to pursue opportunities in the GCC market, one challenge will be to find a marketing strategy that fits your business. In this chapter, we discuss paths that other multinational firms have chosen and draw lessons from their experiences.

FOUR DEGREES OF ADAPTATION

Multinationals have approached the GCC market with varying degrees of planning and preparation. Some firms, such as oil and gas companies, have long operated in the GCC countries through linkages with Gulf governments and their foreign allies. Others have been introduced to the region through enterprising local distributors or agents, and with little or no attention paid to their entry by the global head office. Another set—like Gap and IKEA—have been more deliberate about their market entry and their local market strategy, negotiating terms carefully and monitoring the performance of local franchisees with rigor. Some companies have made the GCC a strategic priority and have entered the market directly or in joint ventures with local partners. To say, therefore, that firms' marketing approaches have always been deliberate would not be entirely accurate.

Nonetheless, there are patterns to the ways multinationals have approached the region. When one looks at the range of customization strategies, four distinct stages can be identified, as illustrated in Figure 6.1.

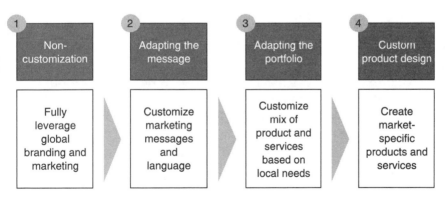

Figure 6.1 Four Degrees of Adaptation

The first degree of adaptation—noncustomization—is the simplest. Under this model, global firms use the marketing and branding approaches they use everywhere and apply those to the GCC markets. The second degree—adapting the message—is the most common route. This option involves using the Arabic language and some customized themes or taglines for the region, while leaving the underlying product unchanged. The next degree is adapting the portfolio: selling the same products in the Gulf that you sell elsewhere, but changing the mix to emphasize elements that have greatest appeal to buyers in GCC countries. The fourth degree of the framework, which involves the greatest effort but can at times yield the greatest reward, is to create products and services specifically for the GCC market.

Higher degrees of adaptation are not always better: the right level of customization depends entirely on your firm's customer base, product characteristics, and business economics. Each degree on the scale has its benefits and drawbacks and suits companies that face a particular set of circumstances. Thinking through the various options at the company's headquarters is important for enabling your firm to oversee its marketing strategy in the GCC for optimal effectiveness.

NONCUSTOMIZATION: MERITS AND DRAWBACKS

One axiom to global marketing, long acknowledged by academics and executives alike, is that standardization is the key to success. The argument for standardization is closely tied to the competitive advantage enjoyed by global corporations: the advantages of scale and of possessing cross-market expertise. What makes a global firm successful, the theory goes, is that it has found a way to make the same message resonate across the world. This message is the essence of the brand and changing it from country to country would reduce the value of the firm and the global appeal of the message. Furthermore, global marketing messages benefit from economies of scale: creating an ad, crafting a logo, and developing a tagline in your home language are fixed costs that should be extended to include as wide a base of customers as possible. Therefore, some argue, the default approach to a new market should be to apply to it everything that is used globally, and in the same way, and only to modify this if absolutely necessary.

In a well-supported argument, Harvard Business School professor Theodore Levitt asserted that "global companies must forget the idiosyncratic differences between countries and cultures and instead concentrate on satisfying universal drives."[2] Many of the world's leading consumer brands have pushed toward standardization and universal marketing as much as possible. Pepsi, for example, used Michael Jackson for worldwide endorsement of its wildly successful "Choice of a New Generation" campaigns in the 1980s. Nike previously used Michael Jordan as a world-renowned symbol of achievement and athletic performance; later it engaged Tiger Woods for the same purpose. The fragrance and cosmetic firm Coty has featured Jennifer Lopez as its global representative, and has used her image widely to promote its products. The underlying belief behind all these endorsements is that a single archetype can act as a universal representative of the brand concept: be it youth and vitality, athletic performance, or beauty and grace.

Within the context of GCC markets, there are circumstances in which complete noncustomization can make sense. High-end luxury goods—especially perfumes and handbags—are often advertised in women's magazines using French or English. The perfume ad in Figure 6.2 from the Saudi magazine *Laha* ("For Her") is entirely in French and uses European-looking (though dark-haired) models.

The rationale for such marketing appears sound: the brand is elite and global, and the experience offered is one of European sophistication or beauty. Using the Arabic language in the ad could dilute the "elite" status of the product and reduce its European look and feel. Another example, from the realm of financial services, would be in the context of high-end private banking and asset management. Firms that seek to emphasize their global presence, world-class systems and services, and international standards may prefer to use English in their advertisements to reinforce this positioning.

It is also crucial to remember that some products may target expatriate buyers, for whom the home language and brand positioning are in fact sources of comfort that reinforce the product's appeal. As discussed earlier in this book, half the GCC states—the UAE, Qatar, and Kuwait—are majority-expatriate. While political power, economic influence, and institutional decision-making rights tend to be squarely the province of the GCC country's national community, expatriates represent a huge segment of the market.

Figure 6.2 French perfume ad, Saudi women's magazine

The importance of expatriate buyers is especially clear with respect to consumer products and basic packaged goods, as the demand for these items is linked more to population numbers than to wealth. According to a study by the National Bank of Dubai, Asian expatriates alone account for over 60 percent of consumer spending in the UAE. UAE national spending would be overrepresented in categories such as luxury goods, high-end financial services, and automobiles, but not as much in consumer products. Considering the demographics, it is not surprising that one finds radio stations in the UAE broadcasting in English, Hindi, and other Asian languages in addition, of course, to Arabic.

Marketing to expatriates in the GCC states—at least those in the middle class and above—is an English-language affair. Although their native languages are diverse, almost all professional expatriates are expected to speak English in the workplace, and therefore their language proficiency is a threshold requirement for being hired. Marketing materials—and even government forms and applications—are usually in both Arabic and English. When dealing with expatriates and foreigners, salespeople and even government officials expect to use English. In fact, I once had an amusing experience with a Saudi customs officer as I entered the country on business. I had filled out the landing card in Arabic, but because I was traveling on a US passport he insisted I complete a new one in English. Go figure.

Some goods, such as foods and restaurants, having a special appeal to certain ethnic groups may be marketed in other languages, but only when the target audience is fairly narrow and/or lower income. Many working-class people in GCC countries do not speak English fluently, but can read basic signs and communicate in English if necessary. This demographic also has limited disposable income and often remits the bulk of this income to the home country. Multinational firms, therefore, can reach nearly all their relevant expatriate customers through English.

Institutional sales are another area in which a noncustomization strategy may be optimal. Institutional buyers tend to be sophisticated purchasers intent on global credibility and world-class performance. Purchasers of software and technology systems, for example, will almost certainly be English readers and will generally look for products and services that have been tried and tested in other markets. They will therefore expect the pitch to be in English and to reflect the global track record of the firm and its products. Some customization for individual users may be considered later on, but for the firm to prove itself as credible it needs not to stray from its global messages and branding materials. Trade shows and conventions for specialized goods are typically conducted in English, and Arabic speakers have become accustomed to the bilingual environment. In fact, Arabic speeches are typically translated into English at major conferences.

CHRISTMAS IN DUBAI: SERVING EXPATRIATES AND TOURISTS

Dubai's Deira City Centre shopping mall, perhaps the city's most popular attraction, is a place where one sees a whole spectrum of marketing strategies being pursued. Hundreds of multinational brands are on display, including US, European, and Asian labels. Naturally, each multinational has taken its own unique approach in customizing for the market, and some customize much more than others.

Much of Deira City Centre—in fact, much more than one sees in other GCC cities—caters to expatriates and tourists. Stores display, for example, risqué "club gear" of interest to expatriates and tourists partaking of Dubai's uncommonly liberal nightlife. Stores here also feature more sweaters and heavy coats than are seen elsewhere, likely targeting tourists from colder climates who are passing through. Few store names are in Arabic alone: this mall is clearly a bilingual place.

The photograph in Figure 6.3, taken in December 2006, illustrates the extent to which the mall seeks to make expatriates and tourists feel at home. The large Christmas tree clearly caters to tourists on winter holiday: only a small proportion of UAE residents (including expatriates) celebrate Christmas. Tourists from the UK, Australia, and continental Europe most certainly do. Elsewhere in the mall, one would see promotional staff dressed as Santa's helpers. Considering Dubai's shopping demographics, these distinctly non-Arabic measures can make business sense.[3]

A noncustomization strategy can be a sound approach if a multinational's target audience in the Gulf does not require Arabic and if the brand appeal is already so deeply tied to foreign affiliation that using the Arabic language would be counterproductive. Noncustomization is, of course, convenient and cost-effective: it requires no incremental marketing design. This efficiency is especially helpful when either (1) a great deal of money has been spent on fixed costs such as global promotions (e.g., very expensive celebrity endorsers) and other global expenses (print advertising, shipping, etc.) or (2) the estimated market demand in the GCC countries is too small to justify spending meaningfully on marketing. Very minor adjustments, however, such as those involving language, can be done at a fairly low cost.

While noncustomization has its merits, it also has significant drawbacks and limitations. The most fundamental of these is that it can make the multinational seem too foreign and therefore a misfit for the region. This risk appears principally in consumer-facing goods, where a sense that such goods belong in a community is

Figure 6.3 Christmas tree, Dubai shopping mall

crucial. Local competitors can gain an edge over global firms if the global firms seem indifferent to or disinterested in local needs. Restricting oneself to the multinational's home language also limits the breadth of the market to which the message is accessible: bilingual strategies have greater reach. Noncustomization can also be a cue that the global firm will not make a special effort at customer service: for example, that it won't have salespeople who speak Arabic. These drawbacks are prohibitive for many firms that seek deep penetration into the GCC market. The most common approach, therefore, is not noncustomization but rather the next degree further: adapting the message.

ADAPTING THE MESSAGE

The majority of global firms and their local distributors see some degree of customization as crucial for connecting with

GCC-country buyers. The most basic form of this is product labeling: using Arabic on product packages to make it easier for non-English speakers to identify and purchase products. Most consumer product companies have taken this simple step—from giants like Coca-Cola and Sprite[4] to smaller companies like Snapple (see Figure 6.4).

Figure 6.4 Bilingual packaging is common in the GCC countries

As is visible on the Crest box, the norm is bilingual packaging—not Arabic-only. The packaging can therefore be understood by almost the entire target audience. In print and television advertising, the most direct way to customize is to take global ads, taglines, and brand messages and translate them into Arabic. Often this is the most effective way to maintain consistent brand messages across markets. Table 6.1 illustrates how HSBC, McDonald's, and others—all of which invest heavily in creating globally consistent brands—use Arabic-language taglines in the GCC that are identical or similar to their global taglines.

HSBC and McDonald's have taken their global taglines and translated them, with slight modification to reflect grammatical norms and linguistic elegance. Ford's adaptation captures the non-technical connotation of the word "drive," in order to reflect the spirit of the brand message more. Snickers and Gillette likewise adapt their taglines to convey the sense of the original message using quite different words.

TABLE 6.1

Global and GCC Taglines

Company	Global Tagline	Arabic Tagline	Literal Meaning[5]
HSBC	"The world's local bank"	"Bank al-'alam al-muhalli"	"Local bank of the world"
McDonald's	"I'm lovin' it"	"Ana uhibbuhu"	"I love it"
Ford	"Drive"	"Taw alla al-qiyadah"	"Take the lead"
Snickers	"Hungry? Grab a Snickers."	"Iqhar ju`ak"	"Conquer your hunger"
Gillette	"The best a man can get"	"Ma yastahiqquhu al-rijal"	"What men deserve"

Coca-Cola and Pepsi, in their regional marketing, have both engaged Lebanese pop stars (Nancy Arjam and Elissa Khoury, respectively) to endorse their products. Pepsi's Elissa ads have been likened at times to its global ones with Christina Aguilera, although the Middle East ads are somewhat less provocative. Frito-Lay, in its Doritos ads, uses the signature *crunch* and upbeat, young actors. The Coke, Pepsi, and Doritos ads all seek to convey the universal brand messages of youth and enjoyment—wrapped in the local language and with local music. For their target demographic, these companies have apparently found that the universal conceptual messages convey the spirit of the brand most effectively. Local actors and the local language, however, are believed to connect better with the GCC country's youth segment being targeted. Taking global advertising scripts, translating the ad into Arabic, and hiring Arab actors for the shoots can be an appropriate strategy but does have its risks. The norms of GCC advertising, which in turn are linked to the culture of the various GCC countries, often call for adaptation of the motifs and messages beyond a switch to the Arabic language.

Gulf Advertising Norms Call for Deeper Adaptation

Advertising norms in the Gulf, and in the broader Middle East, are significantly different from norms in the United States and Europe.

Local advertising agencies—whether they are local offices of global firms or independent local companies—certainly appreciate this phenomenon and can guide multinationals accordingly. From a global headquarters perspective, however, it is imperative that marketers understand that genuine adaptation for the Gulf will often require changing much more than just language.

In a seminal study published in the *International Journal of Advertising*,[6] Kiran Karande, Khalid Al-Murshidee, and Fahad Al-Olayan analyzed advertising in the UAE and recorded some highly noteworthy findings, a few of which follow:

- Of the UAE ads analyzed, 24 percent were for cosmetics and 28 percent were for jewelry. In other words, over half the ads analyzed were for largely feminine luxury or specialist products.
- Eighty-one percent of the ads featured women in long clothing. In a 2000 study, Al-Olayan and Karande had found that only 29 percent of US ads featured women in long clothing.[7]
- An overwhelming majority of the ads—90 percent— showed women with the relevant product. Remember, though, that only about 50 percent of the ads analyzed were for cosmetics and jewelry.
- Only 6 percent of ads were comparative in nature (showing two or more products), whereas the 2000 study showed that 26 percent of US ads were comparative.
- Only 8 percent of the ads had five or more informational cues; in the United States, 32 percent of ads did. The US ads were therefore more information-heavy than the UAE ones.

The findings above are highly instructive for global marketers who wish to know how to adapt their messages for the GCC markets. One clear lesson relates to showing women in long clothing: the norm in the GCC countries is for women to dress more conservatively than they do in the United States and other Western countries, and the ads reflect this. Besides any concerns about censorship or public rebuke (much more of a concern in Saudi Arabia than in the UAE, where the study took place), there is a more basic point: the audience can apparently relate better to women in long clothing because they, too, wear long clothing. Savvy global firms are catching on to this understanding: the cosmetic and fragrance company Coty reportedly shot a special ad campaign for the Middle East. The ad shows only the face of Jennifer Lopez, in stark contrast with ads shown in other markets that are more sensual and revealing.[8]

A second key message relates to the depth of information provided and explicit comparison with competitors. Gulf ads are typically concise and direct rather than deeply informative. Even firms selling complex products like mobile phones and electronics may be well served to focus their advertisement on the brand attributes and lifestyle they wish to communicate, as opposed to product specifications and technical details. That information, if conveyed at all, could be communicated at the point of sale or elsewhere.

The finding that explicitly comparative ads are far less common in the GCC states than elsewhere has evoked no shortage of hypotheses seeking to explain it. One is that the buyer in a GCC market is more concerned with exclusivity and being "special"; therefore reference to other products is counterproductive. Another theory, which I feel would apply to luxury categories, is that the buyer may be less price sensitive and, therefore, the product's being a "better buy" (i.e., less expensive) than its competitors' matters less. Yet another theory, which seems too vague and broad, is that the Gulf is consensus oriented and, therefore, direct negative comments about competitors are seen as insensitive or even unethical. While none of these explanations seems particularly compelling, the observation that comparison ads are less common than in the United States is an important one for marketers to bear in mind.

Good for the Goose, Not for the Gander

While, for the purposes of this book, we discuss "Gulf advertising norms" as a common set of principles, styles and tastes certainly differ from market to market. UAE ads, as confirmed in the *International Journal of Advertising* study, do tend to feature women in long clothing, but more provocative ads can sometimes be shown.

In the course of our research, we looked into the differences in advertising norms among GCC markets. One market insider and expert pointed us to a European ad that, in her experience, would be acceptable in the UAE but certainly off-limits in Saudi Arabia[9] (see Figure 6.5).

Figure 6.5 Acceptable in the UAE, questionable in Saudi Arabia

By Western standards, the ad is not risqué: the model is wearing long sleeves, and her skirt nearly reaches her knees. Yet in the
socially conservative Saudi market, we were told, the ad would be
considered inappropriate and would attract criticism. Marketers
are thus left with a dilemma: whether to use different ads for different Gulf markets or to develop materials that can be deployed
across the region. Especially if customization of ad content or language is called for, economies of scale suggest that firms are often
better off avoiding the controversial and finding other ways to communicate the edginess of their brand.

The *International Journal of Advertising* piece cited above also
confirms a fundamental market reality that we discussed in
Chapter 2, on misconceptions. Female buyers in the Gulf, like
female buyers everywhere, make the majority of purchase decisions and are therefore the target audience for savvy marketers.
Women in the GCC countries decide not only what household

products such as food, children's goods, and furniture will be purchased, but also which of the increasingly important luxury goods. It is noteworthy that over half the ads in the researchers' sample were for cosmetics and jewelry. One reason why female shoppers in the GCC countries may have more disposable income than their counterparts elsewhere is that young professional women tend to live with their parents until they are married and, therefore, do not need to spend on rent and basic household expenses. Even after they marry, there is far less expectation that a professional woman will spend her income on sharing the rent or mortgage or other basic costs of living. It should not be surprising, then, that 90 percent of ads reviewed featured women with the relevant product.

McDonald's: Healthy, Halal, and Family Oriented

McDonald's and its local franchisees have long understood the importance of customizing messages for the local audience. The advertisement in Figure 6.6, from the UAE, is a prime example of customizing a message beyond language alone. The slogan at the top of the ad can be translated to read: "High quality is our sole standard."

A close look at the ad shows that it is tailored for the Gulf market in multiple ways. One basic message, communicated through the image and not through words, is that McDonald's is a family-friendly place. The young family in the front is our focus, but behind them are other couples. Both men and women are dressed in traditional Gulf clothing. Perhaps unlike their positioning in other markets, where McDonald's ads may emphasize being young and hip, this UAE ad presents McDonald's as a family restaurant.

The text reveals further market sensitivity. While the thrust of the ad is on nutritional quality (perhaps a top-of-mind concern in the wake of the recent mad cow disease outbreak and other high-profile health issues), the text also makes reference to all the meat served being halal—permissible by Islamic law. The first sentence in the ad reads: "The meats used by us are halal and are the highest grade of 100 percent pure beef without any additives or preservatives." Local marketers have therefore combined the health message with reassurance that the meat is halal—an important concern in the Gulf region.

Figure 6.6 McDonald's customizes its message

Clearly, the ad is tailored to this specific market, not just in terms of language, but in terms of tone, content, and messages. This level of adaptation makes McDonald's a far more rooted franchise than many other multinational firms in the region.

While adapting the message for the GCC market is an important step in connecting genuinely to Gulf buyers, some firms take customization one step further. These companies adapt their product mix for the region in an effort to better suit the local needs and preferences.

ADAPTING THE PORTFOLIO

Adapting the portfolio for the GCC market is a simple but powerful way to better connect with the market without needing to invest in unique product development. The concept is straightforward: Examine your company's global product portfolio, and identify the products and services that seem most relevant. Then, stock a greater proportion of those items at locations in your GCC countries than you do elsewhere. If, for example, advanced mobile phones appeal more to buyers in GCC countries than to buyers elsewhere, devote more retail space to phones in Qatar than you do in, say, Istanbul or Sarajevo. At first glance, the concept seems so obvious that you'd expect everyone to use it.

Executing a portfolio adaptation, however, can be much more challenging than it seems. One implication of a customized portfolio is that it will differ from other retail locations worldwide. Regional managers need to be able—and empowered—to adopt a merchandising strategy that differs from the global head office's international vision. Perhaps the hot item that global marketing seeks to push worldwide this year simply won't fit the Gulf market. The general manager in each GCC locale must have the latitude to assert a strategy he or she feels is effective and must be supported in procuring inventory that may vary from the global guidelines. Another challenge in executing this approach is that of acquiring reliable and analyzed data. While modern inventory and purchase scanning technology makes capturing this information possible, the difficulty lies in accurately analyzing the data (at the distributor or franchisee level or at the global headquarters) and communicating the analysis between the main office and the region alone. From my experience advising retail clients, I can assure you these things are more easily said than done.

One sector in which portfolio customization can frequently be found is the apparel industry. Especially in women's fashions, international retailers are discovering more about local market needs and highlighting the products in their global portfolios that best meet those needs. Among the distinct needs of the GCC market are, according to expert analysts, "a steady flow of new products which are well-designed, use lightweight fabrics all year round and offer long sleeve and skirt options for those wishing to cover up."[10] Good design, of course, is a competency to which all fashion retailers would wish to lay claim. The other aspects of this target business model are not a perfect fit with every retailer.

A steady supply of new products, according to industry analysts, is perhaps more important in the Gulf than elsewhere, because of the youthful demographics of the region. Teenage girls everywhere, of course, like new clothes. The reason this matters more in the GCC countries is that teenage girls compose a larger portion of the total market than they do elsewhere. Lightweight fabrics fit the global style of some firms—H&M, for example—more than they do of others. And while most retailers will have some long skirts and long-sleeve shirts, these items will often use designs targeting older women (as older women are the ones who dress more conservatively in most other markets) and will likely make up a relatively small proportion of the total clothing line.

One retailer whose global capabilities and regional savvy have enabled it to execute an adapt-the-portfolio strategy with great success is the Spanish retailer Zara. Its competencies gel with the tastes of the Gulf region, and its local management has apparently understood the opportunity well.

Zara: Fashion That Fits

Zara, the Spanish retailer, is a success story now sweeping the fashion industry. The firm, known by consumers for its trendy fashion at reasonable prices, now has more than 650 stores and has reached more than four dozen countries.[11] Zara has become a prominent global brand and is, in some ways, Spain's global ambassador of style. It also turns out that the attributes that drive Zara's global success are a very strong fit with the booming GCC market.

Zara's unique operating model has been summarized by Harvard Business School researchers as "new products in small quantities,"[12] and the company's ability to execute this model has been widely seen as its core competitive advantage. Zara has a team of 200 designers working on the premises of the production facility, helping churn out new fashions at a remarkable rate. These designers are typically women in their 20s, exactly the same demographic as Zara's target audience worldwide and in the Gulf. The mandate of the design team is to innovate . . . and to do it fast. According to the Harvard researchers, Zara's designers mock up 40,000 new designs each year, of which 10,000 are actually produced. These are produced in small quantities, allowing for greater experimentation at lower risk.

The needs of the GCC market fall squarely within Zara's skill set. The GCC market seeks new and trendy items, and that's what

Zara delivers. The GCC market is young—exactly Zara's core audience. And, equally important, Zara's ability to develop a wide range of products without undertaking huge production runs lets the firm deliver products to the Gulf that suit the region's needs. Zara stores in the GCC countries feature, for example, many more long skirts and long-sleeved shirts than Zara stores elsewhere. And while these items may not sell as much outside the GCC market, Zara's business model does not inhibit niche products. In fact, the high-innovation culture of Zara values the creation of niche products that resonate with some consumers but may not become global bestsellers.

Zara has 47 stores in the Middle East, of which 29 are in GCC countries. In these stores, new items are put on display each week and attract large numbers of buyers. Moreover, Zara's Mediterranean roots serve it well in the Gulf region, where lightweight fabrics for warm weather are valued. Local managers, with the support of Zara's renowned inventory and stocking system, have apparently been able to monitor sales closely and keep requesting the goods that move. Zara does not even need to create anything especially for the Gulf; it needs only to make sure that products with GCC-appeal find their way to the region. From the Gulf buyer's perspective, Zara represents fashion that fits.

Adapting the product portfolio need not be expensive. It requires some analysis, but not the most advanced systems in the world. Achieving the third degree of adaptation is more a matter of mind-set and of empowerment than of cost. And the benefits, when executed effectively, can be remarkable.

CUSTOM PRODUCT DESIGN

The fourth and highest degree of adaptation goes beyond customized marketing and a customized product mix—it takes the notion of customization down to the product level. Firms that pursue this strategy develop products or services especially for the GCC markets, investing in the design of these offerings with the belief that incremental sales will more than cover the costs. Taking this step requires careful consideration, but can be warranted when it leads to deeply compelling customer propositions.

McDonald's, which has over the years developed a knack worldwide for balancing its global brand with small local touches, has reached this fourth degree of adaptation with its distinctive "McArabia" sandwich. The sandwich consists of two pieces of grilled chicken wrapped in Arabic bread, dressed with lettuce, onions, tomatoes, and a yogurt-tahini sauce. As noted by observers, the McArabia is both an adaptation of the Big Mac–chicken sandwich and a response to the *shawarma* (gyro) sandwich, which is a highly popular and low-cost meal in the Arab world.[13] While the shawarma itself traces its roots to the Levant (not the Gulf), its widespread consumption in the GCC countries has made it very much a local food.

McDonald's is no stranger to the GCC market. As illustrated in Table 6.2, the American franchise has been in all six GCC countries since the 1990s. Its franchisees are some of the most influential businesspeople in the Gulf region, including a descendant of the former Saudi monarch, King Faisal.

T A B L E   6 . 2

McDonald's in the GCC

Country	Year of Entry	Franchisee	Number of Locations
Saudi Arabia[14]	1993	REZA Food Services Co. Ltd. (Western Province); Riyadh International Catering Corp. (Central and Eastern Provinces)	96
UAE[15]	1994	Emirates Fast Food Corp.	44
Kuwait[16]	1994	Al Maousherji Catering Co.	46
Bahrain[17]	1994	Fakhro Restaurants Co.	10
Oman[18]	1994	Al Daud Restaurants LLC	5
Qatar[19]	1995	Kamal Al Mana	9

It is important to bear in mind two factors when considering McDonald's' ability to develop the McArabia sandwich for the Gulf market. First, the franchise has capabilities and a precedent worldwide for developing market-specific items such as rice burgers for Taiwan and Japan, shrimp burgers for Korea, McCurry Pan for India, and DeliChoices for Australia.[20] McArabia, therefore, is simply an extension of a global capability and best practice into a new region. The second factor is one of cost or scale economics.

While product development and launch of the McArabia burger was managed from Kuwait, the sandwich has appeal far beyond the Gulf. In fact, the sandwich is now marketed elsewhere in the Middle East and even in Indonesia, a nation of 240 million. Any fixed product development costs have therefore been spread over a much wider base of customers than could be accessed in Kuwait alone—or in the entire GCC market.

These two factors—capabilities and cost—are fundamental issues that firms must consider when weighing the option of reaching the fourth degree of adaptation. Firms that do not customize products anywhere in the world—presumably for reasons of efficiency and standardization—will naturally have difficulty doing so solely for the GCC market. Further, product development costs in some sectors, especially those that require sophisticated engineering or intense research and development, may make customization unprofitable. Heavy industry and pharmaceuticals, for example, are two areas in which developing a product exclusively for the Gulf market may prove neither financially viable nor necessary if a customized product mix is possible.

When appropriate, however, product-level customization can have a significant impact in making a global firm's appeal to a GCC market more genuine. The McArabia sandwich is a bestseller, and its presence—along with many other signs of cultural awareness and sensitivity—enhances McDonald's position as highly connected to the local community. Perhaps this is one reason why, despite deep-seated opposition to US policy in the Middle East, McDonald's restaurants have continued to thrive in recent years. Consumer demand has remained strong even as political tensions have ebbed and flowed.

HELP FROM A FRIEND

While the challenges of marketing to GCC buyers may appear somewhat daunting, multinationals can take comfort in the fact that nearly all leading global marketing firms—including the world's top six in earnings—are active in the Gulf and able to support local activity.[21] The global firms often work through local affiliates, who adopt the high standards and best practices of the global parent. Table 6.3 illustrates the presence in the Gulf countries of leading global marketing firms, including marquee ones.

T A B L E 6 . 3

GCC Presence of Top 6 Global Marketing Firms[22]

Group	Firm	Subsidiary	KSA	UAE	KWT	BHR	QTR	OMN	Representative Clients
Omnicom (USA)	BBDO Worldwide	Impact BBDO	HQ						Pepsi, IKEA, Hitachi
	TBWA Worldwide	TBWA Raad, Tequila Raad							Al Jazeera, Adidas
WPP Group (UK)	Grey Worldwide	Grey Worldwide Middle East, Blu Grey							GlaxoSmithKline, Nokia
	JWT	JWT							HSBC, Orascom Telecom, Nestle
	Ogilvy & Mather	MEMAC Ogilvy, Ogilvy One Middle East							Gulf Air, Unilever, Volvo
	Y&R Advertising	Team/Y&R		HQ					DHL, Etisalat, Philip Morris
Interpublic (USA)	FCB Worldwide	Horizon FCB							Kraft, Swatch, Dow Chemicals
	MCN	Promoseven Network, Universal Media, LOWE							McDonald's, Kingdom Holding

			HQ HQ	
Publicis Group (France)	Leo Burnett Worldwide	Radius Leo Burnett, Targets Leo Burnett		P&G, Philip Morris, GM
	Publicis Worldwide	Publicis Graphics		British Airways, L'Oreal
	Saatchi and Saatchi	Akeel/Gulf Saatchi and Saatchi		Lexus, General Mills
Havas Group (France)	Euro RSCG Worldwide	Euro RCSG Furness, Euro RSCG Promopub		Airbus, Microsoft
Dentsu (Japan)	not available	not available		not available

It is evident from Table 6.3 that all firms with a presence in the Gulf have offices in both Saudi Arabia and the UAE, and some in places beyond. This phenomenon reflects the simple but powerful reality that, in consumer terms, Saudi Arabia is the core market of the GCC. No credible consumer marketing firm can ignore it: its population is twice the size of that of the other GCC states combined, and its $400 billion economy is half the GCC states' total. On the other hand, restrictions on creative expression and experimentation throughout all media in Saudi Arabia mean that the UAE, with its business- and expatriate-friendly environment, is a natural choice for a headquarters location, as we will discuss later in this book.

The GCC represents a major growth engine for marketing firms. Local marketing talent is in high demand, and global firms are investing in people, infrastructure, and research in order to strengthen their regional propositions. WPP, the world's second-largest advertising company, reported in its April 2007 earnings statement that "the Middle East continues to be the fastest-growing area."[23]

Multinationals with strong global brands often engage one of the leading marketing firms with a global mandate. Pepsi, for example, works with Omnicom to maintain brand consistency and leverage best practices worldwide. The fact that the marketing agencies are now equipped to serve clients in the GCC states is another enabling factor that makes entry and growth in the region more feasible.

KEY LESSONS

- In marketing to GCC buyers, multinationals must choose from *Four Degrees of Adaptation;* no single strategy will work for all companies.
- *Noncustomization* can be effective when the value proposition of the product or service is international or global in nature.
- *Adapting the message* can be crucial for consumer propositions and spans beyond mere translation to culturally appropriate images, themes, and approaches.

- *Adapting the portfolio* is an important and effective strategy by which multinational firms can selectively choose which products from their global suite they emphasize in the GCC market.
- Some firms invest in *product customization and design* for specific GCC countries—a strategy that can win customer acceptance and loyalty but requires careful cost-benefit analysis.
- *Global marketing and advertising firms* have developed their presence in the GCC region and are available to serve multinational clients in a manner consistent with their global positioning.

CHAPTER 7

Building Your Team: Human Capital Strategies for the GCC

INTRODUCTION

Not long ago, a leading global professional services firm was faced with a peculiar challenge. Companies from the Gulf were actively seeking the firm's services, sending requests for proposals and contacting offices directly. The work being requested was exciting and well within the firm's areas of expertise. The prospective clients were fast-growing institutions more than able to pay the firm's hefty fees: exactly the type of client professional services firms love to serve. All signs pointed to an opportunity to grow a practice in the Gulf region in short order.

What, then, was the problem? As the firm scanned its database of staff worldwide—a staff that numbered in the thousands—they realized that hardly more than a dozen professionals could speak Arabic. Thankfully, most clients in GCC countries did not require Arabic-speaking employees. To build a long-term franchise there, however, the firm needed to identify and recruit staff with an affinity for the region. Within a year of realizing this, the firm had opened offices there, and the new offices were booking more clients at a remarkable rate.

For fast-growing companies and industries, human capital is often the biggest constraint limiting expansion. Business ideas and funding may be abundant, but people with the skills and motivation to turn these ideas into realities are not easy to find. When firms do find them, they discover that these people are in great demand, expensive, and difficult to retain. Certainly this is the case with talented staff who know the GCC market—as opportunities have multiplied, so have the challenges in attracting and retaining a world-class team. Unlike many emerging markets, where jobs with multinational firms are the most coveted by locals as a step toward greater prosperity and mobility, the Gulf is a place where multinationals must compete with public sector and local firms that can often promise greater comfort, stability, and wealth-creation opportunities—especially for GCC country nationals.

Since the boom in prosperity 1970s, the Gulf has been deeply reliant on expatriate talent. Expatriates have played leading roles at many levels of the talent market: bringing board-level executive skills, providing technical and management expertise, and serving as the basic labor supply across all sectors of the economy. Reliance on foreign workers, viewed by insiders as a necessary evil, has had demographic implications that few Gulf governments would have expected 50 years ago—half the GCC states today are majority expatriate. Governments have crafted immigration policies that minimize the political impact of expatriate workers, yet their centrality to the Gulf economies must be understood by employers, marketers, and policy makers alike. While demographic shifts and population growth have made "localizing" the workforce (that is, hiring GCC nationals) a political imperative, practical realities dictate ongoing engagement of expatriate staff for the foreseeable future.

Savvy multinationals, in crafting their human capital strategy for the Gulf region, should take a multistage view. In the short term, the imperative is to recruit and empower expatriate talent with expertise on and affinity toward the region. In the medium term, firms should seek to attract and retain high-caliber GCC national executives at the early stages of their careers. Longer term, multinationals with serious ambitions in the region have little choice but to invest in human capital development there.

While the Gulf represents a highly attractive commercial opportunity for many multinationals, capitalizing on the opportunity is impossible without having the right team. This chapter will explore the critical question of human capital—a matter that savvy firms must weigh carefully in designing their approach to the region.

INEVITABLE RELIANCE: WHY THE GULF HAS NEEDED FOREIGN WORKERS

Gulf labor markets are, to outside observers, anomalies. The majority of the population of three of the six GCC states—the UAE, Qatar, and Kuwait—are expatriates,[1] and the expatriates' role has been unambiguous: to provide labor. This labor pool has included senior executive and other management and professional functions, as well as basic work such as manual labor and unskilled services. Spend a day in almost any Gulf country and you will come across a great number of foreign workers—including hotel staff, taxi drivers, clerks at fast-food and grocery counters, the people pumping gas at the corner service station, you name it. Visit a hospital or clinic and you will find expatriate doctors, nurses, and support staff. Go to a school or university and many, if not most, of the teachers will be expatriates; even in Arabic-language schools, many teachers are Egyptian, Lebanese, Syrian, or Iraqi. And don't forget the "invisible" expatriate workers such as domestic help and construction workers, without whom neither the economy nor many people's homes could function. Few who live in the GCC states, in fact, could imagine life without the expatriate labor on which the countries rely. But how did the Gulf end up with such peculiar labor dynamics?

The answer lies in the unique circumstances of the GCC's economic development (see Figure 7.1). The oil booms of the 1970s raised GDP per capita abruptly and caused Gulf economies to leapfrog, in terms of wealth, ahead of other developing countries without the requisite intermediate steps. In the course of a single decade, for example, Saudi Arabia's per capita GDP went from less than one-fifth of that of the United States to more than one-quarter higher than the US level—representing a tremendous compound annual growth rate of 33 percent.

Most countries that have attained prosperity have done so through more gradual and conventional means, such as building

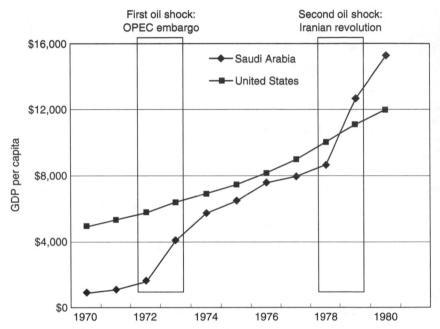

Figure 7.1 Saudi GDP per capita spiked and surpassed the United States' in the 1970s (Source: United Nations)

up industrial infrastructure, educational infrastructure, and the commercial sector through centuries of institution building. This has not been the case in the Gulf, where wealth came quickly but institutions were scarce. GCC states were therefore faced with a peculiar situation: prosperity without infrastructure. Elsewhere, institutions preceded wealth; in the Gulf the sequence was largely reversed.

Figure 7.2 illustrates the phenomenon by which GCC economies found themselves needing to "backfill" institutional development to match their level of prosperity.

Without the benefit of sustained institutional development, GCC states have faced an imperative to build institutions in the wake of their abrupt rise to prosperity. In essence, they have needed to backfill, or catch up on, infrastructure development in order to be on a par with other countries at similar levels of wealth.[2]

The human capital implications of this backfill imperative have been profound. GCC government and private-sector leaders

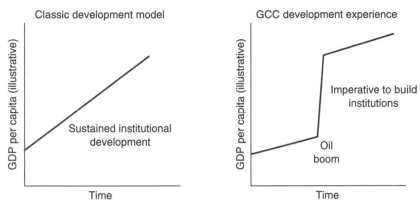

Figure 7.2 Prosperity without institutions: the backfill imperative

needed to embark on an ambitious infrastructure development agenda in the wake of the oil boom, for which the local labor market was not sufficient. A first issue was simply one of scarcity: the sheer number of people needed across all sectors was far more than were locally available. A second, more delicate issue was one of skills. In the 1970s and preceding decades, educational and training facilities in the Gulf were not nearly as plentiful—or as sophisticated—as were needed as the GCC economies developed. The engineers needed for massive infrastructure projects were few and far between; the educators needed to staff schools and colleges were scarce; the managers needed to run larger institutions and businesses were simply not available in the domestic market. Expatriate talent was the only option.

Fortunately for the GCC states, labor from nearby, less prosperous countries has been readily available. The Gulf, as discussed earlier, has been a magnet for Arab talent and represents the most attractive workplace in the Middle East region. Between 1975 and the early 1980s, the number of Arab expatriate workers in the Gulf states nearly doubled.[3] Since then, there has been a steady stream of Arab talent flowing to the region—drawn by its opportunities, proximity, and linguistic and cultural compatibility. South Asia, with a population well above 1 billion people, is another natural pool of talent for the Gulf and has rapidly become the largest source for expatriate workers in the GCC. Manual labor such as construction work and janitorial services is carried out largely by

South Asian expatriates. Although few South Asian expatriates speak Arabic fluently, many are Muslims and therefore feel a greater identification with Gulf culture than workers without this background do. South Asian expatriates also tend to form communities of common origin, in which they speak their native languages, wear their traditional clothing, and eat their traditional foods. They therefore are able to enjoy many of the comforts of home while working abroad and earning far more than they could in their native market.

Expatriates from the West and OECD (Organization for Economic Cooperation and Development) world, though not nearly as numerous, have played a crucial role in providing executive leadership and technical expertise over the past decades. British expatriates and political officers have long wielded influence in the region, in the days of the Trucial States and as early as the nineteenth century through treaties with local rulers. Since the 1970s, GCC institutions have employed OECD staff in senior roles, often in areas requiring sophisticated technical analysis (e.g., engineering and finance) or in areas that involve international relations and cross-border activity (e.g., law and public affairs). The prevalence of expatriate workers from the West and from Asia, along with the legacy of British influence over the region, has led to a business culture in Gulf private-sector firms in which English is the language of the workplace, and most workers are not required to know Arabic. In the public sector, of course, Arabic is much more crucial.

Among GCC leaders, regard for Western education and training is very high. Western institutions of learning are viewed as world-class and as having the highest standards. This is one reason why Western and OECD expatriates enjoy high status and high compensation in the Gulf. Another consequence of the high regard for Western education—in addition to local educational facilities being new and still catching up with global leaders—is that a remarkably high proportion of senior Gulf leaders have been educated or trained in the West. Over the past three decades, the Gulf states have sponsored tens of thousands of undergraduate and graduate students each year to study in the West and especially in the United States. In recent years, fiscal pressures due to population growth have made the sponsorship process for Gulf-country students seeking to study abroad more competitive than before. At the same time, less welcoming visa policies, government practices, and public sentiment in the United States (and, to a lesser degree, the UK) have somewhat diminished the appetite of GCC-state students for studying in the West. Nonetheless, the United States and other developed countries remain a key training ground for top-notch GCC talent.

Consider, for example, the backgrounds of the senior management team at Saudi Aramco—Saudi Arabia's national oil company and by far the most important business in the country. All nine executives on the top team have US educational credentials, as illustrated in Table 7.1.

TABLE 7.1

Saudi Aramco's Top Team: US Educational Credentials[4]

Role	US Educational Credentials
President and CEO	Executive Education, Harvard Business School
Senior Vice President (SVP), Engineering and Project Management	Bachelor's degree, University of Tulsa; Executive Education, Harvard Business School
SVP, Industrial Relations	Bachelor's degree, Texas A&M
SVP, Refining, Marketing, and International	Bachelor's, master's, and MBA degrees, University of California; Executive Education, Wharton
General Counsel and Secretary	Bachelor's degree, University of California Santa Barbara; JD, University of Southern California; Executive Education, MIT
SVP, Finance	MBA, MIT
SVP, Gas Operations	Executive Education, Cornell
SVP, Exploration and Production	Bachelor's degree, University of Oklahoma; Executive Education, University of Pittsburgh
SVP, Operations Services	MBA, University of California Riverside

The credentials gained from the United States on technical matters (e.g., engineering and law) and executive management (executive education and MBA degrees) reflect the core knowledge domains for which Gulf executives admire Western training.

"I JUST WORK HERE": TERMS OF ENGAGEMENT FOR EXPATRIATE WORKERS

There is an irony of sorts in the norms of expatriate worker engagement in the GCC countries. Precisely *because* expatriate workers are so crucial to the GCC economies, they are engaged—through regulation and through the local management norms—at a distance and treated very much as foreigners. In numerous ways, expatriate workers are reminded time and again that the Gulf region is not their home and, almost certainly, never will be. This approach is quite striking and fundamentally different from how migrant workers are typically engaged elsewhere, especially in the Western world.

Consider the life of an expatriate worker. He or she is employed on a contract basis and could be sent home after a couple of years if the employer chooses not to renew his or her contract. If he is a low-wage worker, his family is not granted visas, and therefore he sees his wife and children only a couple of times each year (at best), and perhaps not at all for several years if he is trying to maximize savings and remittances. If the expatriate is a professional-grade worker, his or her family will be together but quite likely only one of the spouses (usually the male) will have a work visa, and the other will not be legally employable. The children will most likely attend a school linked with the home country's system and attended by youngsters of the same cultural or racial background: British children generally attend British schools; Indians, Indian schools. Should the family have a child born in a GCC country, the child will not be a national of that country. The child will inherit the parents' nationality, even if the child has never been to that country. One could live in the Gulf for decades, working loyally for an employer, and be forced to leave upon retirement to return to a country with which one is out of touch.[5] Citizenship laws in the region make naturalization practically impossible for most expatriate workers.[6]

In many ways, the alienating fashion in which expatriate workers are engaged seems unfair or even cruel. In private, business and government leaders will acknowledge that the practices have disturbing effects. The rationale for such policies is basic protectionism: the local workforce, it is argued, was not in a position to compete with foreign workers at the time of the oil booms because the schooling and training systems were simply not in place. As mentioned previously, the sheer volume of projects and economic development begun in the 1970s required massive levels of foreign workers. If these workers were given a path to naturalization, the argument runs, the local community would have been quickly crowded out and would have lost control of their own country. Certainly in the countries with expatriate majorities, naturalization would have had a fundamental impact on the political landscape and would potentially threaten the local dynasties. A further problem with naturalization would be its impact on the states' ability to provide generous welfare packages to citizens— something that becomes much harder if the number of citizens is increased manyfold. Just as relying on foreign workers has been a "necessary evil" in the GCC countries, insiders argue, alienating labor practices have been necessary for locals to retain control of their countries.

Multinational firms doing business in the Gulf cannot, of course, easily influence the labor practices of the region. They can recognize, however, the business and human resources implications of such practices. One such implication is that expatriate communities tend to remain connected to their country of origin and are therefore more apt to seek goods and services linked to their home country. For example, expatriates will often bank with financial institutions linked to their home country such as Citibank or HSBC, and savvy multinationals can market to the expatriate community in targeted ways using home-country to reinforce their allegiance to their homelands.

From the perspective of human capital, there are both tactical and strategic challenges presented by the engagement norms of the GCC countries governing expatriates working in the Gulf. The tactical challenges include such things as knowing how to draft and manage employment contracts by using defined durations (e.g., of two or three years), having to secure visas for staff and families (itself a major competency of any multinational's GCC human resources team), and helping to secure admissions for their children into the relevant schools (e.g., the British or American schools). Also, benefits packages for professional staff typically include tickets to the home country each year, generating significant paperwork in the processing of these visa applications to other countries on which the employer may be asked to declare "no objection." These tactical matters, though they create an administrative burden, can be effectively managed given adequate resources and planning.

The strategic challenge, however, is more fundamental. How can multinationals foster a sense of commitment—and a long-term outlook—among expatriate staff when the staff is reminded each day that they are foreigners in the Gulf and that their home country is elsewhere? How can firms avoid a short-term, exploitative take-the-money-and-run approach by expatriate staff?

The first safeguard against such attitudes lies in the firm's core values and ethics. Most leading multinationals now make explicit such values as long-term client commitment and responsibility to communities served. HSBC's celebrated chairman Sir John Bond, for example, would note to staff that "we are guests in the countries we serve" and therefore have a responsibility to look after the countries' well-being. Being invested in the success of a market is a critical value for firms to consciously adopt and communicate, especially in the GCC context.

A second safeguard lies in the performance management systems used for both the institution and individual staff. If professionals are brought to the Gulf on a rotational basis, their performance there should be measured in terms both of short-term results (e.g., revenues, growth, profits) and of strategic metrics that speak to the long-term health of the business and that reflect investment in long-term assets: market share, customer satisfaction, number of new clients, brand equity, etc. Firms that have long traditions of rotating professionals around the globe, such as professional services firms and energy companies, are good sources for best practices in managing the mobile employee for long-term success.

The shortsighted "take-the-money-and-run" attitude of some expatriates has, unfortunately, been a chronic problem in the GCC countries. A Qatari friend recently recounted the story of an expatriate academic brought to Qatar on a multimillion-dollar annual package to head an important institution. The expatriate stayed for a few months, saved his generous earnings, and promptly resigned to return to his home country and build a retirement home.

GCC insiders can relate many such stories and are increasingly wary of noncommitted expatriates. While such exploitative behavior is clearly blameworthy, GCC leaders must also acknowledge that the alienating labor practices of the Gulf have a hand in fostering a short-term outlook on the part of expatriate workers.

THE LABOR CRUNCH: NATIONALIZATION PROGRAMS ROOTED IN DEMOGRAPHIC PRESSURES

Demographic change is one of the key drivers that make the GCC market more attractive than ever before. Population trends have led to a vibrant GCC market that includes a growing number of youths and young adults. The GCC consumer is more sophisticated and better educated than before, with access to global information and brands. As we have argued throughout this book, attractive demographic shifts represent a core element in the Opportunity Formula for multinational firms operating in the Gulf.

One tool often used by demographers to analyze population shifts is a graph called a "population pyramid." A population pyramid graphs the number of people within each age group (ages 0–4, 5–9, etc.) and reveals which age groups are more highly represented within the population. Figure 7.3 depicts a population pyramid for the United States, based on 2005 census data.

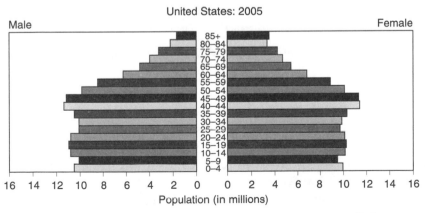

Figure 7.3 United States population pyramid, 2005 (Source: US Census Bureau, International Database)

In this graph, one can see, for example, a strata that represents the "baby boom" generation of post–World War II births composed of people now in the age range of 40–59. The number of people in this generation is significantly larger than in the cohorts immediately surrounding it: note, for example, the steep difference between the number of people aged 55–59 and the population aged 60–65. The 60–65-year-olds were born during the war; the 55–59-year-olds were born immediately thereafter. One can also gather from the graph the impeding strain on the US Social Security system as the 60–64-year-old (on the cusp of Social Security eligibility) and 55–59 year old bands are significantly larger than the bands above them. The largest single age band in the United States, per Figure 7.3, is ages 40–44.

For a sense of the demographic situation in the GCC countries, let us turn to one country as an example. Figure 7.4 features a population pyramid for Oman, based on 2005 population figures.

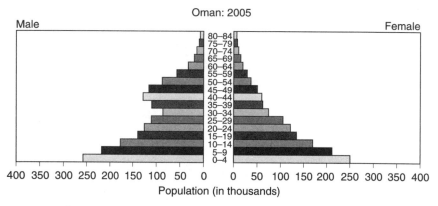

Figure 7.4 Oman population pyramid, 2005 (Source: US Census Bureau, International Database)

It is immediately striking how the population of ages 29 and below is significantly larger than the population of ages 30 and above. A remarkable 52 percent of the population is 19 years old or younger. The largest age band is 0–4, and children of ages 0–9 make up an astonishing 31 percent of the total population. Almost one-third of people in Oman, therefore, are of primary school age or younger! Another point of note is the gender breakdown of the population aged 35–64: these bands are significantly skewed toward males. One major reason for this skew is that the families of male expatriate workers are not counted, presumably because they have remained in the home country and not migrated to Oman.

The key conclusions to be drawn from this GCC population pyramid point to the issues of job creation and the educational needs of the young. These issues are in stark contrast with those existing in many OECD markets, where the population pyramids indicate looming pension and health care crises among retirees. As three of the six GCC states—Bahrain, Oman, and Saudi Arabia—already have double-digit unemployment, the pressure to create employment opportunities for GCC nationals is immense. Moreover, many employed nationals hold jobs in public-sector entities in which workforces will likely need to be trimmed if and when they are privatized, which adds further urgency to the challenge of employment. Policy makers are rightly concerned about creating and freeing up jobs for young nationals either out of work today or soon to be completing their education.

One policy that has been adopted by the governments of GCC countries regionwide is that of "nationalization" of the workforce. The purpose of this policy is to transfer jobs from expatriates to nationals in order to alleviate the current unemployment crisis. While nationalization policies have been adopted and reformed in various Gulf countries for decades now, crafting truly effective policies has been a challenge. The objective is well understood, but the implementation has been fraught with obstacles.

The typical approach taken until now by the governments of Gulf countries to nationalize the workforce has been to dictate quotas. For a given sector or industry, the governments have enacted regulations declaring what percentage of staff must be local nationals. The quotas are meant to force change in the private sector, as public-sector institutions tend already to be heavily nationalized. In fact, a secondary objective in nationalizing the private workforce is to encourage citizens to take private-sector jobs and thereby relieve some of the overstaffing and inefficiencies of many government-linked institutions.

Table 7.2 provides a few examples from each GCC country of policies or objectives that are in place in the effort to further nationalize the private sector. The list is by no means comprehensive, but is meant to illustrate the types of measures being adopted by local governments.

TABLE 7.2

Nationalizing the Private Sector: Policy Measures

Country	Sample Policies to Nationalize Workforce
Saudi Arabia	• 2001: Goal set of 25% Saudization in private sector by 2002 • 2003: Nearly 10,000 banking jobs Saudized on accelerated basis by government decree • 2005: Law passed raising Saudization targets • 2007: Target date of 2007 set for achieving 70% Saudization of overall workforce, with faster Saudization in some sectors[7]
UAE	• Companies with 50 or more employees to increase citizens' share of workforce at 2% annually; targets of 4% and 5% respectively for banks and insurers[8] • 2006: No new work permits for foreigners seeking secretarial jobs; existing secretaries allowed to serve out the duration of their work permits, but permits not to be renewed[9] • December 2007: Deadline for HR and personnel managers in private sector to be UAE nationals; 18-month grace period for companies trying to replace foreign managers with local ones • Government actively promoting entrepreneurship by nationals, through measures such as SME (small and medium-sized enterprise) funding in Abu Dhabi and the Mohammed bin Rashid Establishment for Young Business Leaders in Dubai[10]
Qatar	• Strategic Qatarization plan calls for a 50% nationalization of the "energy and industry" sector of the economy[11]
Bahrain	• Bahrainization accounts for 90% of public-sector jobs and cannot count on more jobs coming from public sector[12] • Desired results not delivered by previous quota-based system[13] • Recent switch from quotas to more market-based system, charging a fee on foreign-worker visas and applying the proceeds to a fund investing in local human capital[14]
Kuwait	• 2003: Kuwaitization program for private sector established, but application of guidelines not flexible[15]
Oman	• Since 2000, certain low-skill job categories (e.g., driving taxis) are reserved for Omani nationals • Oman recently added 24 more categories to the list[16] • Foreign staff capped at 20% in certain industries; expatriate work visas granted for 2 years, renewable for up to 4 years[17] • Firms not meeting the Omanization target of their sector required to hire one Omani to get a work permit for a new expatriate worker.[18] • Since 1994, a fee equal to 7% of the worker's annual salary imposed on the use of foreign labor; fee revenues used as "training contributions."[19]

Not surprisingly, the most robust nationalization policies being pursued are those of Saudi Arabia, Oman, and Bahrain—the countries that face the greatest unemployment challenge today. As more young people come of age and enter the workforce, however, no GCC state will be able to ignore the need for job creation.

THE BEST-LAID PLANS: CHALLENGES OF NATIONALIZATION PROGRAMS

Despite the laudable objectives of nationalization programs, their implementation, as already stated, has faced many difficult challenges over the years. Insiders and astute observers point out that, although quotas can force certain changes, they are a blunt tool, and the issues underlying local unemployment remain unresolved. While the private sector—and especially foreign companies—have had limited say in the formation of nationalization policies, some private firms have found creative solutions to the nationalization challenge. Their concerns and objections are also now being discussed more openly than before, which is a good sign of increased policy dialogue in the region.

In an important 2007 paper on Gulf labor policy, consultants from McKinsey & Co. gave voice to many of the concerns that private-sector leaders have long had about nationalization quotas but none dared to say publicly. Private-sector leaders have long argued—behind closed doors—that the local education system simply does not prepare many nationals for work in top-notch professional environments. As McKinsey notes, the mathematical skills of Saudi eighth-grade students are near the bottom of international rankings, in the same league as Botswana and Ghana.[20] Private-sector leaders have repeatedly told me that they are happy to hire local employees but can't find the necessary caliber of talent in the market and are unwilling to lower their hiring standards. Local nationals also have significantly higher salary expectations than do many expatriates, making the cost of hiring them substantially greater.

Private-sector firms have managed compliance with nationalization quotas in a number of ways. At times, exemptions can be won from the government due to "exceptional" circumstances. Some simply view the quotas as a form of taxation and therefore add nationals to the payroll while expecting little or no productivity from them. This approach is, of course, corrosive to overall morale and to any sense of fairness in the company. Another approach is to engage expatriates through what McKinsey calls "ghost companies"— firms that exist only to import workers and pass them on to other companies. McKinsey estimates that 25 to 30 percent of the GCC expatriate workforce may be "ghost-company" staff.[21]

For leading multinationals with stringent global standards, none of the "creative" solutions cited above—except the direct negotiation of exemptions—will be appropriate. Compromising integrity is not an option, and the risks of evasive behavior are too large for a global franchise. Some sectors require large workforces at variable skill levels, and in those cases complying with the quotas is less difficult. Many companies will choose to register in free zones, where the quotas either don't apply or apply at a reduced level. The new Dubai International Financial Centre, for example, is completely exempt from local labor laws and nationalization quotas.[22]

Observers have cited recent reforms in Bahrain—one of which requires a fee to be charged for foreign work visas that is then used to fund investment in local human capital—as a breakthrough innovation of much significance. Market-based approaches like Bahrain's are more likely to fit the needs of multinational firms. Leading global firms are willing to bear additional financial costs if needed but will not compromise their global hiring or compliance standards. Doing so can put the company's worldwide reputation at risk.

HIRING BALANCING ACT: MANAGING THE MIX OF EXPATRIATE AND LOCAL STAFF

For multinational firms operating in the Gulf, finding the balance in the hiring of expatriates and local workers is a delicate matter. Expatriate talent brings expertise and other benefits, but also imposes limitations. Local talent is crucial for long-term success, but recruitment and retention are real challenges. Figure 7.5 captures some of the key elements of the balancing act that global firms must manage.

Expatriate talent brings global expertise into the region, including training received and skill sets developed from working

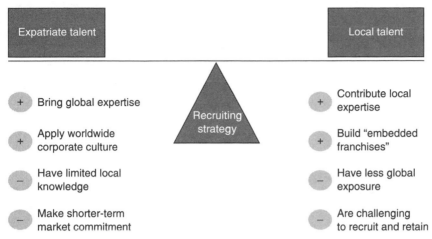

Figure 7.5 The hiring balancing act

in other markets. As the GCC market is rapidly evolving and adopting norms from other regions, an understanding of outside markets is becoming absolutely critical to strong performance. Global expertise is especially critical in the more technical aspects of work such as financial analysis, technology, and marketing execution. Expatriates, who are part of the same global firm and are brought to the region through transfers from other markets, bring with them the company's worldwide corporate culture. By "culture" I mean both concrete best practices such as credit assessment and document formatting and more intangible elements such as expertise in client focus and cross-functional collaboration. While the concrete aspects are easier to impose from outside, the more intangible ones generally require a core group of staff who have experienced the culture of other offices and bring those cultural values with them.

Expatriate hires will, however, typically have very limited knowledge of the GCC market. Arabic language skills, except of course among Arab expatriates, will generally be limited. A firm's expatriate talent pool will generally need quite intensive training and orientation in the market dynamics of the Gulf in order to be fully effective in the region. Over time, expatriates will likely develop a deeper understanding of the market through their own experience. Savvy firms will take measures to ensure that they don't lose all their expatriate talent—through a transfer to another region at the end of a rotational cycle—precisely at the time they really start understanding the market. It is generally after two or three years, in fact, that expatriates become most valuable to the global firm. Sending them away—especially if they have held senior, client-facing roles—is a mistake firms make all too often.

A second drawback of expatriate talent is the short-term outlook that often comes with temporary postings. As discussed earlier, firms must take measures, both in terms of corporate values and of the performance-management process, to ensure that they promote and reward a longer-term view. Expatriate staff should view a GCC posting as a chance to leave their mark and build a legacy, even if they will subsequently move on to another business in another region.

Local talent, on the other hand, brings several of the competencies that expatriate staff lack. Chief among these is expertise in and insight into the ways of the local market. In this sense, the GCC region is no different from any other part of the world: people who live in a region their entire lives, and are thoughtful about their experiences, will have an intuitive feel for market needs, norms, and trends. Through their families and their social networks, they will have direct access to local consumers of various ages. They will also possess insight into latent needs and what people want to see next. Without locals on your team, direct understanding of where the market is—and more important where it is heading—is almost impossible.

Local staff is also pivotal for building a long-term "embedded franchise"[23] in the GCC market. One powerful way that global firms build deep connections with communities is through long-term employment. Having local staff, especially in customer-facing roles, sends a strong signal that your firm is not a "foreign" entity unconcerned about the region. Long-term service at the company's GCC offices—which generally suits the personal preferences of local staff more than those of expatriates—is a vital way to preserve institutional memory. In the eyes of institutional clients and external stakeholders such as regulators and industry bodies, committed local staff members contribute a tremendous amount of value and credibility. The local business community of Abu Dhabi, for example, is a very small and interconnected circle. Local staff members and institutional salespeople can be crucial for understanding the best way to approach clients and to close major deals. With regulators, they communicate your firm's sense of commitment and belonging.[24]

A few years ago, I met with a prominent UAE national (from Dubai) who was a lifelong employee of a major multinational corporation. Having reached a very senior role, much of his work involved interfacing with public officials and external stakeholders, representing the multinational on public initiatives. As Dubai was booming and opportunities for senior executives like him were both abundant and lucrative, I asked him privately why he was still with the multinational. The firm, he replied, "was my school. When I came to work here [decades ago] I could not read or write. The [firm] taught me." This senior local felt a great deal of loyalty to the company that had shown its loyalty to him. This loyalty was a huge asset and testament to the firm's local commitment.

One challenge for global firms regarding their local staff, is that of ensuring they acquire adequate global exposure. Unlike expatriates who transfer to the GCC from other offices, local staff usually do not have much experience working abroad. Receiving training in the firm's global standards and norms is essential. Also, for high-potential hires, rotational exposure to other offices can be tremendously valuable. This exposure will allow them to experience international practices firsthand, for application in their home market later on. And unlike rotational programs for high-potential staff from other emerging markets, GCC-country nationals are far less likely to switch to another employer in order to stay in the OECD market they rotate through—their quality-of-life and career prospects at home are usually too promising to pass up.

The most difficult aspect of local hiring, as mentioned before, is finding and attracting locals to join multinational firms. Local educational facilities have been of variable quality, but recent initiatives such as Dubai's Knowledge Village and Qatar's Education City are increasingly bringing world-class academic institutions into the region. These ventures bode well for the medium and long terms, but are less helpful immediately. Multinationals must also compete with public-sector jobs, which tend to offer significantly lighter hours and more days off per year. Public-sector jobs promise stability and pensions that few multinationals want to match. Add to this that public-sector and local firms can generally offer locals an Arabic-speaking workplace as opposed to an office in which they will need to use English, and the challenge of attracting local talent seems even more daunting.

Multinational firms must acknowledge that their employment proposition appeals to a certain subset of the local community: those who seek international exposure, enjoy using English, want to learn global best practices, and value the standards and traditions of multinational businesses. Not every GCC national fits this mold. The good news, however, is that many do—especially early on in their careers. Often that is the time to bring local talent on board.

Village and City: Competing for Global Education Partnerships

As the need—and market—for world-class educational facilities in the region has intensified, Gulf states have begun actively competing to bring in leading academic institutions. Two prime contenders in this healthy rivalry are Dubai, largely through its Knowledge Village, and Qatar, through its Education City. Both have managed to attract a diverse set of international institutions to establish official, degree-granting branches in the Gulf states.

Dubai Knowledge Village's "Partners" come from a remarkable range of countries including the UK, Australia, France, Belgium, India, Pakistan, and even Russia. The diversity of degree programs is likewise impressive: business, technology, engineering, management, and even fashion are among the disciplines in which students can study in Dubai and receive accredited degrees from global institutions.[25] The Dubai International Financial Centre (DIFC) has formed a partnership with the Cass Business School in London for an Executive MBA program in Dubai. Besides a general MBA, students can choose to specialize in Energy or in Islamic Finance, two fields of immense interest in the region.[26]

Qatar's Education City has taken a different approach, focusing on highly regarded US institutions. Qatar has attracted Weill Cornell Medical College, Carnegie Mellon, Texas A&M, the Georgetown School of Foreign Service, and the Virginia Commonwealth School of the Arts to establish degree-granting branches in their respective areas of core competence. The Qatar branches follow the same rigorous curricula as their international partners.[27] As Qatar's local population is too small to sustain so many institutions, Education City aims to attract talent from elsewhere in the Gulf and MENA regions, acting as a regional hub for developing human capital.

The competition between Dubai and Qatar to build educational facilities has multiple winners. At the top of the list are the local talent pool and the companies—both local and international—that seek to hire them.

CHARTING YOUR WAY

Human capital issues in the Gulf, as we have now seen, are by no means simple and straightforward. They pose a set of interesting and complex challenges—challenges linked to the market, to the infrastructure, and to regulations. What, then, is the path ahead?

In thinking through human capital, global firms need to take a sophisticated view involving short-, medium-, and long-term strategies. In the short term, expatriate talent remains crucial but should be attracted based on fit with the GCC market. In the medium term, attracting high-caliber GCC local executives at the early stages of their careers is central. And in the longer term, there is no substitute for investing in human capital development in the region. This exact path may not suit every global firm, but as a general approach it fits the needs of a great many multinational firms intent on conducting long-term operations in the Gulf. (See Figure 7.6.)

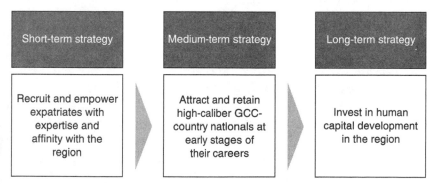

Figure 7.6 Human capital: a path ahead

SHORT-TERM STRATEGY: EXPATRIATES
WHO FIT

In the short term, multinationals need to attract expatriates who bring more to the region than the basics. Too often in the past, postings in the Gulf have been for executives who are average or even lackluster performers. One reason for this has been the policy of keeping the top-notch staff close to the multinational's main office and in large OECD markets, sending second-tier talent to emerging markets like those of the GCC countries. This approach is shortsighted, however, as the opportunities and challenges in the Gulf today are complex and rich, calling for some of the best minds a firm can deploy. Further, the dynamic nature of the GCC market provides an outstanding proving ground in which junior executives can learn and grow and senior management can generate results and demonstrate high-level leadership qualities. The world's leading global firms have all understood by now that the Gulf is no backwater, and should not be used as a posting for second-rate talent, and that not staffing appropriately can cause your firm to miss out on the potential of booming markets.

The Gulf is also, generally speaking, not a good place to send staff for involuntary or compulsory rotations if they are averse to the move. Bringing executives to the market who have a distaste for it is a recipe for disaster. Their resentment will be apparent to colleagues (destroying morale) and, even worse, to clients. No one likes working with, or being served by, someone whose heart is elsewhere. Staff who are posted against their wishes will be most likely to have a short-term, exploitative, take-the-money-and-run attitude in their dealings. Also, in the present environment, there should be no shortage of qualified candidates who recognize the Gulf for the opportunity it is and therefore seek postings there willingly. They can be found, with a little bit of effort.

The right kind of expatriate for the GCC countries today brings a combination of experience, skills, and genuine passion for the region. All three are important for success. Table 7.3 provides a basic checklist to consider when recruiting expatriates—either through an external search or through an internal transfer process.

TABLE 7.3

The Right Stuff Checklist for Expatriate Recruiting

Domain	Sample Criteria
Experience	• Experience in high-growth markets
	• Experience in rapidly changing business environments
	• Leadership in challenging environments
	• Leadership of diverse teams
Skills	• Analytical prowess
	• Technical proficiency in area of focus
	• Communication skills
	• Leadership and management skills
	• Ability to manage growth and change
Passion and Affinity	• Genuine passion for the Gulf/Middle East region
	• Interest in economic and commercial development of the region
	• Arabic language skills
	• Openness toward local culture

Many firms pay adequate attention to the first two domains but overlook the third: passion and affinity. Through years of observing expatriates in the Gulf, I have seen time and again how crucial passion and affinity are and how they often represent the difference between mediocre and stellar performers.

While passion and affinity need not be—and very often are not—linked with country of origin, certain countries do tend to have more professionals with genuine interest in the Gulf. Chief among these are other Middle East and North Africa countries (e.g., Egypt, Lebanon, etc.), for whom language, proximity, and culture all fit well with the GCC states. Next are the markets of South Asia (India, Pakistan, Bangladesh, and Sri Lanka), as South Asian expatriate communities in the Gulf often create a home-away-from-home environment. This is especially true for the UAE. Filipino expatriate communities in the Gulf are also sizable, making it easier to recruit additional talent from the Philippines. Talent from the broader Muslim world (e.g., Malaysia, Indonesia, Muslim Africa, etc.) is another important affinity pool, as many (though certainly not all) Muslims are attracted to the Islamic environment and facilities of the GCC countries. The same holds for a sizable number of Muslims living in the West—in fact several prominent firms have brought in Muslims from the West or other OECD markets to lead their GCC businesses.

As awareness of the Middle East and the GCC grows around the world, an increasingly wider range of people will develop genuine passion and affinity for the region. In 2005, for example, nearly 100 students enrolled in Harvard University's "Arabic A" elementary language course—about double the number who did so 10 years prior.[28] The high volume of interest at universities is likely to be sustained as the Middle East region remains headline news, attracting students from all backgrounds. Leading executive-search firms, in recent years, have been rapidly expanding their GCC capabilities, reflecting the demand for top-notch talent in the region.

BRIGHT AND EARLY: MEDIUM-TERM STRATEGY

For the medium term, multinationals should strive to attract and retain high-caliber nationals from GCC countries in the early stages of their careers. Experienced senior and middle managers of Gulf origin are extremely difficult to attract to multinational firms, because their opportunities in the public sector and in local business in the Gulf are simply too attractive. The Emirati national talent pool provides no shortage of examples. A midlevel staffer whom I met at the office of Sheikh Mohammed bin Rashid (then Dubai's Crown Prince, now its ruler) in early 2003 was, less than three years later, put in charge of a large-scale capital project far more ambitious than anything a multinational firm could offer him. An Emirati alumnus of the Harvard Business School, with prior experience at a leading global energy firm, found it more worthwhile to attend to his family business in the UAE than work elsewhere. His firm subsequently raised an unprecedented amount of capital in a wildly successful 2005 IPO.

One sector from which multinationals could draw local talent with experience in best practices is that of leading professional services firms. Worldwide, these firms—whose core assets are their people—have differentiated themselves by attracting the very best talent from elite universities very early in their careers.

Their proposition is compelling: work with us and you'll build a superb skill set that you can take almost anywhere and become a leader. These firms don't promise lifelong employment or immediate wealth; they promise unmatched development opportunities.

Development Covenant: The Professional Services Approach

The world's leading professional services firms—consultancies, investment banks, accounting firms, law firms, marketing agencies, and the like—have refined the practice of high-caliber recruiting to an art. Since the quality of their staff is the key value proposition they bring to clients, these firms see attracting the best and brightest as fundamental to their success. These firms have, over the decades, come to understand that the optimal time for them to attract talent is early in their careers—often directly from university.

Some of the tactics employed by leading professional firms include aggressive on-campus recruiting, proactively inviting especially bright students to private dinners with senior staff, and sponsoring student activities such as business plan contests. These tactics, along with decades-long track records of attracting talent from the same or similar universities, position the professional services firms as the natural next step for bright students. It's not surprising, then, that up to half the graduating class of leading business schools often join management consulting, investment banking, or similar professional services firms.

The promise made by professional services firms to young talent could be called a "development covenant." Among the key elements of this covenant are:

- Providing an unmatched skill set, built rapidly and efficiently
- Offering a development-focused culture, with frequent training and feedback
- Mentorship by senior staff with similar "star" backgrounds
- A brand on the résumé that will lead to abundant future opportunities
- The chance to work with leading clients and their senior managers

- An "alumni" network of former staff in leadership positions worldwide

Top-notch professional services firms cannot—and need not—offer lifelong employment. Competition for promotion within these firms is intense and merit based. Simply starting one's career there is seen as sufficient grounding for ongoing success. For under-graduate recruits, the period of employment is frequently defined as two years, after which the firm may sponsor graduate education on the condition that the staff member return after graduation.

Leading firms such as McKinsey & Co., Goldman Sachs, and the Boston Consulting Group have begun targeted recruiting efforts exclusively for their Gulf offices. These efforts have drawn top-notch talent from the region and with affinity to it, giving these firms a deeper understanding of the region and more credibility with clients. Having drawn in such high-caliber recruits, the challenge becomes retaining them by continuing to invest in them in keeping with the company's development covenant.

Actively recruiting young and talented GCC-country nationals is, of course, something that multinational firms can and should begin doing today. Its benefits will become more apparent in the medium-term future (three to five years from today) as these professionals begin taking more responsibility in and having greater impact on the company.

YOU REAP WHAT YOU SOW: LONG-TERM HUMAN CAPITAL INVESTMENT

In the longer term, multinational firms with serious ambitions in the GCC states have little choice but to invest in local human capital. Even as educational standards rise and external training facilities expand, corporate training will remain crucial for company-specific skills and knowledge that firms need to instill in their workforce worldwide. Beyond formal training, internship programs for students and mentorship programs for staff can go a long way in building the human capital base in the firm and in the market. Such programs can also build a great deal of goodwill, as is evident in the experience of multinationals such as Citigroup and General Electric.

In the UAE, Citigroup runs a high-profile initiative called the Citibank Internship Program (CIP). The CIP is a year-long program through which UAE nationals, drawn from universities across the country, serve as interns and are trained in various banking functions. At the end of the year, graduates of the program enter the job market—applying for positions at Citibank but also elsewhere in the financial services sector. Through efforts such as these, Citibank has been repeatedly recognized with the UAE government's Human Resources Development Award.[29]

Programs like Citigroup's are effective and strategic for several reasons. One is that they give firms a "first look" at top students from UAE universities, bringing them on board for a defined period and evaluating them for longer-term employment. Firms can keep the top performers and let the others go out into the marketplace. A second reason is that these programs are designed in a fashion that commits neither the bank nor the student beyond the first year— precluding the unpleasant complications that can arise when an employment contract with a local hire is severed. Third, the programs give firms a chance to interact with a large number of high-caliber locals who can become personal and institutional clients in the long run. Good memories from the internship can lead to significant business flows in the future.

General Electric provides another example of investment in human capital in the Gulf through the large-scale GE Technology and Learning Center it established in Qatar in 2005. The initiative has won significant praise and makes sound business sense for a firm eager to grow its business in the GCC region.

GE Qatar: Good Business and Goodwill

In 2005, GE announced a five-year, $50 million investment in a Technology and Learning Center to be built in Qatar's Science and Technology Park. The center's objectives include technical training for GE customers in the Middle East, Africa, Europe, and Asia, and research and development for key business lines of relevance to the region including oil, gas, and water. When completed, the center should employ about 45 people.[30]

The business case for the center appears to be solid. GE's expansion in the Middle East and nearby regions has brought many new customers for whom Doha is a convenient place to train. Qatar's world-class infrastructure makes it an easy place for training participants to travel to and move around in. Concerning the center itself, the sectors on which it will focus represent a huge commercial opportunity for the firm. In the energy sector alone, for example, Qatar is expected to invest $70 billion between 2006 and 2011.[31] Having a research center in the country can be a big advantage during a competitive bidding process, demonstrating an expertise in responding to local needs and a commitment to the local community. The profits from one multibillion-dollar contract alone can easily recoup the $50 million cost of the center.

On the announcement of the center, Sheikha Mozah Bint Nasser Al Missned—head of the Qatar Foundation and wife of Qatar's ruler—had high praise for GE. "Transferring the expertise and technology of leading companies to the Qatar population is an important part of our strategy," she said, "and GE is showing that it embraces this vision."[32] One can only imagine such accolades as being immensely valuable when seeking to win government business in the country.

Investment in local human capital, when done strategically, can yield tremendous commercial and public relations benefits. It is also critical to building a truly "embedded franchise" with genuine roots in society.

KEY LESSONS

- *Expatriate talent*, largely out of necessity, has played a central role in the development of GCC businesses over the past several decades.
- Demographic shifts, however, have been fueling *initiatives to "localize" the private-sector workforce*.
- Multinationals must manage a *balancing act* in their hiring: being sensitive to both the need for expatriate talent and the imperative for local human capital development.
- In the short term, multinationals should *recruit and empower expatriates* with expertise and affinity with the region.
- In the medium term, multinationals should learn from leading professional services firms and *attract GCC nationals at the early stages of their careers*.
- For long-term success, *investing in local human capital* makes commercial and public relations sense.

CHAPTER 8

Capable Capital: The GCC as a Source of Capital

INTRODUCTION

If dollar bills could talk, a lot of them would speak Arabic. The economies of the Gulf have long been exporters of capital, denominated in US dollars, because energy markets are dollar-based. GCC investors—both public investment arms and private institutions—hold massive amounts of international investments, including hundreds of billions in US Treasury bills.[1] As the US economy runs record-breaking budget and trade deficits, Gulf economies are running unprecedented surpluses and investing those surpluses both at home and abroad. Together, the Gulf states enjoyed a combined budget surplus of about $120 billion in 2006.[2] That's around $3,000 per person who lives there.

The GCC has seen boom times before, but this time its investment strategies are different. In addition to traditional assets like US Treasury bills and OECD equities, Gulf investors are putting more money into alternative investments, such as IPOs and private equity, than ever before. They have also been investing in their home markets with unprecedented enthusiasm: local stock markets increased in value many times over in the first half of the 2000s before a serious market correction brought valuations closer in line with global and historical standards. Some sectors—most notably real estate—have enjoyed a more sustained boom that many expect will cool down (if not crash) before the decade is out. Although investors—especially the most sophisticated ones—still place the vast majority of their assets abroad, increasing their focus on local markets has had a transformative effect on asset values in the region.

The rise of Islamic finance—financial services conducted in accordance with Islamic guidelines—has been a major trend in Gulf markets. The Islamic financial services sector has been a key growth area within the broader financial services industry, has captured a large percentage of total assets and market share, and has attracted the attention of major global institutions like HSBC, Citigroup, Deutsche Bank, and many others. Developing Sharia-compliant (conforming with Islamic law) products is an important capability for any financial institution interested in building a large-scale business in the GCC countries.

Multinationals can increasingly look to the GCC states as a source of investment capital, and the savviest firms already do so. No investment banking or private equity capital-raising campaign can be considered truly global without including a stop or two in the Gulf. In the biggest IPO in history—that of a Chinese bank—the single largest investor was the Kuwait Investment Authority. Major multinationals increasingly court GCC institutional investors for both equity and debt financing. Some Western institutions have structured financing deals in a Sharia-compliant way in order to tap a broader pool of capital. As regulatory environments in the Gulf, London, and elsewhere increasingly accommodate Islamic finance, Sharia-compliant investors will be more central on the global stage.

Savvy firms cannot overlook the GCC in their global capital strategy. The Gulf is more than able to fund local joint ventures and subsidiaries on regional exchanges that are more flexible than ever before. Gulf companies and investors have also become major players in global mergers, acquisitions, and buyout situations. In May 2007, for example, the Saudi chemicals firm SABIC prevailed over several other bidders to acquire GE's multibillion-dollar plastics business. GE is not the first—and certainly not the last— multinational to find itself across the table from a Gulf buyer when negotiating a major transaction.

ENJOYING THE SURPLUS

The source of GCC prosperity is, of course, no mystery. High prices for fossil fuels, in great demand on worldwide energy markets, bring immense wealth to the region. The Gulf's role in global energy markets should not be underestimated: the region holds 40 percent of the world's known oil reserves, and 23 percent of its known gas reserves. The fact that the GCC represents only 22 percent of actual oil production and only 8 percent of actual gas production is a sobering thought for any who might consider competing with them—the Gulf is actually underrepresented in the market considering what impact it could have.[3] At current rates of production, Gulf oil and gas producers can outlast other nations by a significant period of time. The Gulf states' capacity also gives them a huge influence on global energy prices: increasing production will lower prices, holding back will drive them up. Since Saudi Arabia alone possesses about a quarter of the total known reserves, the Saudi oil minister is broadly understood to be the driving force of OPEC (the Organization of Petroleum Exporting Countries) irrespective of who chairs its meetings or acts as secretary-general. Since the days of Zaki Yamani, who held the post during the crises of the 1970s, the Saudi oil minister has remained the single most influential figure in world energy markets.

Two basic facts must be understood to assess the phenomenon of wealth creation in the GCC countries. First, oil resources in the region are firmly controlled by governments and (at the federal level) represent the governments' prime source of income.[4] Personal income and corporate taxes are not necessary to support the state as long as it controls the oil and populations remain small. At the same time, control of energy revenue makes the state the dominant actor in each country's economy. A second basic fact is that energy markets are dollar-denominated exchanges. The revenue that comes in from oil is in US currency (hence the term "petrodollars") and goes straight to government-linked institutions. Largely because of these dynamics, until recently all Gulf countries pegged their currencies to the dollar (i.e., the local currency fluctuates with the dollar), and GCC country–based entities have historically had a propensity to invest in US Treasury bills and other dollar-denominated assets. While the dollar peg has long

made sense for GCC economies considering their dollar-denominated exports, the situation is changing: inflationary pressures, a
slipping dollar, and the increasing importance of Europe as an
import source are causing Gulf states to rethink the peg. In May
2007, Kuwait announced it would end its dollar peg, to reduce what
analysts dubbed "imported inflation."[5] Other states may follow
suit, though Saudi Arabia—the biggest GCC economy of all—
appears unlikely to budge in the near term.

The dynamic of government surpluses is illustrated in
Figure 8.1. Governments plan their spending based on local needs
and their expectations of revenue (mainly from oil). Income generated above this budget creates a surplus, which in turn is used for a
variety of purposes.

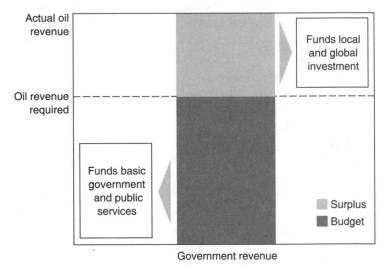

Figure 8.1 Surplus is creating wealth for investment

When energy prices are high, the government surpluses of
GCC states can reach astonishing levels. According to IMF
estimates, in 2007 the region will run a current account surplus of
over 20 percent of GDP and a fiscal surplus (the phenomenon
illustrated in Figure 8.1) of over 10 percent of GDP.[6] In 2006, the Gulf
states enjoyed a combined budget surplus of about $120 billion.[7] In
per capita terms, this amounts to around $3,000 per person living
there. The current boom is not the first time that extraordinary

surpluses have been achieved: by 1980, Saudi oil revenues grew to 25 times the 1973 figure (from $4.3 billion to $101.8 billion), giving the government a huge pool of capital to invest in economic transformation and modernization.[8]

Governments' enormous surpluses are, however, at the mercy of global energy markets. There have been periods, like much of the 1990s, in which deficits resulted because oil income was not sufficient to meet governments' spending. Local planners are, of course, aware of this phenomenon and therefore try to craft their budgets to cover basic government services based on conservative estimates of oil prices. Saudi officials, for example, have historically planned their budget based on a $25 per barrel oil price—less than half the current market rate.[9] When the price is above the planned level—which varies from state to state and year to year—excess capital can be invested in the types of infrastructure projects now common in the GCC countries. Basic government services like public health care, police departments, the water supply, and defense need to be planned in such a way that they can break even if oil revenue is at the planned level.

PREPARING FOR THE MOMENT OF TRUTH

Gulf governments face a stark challenge in the years ahead as they prepare for what could be called the "Moment of Truth." Demand for government services is growing steadily in all Gulf countries as populations increase. Recent prosperity has also prompted governments to launch new programs and services (for example, subsidized investment funds for small businesses started by locals) that would be difficult to cut in the future now that expectations have been set. Oil prices, however, are highly volatile and are expected by many to come down from the $60-per-barrel level to a steady state between $40 and $50 in the medium-term future. Budgets—excluding large-scale capital projects—need to grow steadily while oil revenue does not grow in the same fashion. Figure 8.2 illustrates the challenge.

While oil prices cannot be predicted with certainty, the US Energy Information Administration (EIA) and industry analysts expect prices to fall from the 2005–2007 level of over $60 per barrel to a level between $40 and $50 per barrel for the foreseeable future.

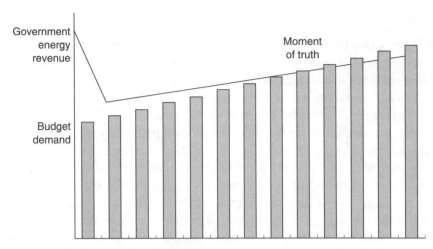

Figure 8.2 Gulf states' budgets likely to face a moment of truth (Source: Based on US Energy Information Administration "Reference Case" for oil prices and author analysis)

Even at $40 per barrel, Gulf governments can continue to run budget surpluses. Over time, however, demands on government budgets can be expected to rise steadily as population increases, and at some point, barring unforeseen circumstances or fundamental changes, Gulf governments are likely to face a moment of truth at which energy revenue alone ceases to provide them with budget surpluses.

Figure 8.2 is only an illustration of the general phenomenon. Each country's situation is different, and some will face budget squeezes long before others will. Saudi Arabia, with its large population and landmass, requires an oil price of around $38 per barrel to maintain a surplus.[10] The UAE, with a far smaller population and substantial oil reserves, needs a price of only about half that amount to balance its budget.[11] The UAE's growth in population means its budgetary demands are climbing very quickly; however, it should have substantial investments to tide it over. Bahrain's oil reserves are very limited and, depending on production strategies, may not last much more than a decade. Qatar's abundant natural gas has put it in a very strong position. Kuwait likewise maintains a strong outlook and has a large savings pool. The moment-of-truth analysis is therefore less applicable in some countries, where its time frame is much more prolonged. Nonetheless, all GCC states are aware that today's surpluses cannot be relied on forever.

There are, of course, many measures that governments can undertake to manage income in the face of rising budgetary pressures. One that is being used heavily is investment in income-yielding securities. GCC states have for decades been applying much of their surpluses to the purchase of US Treasury bills and other fixed-income instruments that guarantee an annual return. They have also been investing in dividend-yielding equities, although this has been with a smaller proportion of the total surplus. The size and clout of sovereign investment arms in the region—as well as their ability to support government spending—should not be underestimated. A prime example is the Abu Dhabi Investment Authority (ADIA), widely acknowledged as one of the world's most important institutional investors, which is single-handedly able to support a huge proportion of Abu Dhabi (and UAE) government spending for years to come if need be.

ADIA's Massive Coffers

The Abu Dhabi Investment Authority (ADIA), established in 1976 by the UAE's founder Sheikh Zayed Al Nahyan, has been a custodian of Abu Dhabi's oil surplus for decades. Although the organization is highly opaque and its inner workings are strictly confidential, experts estimate its assets to be well above $250 billion, and probably over half a trillion dollars. Morgan Stanley believes ADIA's assets to be a breathtaking $875 billion and growing.[12]

Like all massive institutional investors, the ADIA invests in a range of asset classes across multiple regions. Typically, the bulk of such investors' assets tends to be in conservative, fixed-income instruments. To provide a sense of the scale of income the ADIA's coffers could produce, consider the following analysis. Let's assume the ADIA had $750 billion in assets and that two-thirds ($500 billion) was in bonds yielding 5 percent per year. The income from those investments alone would be $25 billion per year—or $6,000 per person living in the UAE. If, in a severe crisis, ADIA was forced to start liquidating its assets, even half of the $750 billion estimated total would provide over $350,000 per UAE citizen. ADIA's assets are, therefore, a tremendous cushion of fiscal security for the emirate and for the broader UAE.

It is not surprising that global bankers sit up and notice whenever the (typically low-profile) ADIA speaks up. In a 2006

Euromoney article, a former HSBC banker acknowledged that the ADIA was one of the few institutions in the world that the bank's most senior executives would drop everything to visit, regardless of what else they were doing.[13] HSBC's bankers are certainly not alone in recognizing the ADIA's clout.

The depth of the GCC states' government investments was apparent in the first Gulf War. When Iraq invaded Kuwait, the Kuwaiti government fled to Saudi Arabia and Europe, and Kuwaiti oil production stopped. Despite having no current source of income, the government easily sustained itself based entirely on its investments. The state was also, according to insiders, able to offer generous support and incentive packages for business families to reestablish their enterprises in Kuwait once the war was over. Such payouts would not have been possible without significant government reserves.

Besides drawing on savings, Gulf states can also issue sovereign debt in the form of conventional bonds and Sharia-compliant Sukuk. Sukuk, often dubbed "Islamic bonds," offer a return profile similar to that of bonds while using a Sharia-compliant structure involving leases or other asset-linked instruments. Credit ratings for all Gulf governments are strong, as control of energy resources provides a solid asset base and source of income. Sovereign debt is therefore a real option for GCC countries as budgetary pressures mount. Another rationale for sovereign debt—even in countries with strong fiscal positions—is that it creates a local benchmark for debt pricing and thereby boosts capital markets.

Another measure that is possible but would be difficult to implement is increasing oil production. As the GCC states make up the dominant bloc within OPEC, increasing Gulf production without OPEC support could lead to large-scale noncompliance with OPEC quotas worldwide. For the cartel to work, the Gulf states—and especially Saudi Arabia—need to demonstrate commitment and compliance.

The other obvious option is taxation—in the form of direct income taxes and less-direct sales taxes, luxury surcharges, highway tolls, license fees, and similar levies. Taxation has been uncommon and hidden in the Gulf for decades now in the form of import duties, hotel taxes, and the like. The basic social contract has been one by which citizens accept a relatively limited role in political affairs in exchange for being looked after by the state through benefits, social services, and not having an income tax. Kuwait, for example, provides citizens with financial rewards for marrying. Introducing an income tax could have profound implications for the social contract and give citizens a greater sense of entitlement in the political arena. Just as the American independence movement was grounded on the principle of no taxation without representation, Gulf nationals could assert greater political claims if they had to pay taxes. Governments are aware of this dynamic and tread gently around the issue of taxation. Taxation, when introduced, begins at the corporate level (Oman already has a corporate tax rate of 12 percent),[14] then spreads next to indirect taxation, and expands only slowly into a personal income tax.

The shift toward greater democratization in the Gulf is already taking place, with active parliaments in Kuwait and Bahrain, and consultative councils elsewhere. Hitherto, all moves toward elected representation have preserved the notion of ruling dynasties. Even when Kuwait's parliament played a role in the succession of the last ruler, its options were limited to two candidates within the ruling family. Increased political representation is a trend that is likely to continue irrespective of fiscal pressures. A need for higher government revenue as the moment of truth draws closer would only bolster or accelerate this process.

A DIFFERENT KIND OF BOOM

The boom of the 2000s has been managed in the GCC quite differently from the booms of the 1970s. While both periods witnessed enormous surpluses for GCC states and unprecedented wealth creation, strategies for deploying the wealth have been quite different. The differences in approach stem from the GCC in the 1970s having been far less developed in terms of local institutions, investment management capabilities, and the regional private sector. Table 8.1 summarizes some of the salient differences between investment strategies of the 1970s and those of today.

During the boom of the 1970s, local capital markets were simply too underdeveloped to absorb the massive liquidity created by oil wealth. Investing the bulk of the money in local markets would have been irresponsible, as there were not enough investment

TABLE 8.1

Contrasting the Booms: Investment Strategies

Element of Strategy	1970s	2000s
Geographic allocation of capital	Primarily OECD markets	OECD and developing markets plus more local allocation
Local investment priorities	Basic infrastructure and institutions	Advanced infrastructure, "knowledge" infrastructure, and centers of excellence
Instruments used	Traditional asset classes	Traditional asset classes plus alternative investments
Engagement of private sector	Minimal	Central component of strategy
Investment management expertise	Overseas	Overseas plus local (including expatriates)

opportunities and the risk of "overheating" the local market was clear. The most prudent investment strategy at the time was to invest in developed markets where the return would be safe, wealth could be stored in dollars, and Gulf investments (sizable as they were) would not disrupt the market. Applying large amounts of capital to small markets would also drive prices up and yields down, as well as limit large investors' liquidity and ability to exit with good returns. Investing heavily in small markets such as the GCC or other emerging markets would have exposed Gulf investors to undue market risk. It is therefore not surprising that GCC investors focused heavily on Western markets, with limited exposure to more developed Asian markets like Japan (which in the 1970s was still not fully developed).

In the boom of the 2000s, however, Gulf investors have taken a broader approach to capital allocation. While the bulk of assets are still being channeled to OECD markets, emerging markets receive far greater attention and consideration. Kuwait's role as the largest subscriber in the Industrial and Commercial Bank of China's 2006 IPO is one illustration of the increased appetite for high-growth Asian markets. Gulf investors and corporations are also investing more in South Asia than ever before—the property developer Emaar, for example, has undertaken a large-scale project in

Pakistan while Dubai Islamic Bank has opened many branches there. Local investors and corporations view emerging markets as an opportunity for growth, diversification, and access to customer pools far larger than domestic GCC markets will afford. While these markets bear additional risk, the potential for reward is enough to warrant a sizable (though still small minority) portion of investors' total portfolio.

GCC markets have seen a significantly greater allocation of capital—especially by private investors—during the boom of the 2000s than during the previous booms. One reason for this is the abundance of attractive investment opportunities, especially in population-linked sectors. The Gulf states now have almost 40 million people, compared with just 10 million in 1975. The real estate market, which most sophisticated observers now see as overheated, has offered phenomenal returns in recent years. Many buyers— especially in red-hot Dubai—purchase properties during the concept phase of development, based on nothing but a floor plan and a promise, and then sell the property for a handsome return before it is even built. Local stock markets also enjoyed phenomenal growth before experiencing a sharp market correction in 2006. Institutional investors, many of whom tread carefully to avoid "bubble" sectors like listed equities, have found solid opportunities in infrastructure investment and large-scale projects in sectors such as energy that promise strong fundamental growth. The flow of capital and high rates of return are mutually reinforcing: more capital raises asset values and creates high returns, which in turn attract additional capital and investors. This cycle has made domestic investment more attractive to GCC investors than ever before.

One hypothesis that appears often in the media is that after September 11, 2001, and the subsequent War on Terror, Gulf investors repatriated their capital due to political and security concerns. While it is clear that the bulk of Gulf investors oppose US policy in Iraq and elsewhere, attributing their preference for local investment to the current political environment is, in my view, an exaggeration. GCC investors, like most investors everywhere, are principally concerned with returns. US equity markets dipped after 9/11 (due to a large number of factors unrelated to Gulf capital) and lagged for years, while GCC markets were booming. At the same time, US interest rates remained relatively low and bonds paid unattractive yields. Rational GCC investors therefore saw more promise in local markets and international markets other than the United States' and decided to revise their investment strategy accordingly. This decision had more to do with return than with opposition to the Bush administration. In fact, the portfolios and acquisition activities of high-profile Gulf investors such as Alwaleed Bin Talal (major investor in the Four Seasons Hotels, Apple, Citigroup, the News Corp., and other global businesses) confirm that the Gulf has not lost its appetite for US and Western assets.

Another important difference between the booms of the 1970s and the 2000s is the diversity of financial instruments used. Whereas petrodollars in the 1970s were overwhelmingly channeled toward traditional asset classes such as fixed income and listed equities, capital in the 2000s has flowed not only into these asset classes but also a wide range of alternative assets such as private equity, real estate, and hedge funds. Alternative assets have been acquired in both international and domestic markets. Abu Dhabi's active investment arm Mubadala—funded by ADIA—has made a number of prominent private-equity investments at home and abroad, including the purchase of a 5 percent stake in Ferrari. The sectors in which Mubadala has invested reflect the core sectors of growth in the region: energy, industry, health care, infrastructure, and education. One of the more interesting portfolio companies is SR Technics, an airplane maintenance firm with Swiss origins and well positioned to service the region's fast-expanding airline market.

International and regional private-equity firms alike have been actively raising capital in the region. Leading private-equity firms such as Blackstone and Carlyle call on Gulf investors frequently and include the region in fund-raising strategies for massive new global funds. Local firms raising funds of $500 million or more include Abraaj Capital of the UAE, Global Investment House of Kuwait, and Bahrain-based Investcorp.[15] Investcorp has a long history of investments in the West, including buyouts and complete turnarounds of luxury retailers like Tiffany's and Saks Fifth Avenue. Between 2005 and 2006, the amount of private-equity investment raised by local firms grew by about 80 percent, to nearly $10 billion.[16] This figure does not include the large investments made by Gulf investors in Western and global private-equity firms, or the direct investments made by institutions and high-net-worth individuals.

The Gulf's enthusiasm for private equity is, in some ways, a reflection of a global trend toward this asset class witnessed worldwide. It is also, however, a sign of the increased sophistication of GCC investors and of their tolerance for the risks associated with private-equity investment.

Unlike in previous booms, government and government-linked institutions now place private-sector development at the core of their investment strategy. This shift in emphasis is exhibited in three ways. One is the development of "soft" infrastructure—such as the UAE's free zones, King Abdullah Economic City in Saudi Arabia, and Bahrain's Financial Harbor—designed to stimulate the private sector and jump-start local entrepreneurial ventures. These ventures reflect governments' objective of providing the private sector all the tools it needs to drive economic diversification and growth and to make the economies more competitive. A second mechanism of private-sector development has been the privatization of state enterprises. One high-profile privatization was the listing of shares in Etisalat, long the UAE's monopoly telecom provider. Etisalat has since gone on to acquire or launch services in other markets, including a wireless carrier in Saudi Arabia and a stake in Pakistan's formerly state-owned telecom company. Insiders view such privatizations as a mechanism by means of which the state can share the wealth created by economic growth while at the same time making companies more efficient and market oriented. A third, and similar, mechanism is state coinvestment in companies floated on exchanges or otherwise made available to private shareholders. Two examples of this are Abu Dhabi's real estate firm Al Dar and air-conditioning company Tabreed—both publicly listed companies in which the state-owned Mubadala keeps a small minority stake. The signal sent by such ventures is that the government will support new enterprises but wants the private sector to drive them forward.

A final—yet crucial—difference between today's investment approach and that of the past concerns the way investment management expertise is utilized. In the past, Gulf institutions were more passive investors who channeled funds to investment managers in New York or London and "managed the managers" from afar. Over the years, however, GCC institutions have taken a much more active role and have increasingly brought expertise in-house.

This approach is driven in part by the increased sophistication of the leadership and managers in these institutions—leadership and managers, who generally tend to have world-class talents, have excellent educations in international business, and have work experience at global firms. A significant number of GCC nationals who have trained abroad and worked in top foreign firms are now bringing their experience to local institutions. In addition, GCC institutions are exploring other ways to develop local expertise: one major institution, for example, has been sending young talent out to work as interns at global banks where it keeps large accounts. The interns gain exposure to the workings of the banks and bring their insights about this home with them.

Another advantage of the strategy of bringing talent in-house is that it has attracted expatriate talent to work directly for the institution, on the ground in the Gulf. Investment managers from around the world, and especially from the UK and Commonwealth countries, can be found in increasing numbers around the region, generally employed by large institutional investors. Whereas Gulf postings were once seen as hardship assignments at unsophisticated institutions, today's expatriates enjoy both a very high standard of living and a rigorously challenging work environment. An investment manager with ADIA or the Kuwait Investment Authority on his or her CV, for example, is now viewed as someone with experience at one of the world's most important institutional investment firms. In fact, ADIA's current head of investment strategy is a Frenchman.

The world's leading investment banks have recognized the potential of the GCC, as well as the value of having a local presence. The Dubai International Financial Centre (DIFC), opened in 2005 and regulated independently through the Dubai Financial Services Authority, had by 2007 attracted well over 300 global firms. Among these are marquee firms such as Goldman Sachs, Merrill Lynch, Deutsche Bank, Barclays Capital, and Credit Suisse. The Qatar Financial Centre (QFC) has also attracted an impressive list of global firms, including Citibank, Standard Chartered, and the Royal Bank of Scotland. Many firms, like Credit Suisse, have a presence in both centers. In an interesting development, DIFC Investments—the proprietary investment arm of Dubai's finance center—became one of the largest shareholders in Deutsche Bank in

May 2007 by taking a 2.2 percent equity stake.[17] Besides being a promising market for clients, the GCC is becoming a significant source of equity investment for financial institutions worldwide.

LOCAL STOCK MARKETS: EXPLOSIVE GROWTH AND MASSIVE CORRECTION

Between 2001 and 2007, the GCC's local stock markets witnessed tremendous growth and a severe market correction. For the first part of this period, local markets went nowhere but up: between 2001 and 2004, total market capitalization in the UAE grew sevenfold while the Saudi market more than tripled.[18] One Saudi firm even had a market capitalization close to Google's at the time. Through 2005 and the early months of 2006, the frenzy continued and "irrational exuberance" akin to the 1990s dot-com bubble on the Nasdaq market set in. The bulk of investors in the market—an estimated 70 percent—were individual investors, of which as many as 90 percent may have been short-term speculators.[19] These were the Gulf equivalent of day traders during the dot-com bubble period—investors with little understanding of or interest in the fundamental performance of the businesses they invested in, but eager to capture returns that could be as high as 5 percent per day. Even local companies found the frenzy too tempting to resist. In 2004 and 2005, for example, it was not uncommon for companies to have more "extraordinary income" from gains on the stock market than operating profits from their core business.

Stock market euphoria in the Gulf got out of hand quickly and reached extreme heights. Some investors sold their cars to finance shares, and banks would lend cash to investors to buy stock and participate in IPOs. Some lending behavior became downright irresponsible. According to the local Saudi press, some lenders could garner 20 to 30 percent returns in a single week by financing shares; the Saudi Arabian Monetary Agency needed to intervene.[20] In Kuwait, lending to purchase shares grew 337 percent between 2000 and 2005.[21] A sign of the times was that some ATMs were enabled with brokerage capabilities so that customers could day-trade as they withdrew cash from their accounts. When a hot IPO was open to investors from around the GCC, it was not uncommon for nationals to drive across borders, sleep in their cars if need be, and stand in long lines to register for shares. Many people quit their jobs entirely when day trading became too lucrative. I recall a striking scene from a visit to the Abu Dhabi stock exchange in 2005. The floor seemed to be in a frenzy, with a buzz going all around, as is common to all exchanges with human traders. Unlike the New York or Chicago exchanges, however, most of the people on the floor were individual investors—not professional brokers and dealers. When the petrochemical company Yansab was listed in Saudi Arabia, almost two-fifths of the Saudi national population—over 8 million people—participated in the IPO.[22] In the United States, by contrast, roughly half of all households own any individual stocks at all, and no single share would be universally owned by all of them.[23]

Figure 8.3 illustrates the performance of the Saudi stock market, by far the GCC's largest and representative of the phenomenon witnessed in the UAE and Qatar as well.

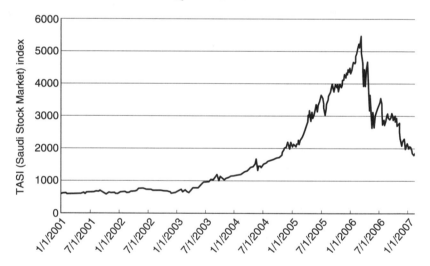

Figure 8.3 Saudi stock market boom and crash, 2001–2007 (Source: Bloomberg)

Stocks continued to climb until March 2006, when they plummeted. Ironically, the crash began at a time when oil prices—and therefore liquidity in the region—were at all-time highs. This is yet another sign that the high valuations were simply a bubble and not based on fundamental economic realities. The correction, which continued throughout 2006, wiped out most of the gains made since early 2005. As of June 2007, however, the market was up around 250 percent from its 2001 level. The investors most hurt by the correction were those who came in at the peak of the frenzy in 2005 and 2006—and these, unfortunately, tended to be the least sophisticated and most vulnerable retail investors.

Table 8.2 shows the change in equity market values across the GCC countries between 2001 and early 2006 (the boom period) and between 2001 and mid-2007. As the data shows, all markets remained well above their pre-boom values even after the correction of 2006—markets in Kuwait, Qatar, and the UAE maintained values several times greater than the 2001 figures.

TABLE 8.2

Change in Equity Market Values across the GCC Countries between 2001 and Early 2006

Country	Market Change, 1/1/01 to 2/1/06	Market Change, 1/1/01 to 6/1/07
Saudi Arabia	629%	186%
UAE	605%	393%
Qatar	682%	491%
Bahrain	91%	77%
Kuwait	453%	589%
Oman	131%	153%
Source: Shuaa Capital		

It is worth noting that market corrections in Kuwait and Bahrain were far less pronounced than those in Saudi Arabia, the UAE, and Qatar. One reason for this is that Kuwait and Bahrain had more sophisticated stock markets—Kuwait's being the first in the region and Bahrain's being heavily weighted toward shares of more stable financial institutions. Both exchanges also enjoy a high proportion of institutional investors, who are less likely to succumb to the temptations of valuation bubbles. Oman's stock market, quite interestingly, grew at a healthy pace in 2006—a sign that it was insulated from the frenzy occurring in the other GCC markets.

While the sharp market correction was certainly jarring for many investors, observers see it as a necessary step and a maturing experience for the region. As of February 2007, average price-to-earnings (P/E) ratios for shares traded on regional exchanges were far closer in line with emerging-market averages worldwide than they had been a year before. In February 2006, Saudi and UAE shares had been trading at unsustainable P/E ratios above 50. Figure 8.4 illustrates market-average P/E ratios before and after the correction, highlighting the percentage change.

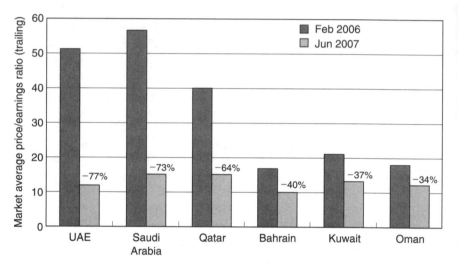

Figure 8.4 Gulf P/E ratios before and after the crash (Source: MSCI, research team analysis)

The pre-correction P/E ratios were, in some cases, four times the average for emerging markets worldwide. While the GCC economies certainly did have—and continue to have—a more positive outlook than many other emerging markets, their growth potential did not warrant such a huge premium. After the correction, valuations are much closer to—and in fact sometimes lower than—those of other high-growth markets. This has several positive implications. One is that GCC-market shares can again be seen as attractive buys—the ratios and fundamentals of the market suggest that valuations should go up again. Winning back investor confidence may take time, but sophisticated investors will see room for an upside in the Gulf. A second key implication is that valuations are at a level where mergers and acquisitions in the region become more viable. In 2004 and 2005, GCC acquisitions were very difficult to conceive (unless the acquiring party was also listed on the same exchange) because valuations were extremely high and difficult to justify. Apart from the regulatory barriers to acquisitions by non-GCC buyers (which are slowly being dismantled), share prices were simply too high to warrant investment by outside parties. As WTO and internal reforms make Gulf markets more open to foreigners, realistic equity valuations are crucial for enabling M&A activity.

Perhaps the most important implication of the market correction has been its effect on local investors' expectations. In boom times, many investors became accustomed to annual returns of 100 percent or more. Solid, fundamentals-based returns of 10 to 20 percent were simply unattractive compared with what they could get on local exchanges. Now that the market has corrected, GCC investors have a more realistic outlook about what is a good market return and are looking globally for opportunities. The most sophisticated investors, savvy about global markets, never lost sight of what a solid return really is. Retail investors, however, are now looking far more favorably at emerging markets and global equity funds with 10 to 20 percent promised returns than they did in 2005. At the same time, institutional investors are even more excited about private equity, hedge funds, and other alternative asset classes that can garner returns of 20 percent or more per year.

ISLAMIC FINANCE: A CRUCIAL TREND

Islamic finance, more precisely termed "Sharia-compliant" finance, refers to financial services conducted in accordance with Islamic legal principles. One of these principles is that a fixed return, without sharing any risk, is considered unjust. Conventional interest is therefore deemed impermissible. Another principle is that Muslims cannot profit from activities considered immoral: investing in casinos, pornography, weapons of mass destruction, and other such sectors is not allowed. One interesting notion is that, according the Sharia (the body of Islamic law), people are not allowed to sell what they do not own—therefore "short selling" is not permitted. A fourth key principle is that, in sales contracts, what is being bought and sold must be clearly understood by both parties. Conventional insurance contracts are deemed to have an excessive amount of uncertainty, and therefore a Sharia-compliant system called *takaful* has been developed to meet needs similar to those covered by conventional insurance products.

The core principles of Islamic finance are in fact consistent with the traditional teachings of other religions, and especially of the other Abrahamic faiths. Judaism and Christianity both also considered usury and interest unjust for most of their histories.[24] The Islamic financial industry has much in common with the fields of "ethical investment" and "corporate social responsibility," both of which are growing in popularity worldwide. People increasingly realize how important it is to be mindful of the source and purpose of their wealth. In fact, we could say that Islamic finance is the largest and most influential branch of "ethical investment" worldwide.

One of the most common Islamic financial instruments is called a *Murabaha*—a cost-plus sale in which one party buys something and sells it to someone else for a profit. This simple arrangement is used commonly, and unlike conventional finance it links lending to an asset and attaches ownership risk to the asset. Other common financial structures are *Ijara*, or leasing, and *Mudaraba* (investment partnership). In *Mudaraba*, investors provide capital to a manager, who contributes his or her time and efforts in exchange for a portion of the return. The practice of *Musharaka* (profit-and-loss-sharing partnership) is viewed by many as the purest form of finance—all parties share the underlying risk. It is also probably the most difficult financing mode to implement. On the investment side, products include equity investment, *Murabaha*-based instruments, and a product called Sukuk, which acts similarly to conventional bonds but involves the financing of identifiable assets.[25]

While Islamic finance has arguably been in existence for centuries, the first modern Islamic financial institutions took root in the 1960s in both Egypt and Malaysia. Early institutions were focused on savings and community banking—Malaysia's Tabung Haji, for example, was established as a savings mechanism for Malaysian Muslims who were planning for their pilgrimage to Makkah. During the booms of the 1970s, Islamic finance gained momentum in the GCC region. The Gulf states were becoming prosperous, had

secured their independence from colonial influence, and were keen
to develop financial institutions consistent with Islamic values.
A number of Gulf-based financial services conglomerates emerged
in the 1970s and expanded in the 1980s, developing new products
and business models to compete with their conventional (non-
Sharia-compliant) counterparts. In the 1990s, Islamic finance was
identified by major global banks as critical to success in certain
Muslim markets. Citibank and HSBC established global Islamic
finance units, after which nearly all major global banks followed
suit. *Euromoney* holds frequent seminars on the topic of Islamic
finance, the Harvard Law School has a research program based on
it, and the Dow Jones Indexes track Sharia-compliant securities in
various markets. According to a World Bank study, there are over
300 institutions offering Islamic financial services today.[26]
The industry has, according to many observers, reached main-
stream relevance and acceptance.

    While Islamic finance is a global phenomenon—HSBC, for
example, offers Islamic retail services in nine countries—the heart
of the market is the GCC countries and Malaysia. In Saudi Arabia,
according to central-bank data and observers' analysis, the volume
of Sharia-compliant banking assets is believed to have surpassed, as
of 2005, the volume of conventional assets. In the Gulf overall,[27]
Islamic financial assets are believed to be 25 to 30 percent of all
banking assets, with the figure expected to reach around 40 percent
by 2010.[28] As Sharia compliance has proven its viability, corporate
entities that otherwise may have been comfortable with conventional finance are facing pressure from customers and shareholders
to eliminate noncompliant practices. A friend whose family owns
one of the largest listed companies in the UAE confided to me that
board members were increasingly pressuring his family to adopt a
fully Sharia-compliant corporate balance sheet. In response to market demand for Sharia compliance—Islamic finance is growing
faster than conventional banking—a number of conventional banks
including the UAE's National Bank of Sharjah and Saudi Arabia's
Bank Al Jazira, have converted their operations to become fully
Sharia-compliant. Other major banks are launching separate brands
and product lines for Islamic finance.

    The rise of Islamic finance has a number of important implica-
tions for multinationals seeking to build business ties with the GCC.

The first applies to financial services firms that wish to expand there: credible Islamic finance expertise has now become essential for large-scale appeal in the Gulf. A second relates to companies whose offerings currently or potentially could include consumer finance elements, such as automobiles, electronics, and other large purchases for which customers might wish to pay over time. Global firms should work with their local franchisees or partners to explore Sharia-compliant consumer finance services (through partnerships with financial institutions), which would ensure access to as wide a customer base as possible. Sharia-minded customers may not have credit cards, and therefore consumer finance options become all the more important. Savvy local partners would, of course, understand the local dynamics.

A third—and increasingly important—implication relates to raising capital through Sharia-compliant instruments. Many GCC investors are either completely Sharia-compliant as a matter of policy or have a preference for Islamic instruments. Caribou Coffee, for example—America's second-largest specialty coffee chain—was acquired by the fully Sharia-compliant, Bahrain-based private-equity firm Arcapita. Ford's $848 million sale of Aston Martin to an LBO consortium involved Sharia-compliant financing because of the wishes of Kuwaiti investors Investment Dar and Adeem Investment Company.[29] Global firms who are serious about M&A activity involving GCC investors need to be open to the possibility of using Sharia-compliant structures and instruments. While these may, at times, involve unfamiliar procedures, flexibility in accommodating Sharia compliance can make a meaningful difference in widening the potential Gulf investor base and capturing the highest possible valuation.

OECD entities, recognizing these benefits, have begun issuing Shariah-compliant Sukuk (bondlike instruments) and attracting Islamic investors. The Sukuk market, expected by S&P to reach $100 billion by 2010,[30] has included issuers far afield of the Muslim world. The German state of Saxony issued the first-ever Western federal Sukuk in 2004, and Japan's central bank, with the Japan Bank for International Cooperation, is planning a $500 million Sukuk issue in 2007.[31] The City of London is positioning itself as a Sukuk hub of the world, and Britain's Prime Minister Gordon Brown's 2007 budget introduced measures to make Sukuk issues easier and more competitive in the UK. Even the United States has now entered the market—with the Texas-based firm East Cameron Gas Company issuing the first-ever American Sukuk in 2006.[32] These entities all saw value in taking the additional steps needed to ensure Sharia compliance.

SOURCING CAPITAL: STRATEGIC OR ACCIDENTAL

There is no shortage of examples of global companies for whom GCC investors make up a meaningful segment of their investor base. Apple and Citigroup, for example, count Alwaleed Bin Talal as one of their largest shareholders. Investor relations professionals at major listed companies may, in fact, be surprised at the number of GCC investors who subscribe to their shares— investors who can often be less vocal than large OECD mutual and pension funds and therefore somewhat overlooked. Gulf investors wishing to avoid media attention may also limit their stakes to under the public disclosure threshold, which is 5 percent in the United States, Japan, France, and Hong Kong, and 3 percent in Britain and Germany.[33]

Private-equity investment and strategic acquisitions have brought GCC buyers into the limelight more than passive owner-ship stakes in listed companies. Some of the high-profile entities that have been or are currently portfolio companies or subsidiaries of GCC institutions are listed in Table 8.3. While the list is far from comprehensive, it captures some of the breadth of companies in which Gulf investors have controlling or large minority holdings.

TABLE 8.3

Prominent GCC Portfolio Companies[34]

Country	Investing Entity	Portfolio Company	Ownership Stake
UAE	Istithmaar[35]	Standard Chartered	2.7%
	DIFC Investments[36,37]	Deutsche Bank	2.2%
		Euronext	3.5%
	Jumeirah International	Essex House (NY)	100%

Continued

TABLE 8.3

Prominent GCC Portfolio Companies—cont'd

Country	Investing Entity	Portfolio Company	Ownership Stake
		Carlton Tower (London)	100%
	Mubadala	Ferrari	5%
	Dubai Ports World	P&O	100%
	Dubai International Capital[38, 39,40]	Madame Tussauds	20% (was 100%)
		Travelodge (UK)	100%
		HSBC ($1 bn)	minority
		DaimlerChrysler ($1bn) (sold)	2%
		Doncasters Group (UK)	100%
	Dubai Investment	Marfin Financial (Greece)	31.5%
	Group	Bank Islam (Malaysia)	40%
Saudi Arabia	Kingdom Holdings / Alwaleed	Four Seasons Hotels (with Bill Gates)	22%
	Bin Talal[41]	Fairmont Hotels	16%
		Canary Wharf	substantial
		Disneyland Paris	17%
		Saks Inc.	10%
		Citigroup	4.3%
		Apple	5%
		News Corp.	5%
		AOL Time Warner	5%
		Motorola	substantial
		Walt Disney	substantial
		Planet Hollywood	substantial
	SABIC	GE Plastics	100%
	Maan al-Sanea[42,43]	HSBC ($6.6 bn)	3.1%
		Berkeley Holdings	29%
		Citigroup	minority
		Bank of China	minority
		Industrial and Commercial Bank of China	minority
Qatar	Qatar Investment	Lagadere	7%
	Authority	ICBC	minority
	Delta Two[44]	J Sainsbury	25%

TABLE 8.3

Prominent GCC Portfolio Companies—cont'd

Country	Investing Entity	Portfolio Company	Ownership Stake
Kuwait	Investment Dar, Adeem Investment	Aston Martin	78%
	Kuwait Investment Authority	Industrial and Commercial Bank of China	19%
		Daimler Benz	7.1%
Bahrain	Arcapita	Caribou Coffee (US)	60%
		Viridian Group	100%
		South Staffordshire Water	100%
		N. Ireland electricity provider	100%
	Investcorp	Tiffany (floated 1987)	100%
		Gucci (floated 1996)	50%
		Saks Fifth Avenue (floated 1996)	100%

While all the above companies have significant stakes by GCC investors, it is not clear how many of them actively sought Gulf capital or saw it as an opportunity. In the cases of P&O and GE Plastics, where the buyers were more strategic than financial in nature, the companies most likely engaged their GCC buyers actively. In the majority of situations, however, it could very well be that multinationals came across GCC investors in an "accidental," opportunistic fashion. Savvy firms should learn from their experience and consider including the Gulf as an integral part of their capital-raising and M&A strategies.

Capital can be raised in the GCC at a number of levels. The simplest is at the global "parent" level, such as the case with Standard Chartered and Deutsche Bank described above. These firms are applying GCC capital to their overall worldwide operations, and in that sense Gulf investors are merely an extension of their traditional shareholder base. No customized documentation or structuring is necessary; investors are buying ordinary stock. To raise capital at this level all that is required is a "typical" road show in which the merits of the firm and its long-term value

are communicated to Gulf principals and their investment
managers.

A second manner in which Gulf capital can be injected is at the
"business unit" level. These transactions, typically involving both
equity and debt, are far more customized and involve in-depth
negotiations. The sales of Aston Martin by Ford and GE Plastics are
examples of such transactions. Structuring such deals may include
accommodation of Gulf investors' particular circumstances and needs,
such as sovereign or semisovereign tax status or preference for Sharia
compliance. Especially when such deals are for strategic and not only
for financial reasons, global firms with business lines to dispose of can
expect attractive valuations from Gulf buyers. Global investment banks
are now more able than ever before to showcase deals to GCC investors.

A third level of capital injection, and one that may become
common as GCC economies liberalize and relax their ownership
restrictions further, is raising capital at the subsidiary or regional
entity level. In some respects, banking joint ventures such as the
Saudi Hollandi Bank—in which ABN Amro retained an equity
stake while taking on local Saudi investors—could be considered
forerunners to this model.[45] Multinationals can explore funding—at
least partially—their Gulf or Middle East operations through raising capital for a region-specific entity from regional investors. A
company could "spin out" its Middle East business or create a new
entity for the region. Capital could be raised through a private
placement or through a local exchange.

The increased sophistication of local exchanges is a positive
development for those seeking to raise Gulf capital. In addition to
general enhancements such as tighter disclosure and governance standards, new exchanges are being created with regulations and operating guidelines based on global best practices. At the forefront of these
new exchanges is the Dubai International Financial Exchange (DIFX),
which is regulated independently by the Dubai Financial Services
Authority. Some of the main differences between the DIFX and extant
"onshore" regional exchanges are summarized in Table 8.4.[46]

The DIFX's approach, in summary, is more "issuer friendly."
The exchange's aspiration is to be a world-class market filling the
geographic and time-zone gap between London and Hong Kong. It
therefore seeks to create an environment by which multinationals
feel comfortable listing there in addition to one or more of the
global exchanges such as New York or London.

TABLE 8.4

DIFX: A Different Kind of Exchange

Attribute	"Onshore" Exchanges	DIFX
Foreign ownership restrictions	Variable, can be as high as 100%	None
Minimum public flotation	Tends to be 40% or higher	25%
Offering price	Negotiated with regulator	Through institutional investor-driven process
Corporate form	Mandated	Flexible

The central importance of GCC investors in global capital markets is a reality likely to persist for years to come. Savvy firms will acknowledge this reality and develop financial strategies that benefit from the participation of Gulf investors and optimize value creation for the global parent company.

KEY LESSONS

- The GCC economies have long been *exporters of dollar-denominated capital* and are significant investors in global capital markets.
- Wealth in the region is fueled by *large government surpluses*, which may face greater pressure over the years as energy prices normalize and budgetary pressures rise.
- The boom of the 2000s has seen *investment strategies that vary significantly from those of previous booms*, though the bulk of GCC capital is still invested outside the region.
- GCC stock markets experienced a *boom and steep correction* in the 2000s, as valuations reached levels far out of line with global norms.
- The *growth of Islamic finance* is an important trend in the region and should be understood by multinationals.
- Savvy multinationals should integrate *the region into their capital strategies*, sourcing funds from the Gulf and even consider financing local subsidiaries from within.

CHAPTER 9

Getting Things Done: Operations Strategy and the GCC

INTRODUCTION

Take a look at Dubai from the air and what you see might surprise you. You might expect, based on what you have heard about the famous hotels, office buildings, and high-profile construction projects, to see a sprawling metropolis studded with glass and steel. Or, having heard the enthusiastic accounts of the fabulous luxury resorts that attract the rich and famous from around the world, you might be expecting to see endless miles of pristine beaches and artificial islands. In both cases, however, you would be greatly surprised. While these landmarks are visible from the air, more visually prominent are a massive port and shipping zone several times larger than the commercial center of the city. The core of Dubai's landscape is not its office buildings or tourist hot spots; it is a gigantic port and industrial area called Jebel Ali, which happens to be the largest man-made harbor in the world.

While much is made of the glitz and glamour of Dubai, at the heart of its success story is its role as a shipping, logistics, and operations center. Other parts of the GCC, which also may be known for their opulence, derive their wealth from the gritty business of oil drilling and energy production, whereas Dubai has little oil left. Developing industrial and operational capabilities has been fundamental to creating prosperity in the Gulf region. The Gulf states have, over the past three decades, had every incentive and means to develop world-class infrastructure.

The world-class infrastructure of the Gulf stands in sharp contrast with less-business-friendly emerging markets and has several major implications for multinationals. The ease of transporting people in and out, along with the strength of business support systems such as telecommunications, adds to the attractiveness of basing offices and holding corporate events in Gulf cities. The ease of transporting goods has caused global leaders like Sony to use Gulf ports as a central staging ground of their global operations. Further, the abundance of industrial inputs and support for industrial activity—not to mention a booming consumer market—has inspired firms like Kraft to see the GCC states as an attractive place in which to establish manufacturing facilities.

While the strength of the Gulf's infrastructure makes operations convenient, there are operational complexities that detract from this convenience. The GCC weekend, for example, occurs on Friday and Saturday or Thursday and Friday and is not aligned with the Saturday and Sunday weekend norm observed by other markets in the world. Running a business in the region also typically involves a significant amount of bureaucratic paperwork, for which dedicated compliance and government relations staffs are needed. Multinationals need to factor in these issues when designing their operational strategies for the region.

Leading firms such as Nestlé and Honda have identified the Gulf as important to their global operations, and in the years ahead many other multinationals will likely follow. The Gulf's advanced infrastructure and operations advantage have also fueled the push toward the global expansion of GCC-based logistics and transport firms such as Dubai Ports World and Emirates Airlines, propelling those enterprises to the forefront of their industries worldwide. When crafting their overall Gulf strategies, operations is an area that savvy multinationals cannot afford to overlook.

INFRASTRUCTURE EXCELLENCE

GCC countries, particularly in their major business cities, have reached an impressive level of infrastructure sophistication. I use "infrastructure" here in a broad sense, including air, land, and marine transportation, as well as utilities and support systems such as electricity and telecommunications. GCC states have generally achieved or exceeded world-class standards in all of these categories.

Investment in infrastructure has long been a theme of GCC government agendas. As oil revenue began creating massive public surpluses in the 1970s, it was crucial both economically and politically for rulers to invest in infrastructure. The business case was clear: strong infrastructure enables economic activity across the full range of industries and enables the private sector to take initiative on its own. Infrastructure gives people some of the tools they need to create thriving institutions. Politically, it was crucial for governments to demonstrate how they were "sharing the wealth" of oil windfalls with the common citizen. The political contract was straightforward: rulers have stewardship of the countries' natural resources and in return are expected to take care of their citizens' needs. Basic necessities like roads and sanitation were to be provided at no cost (neither taxation nor tolls) and utilities like electricity and phone services were to be heavily subsidized and enabled by public-sector investment. If citizens were not looked after with strong infrastructure, governments were not seen to be allocating resources responsibly.

The GCC countries' record of infrastructure excellence is good for business. Some of the core benefits for multinational businesses in particular are illustrated in Figure 9.1.

Airports and transport links have facilitated the flow of people through the region—and especially through Dubai—in an unprecedented and remarkable fashion. The easy flow of goods—also pioneered by Dubai but quickly becoming more common in the region—makes the Gulf an important hub for global trade. The GCC is, as more and more global companies are coming to realize, endowed with remarkable access to the core inputs required for industry and manufacturing—including energy and labor. In addition, the region's infrastructure provides reliable and increasingly business-friendly support systems such as fast Internet access and corporate business parks that facilitate opening offices in the Gulf.

Gulf-state governments, increasingly through partnership with the private sector, continue to invest heavily in upgrading

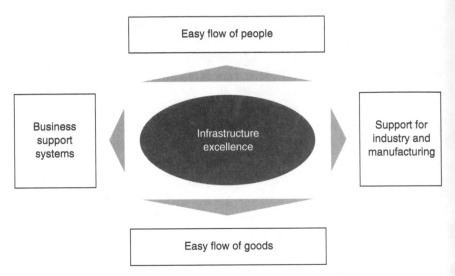

Figure 9.1 Business benefits of strong infrastructure in GCC countries

their countries' infrastructure and preserving their infrastructure excellence. The number of "megaprojects" planned for the region, across a wide range of infrastructure sectors, is striking. Mentioning them all would be tedious if not impossible. As we discuss each of the benefits to business illustrated in Figure 9.1, select examples of existing facilities and investments being made will suffice to describe the scale of resources being allocated to infrastructure in the region.

FLOW OF PEOPLE: EASY IN, EASY OUT

Accessing the GCC region—and especially Dubai—has become remarkably easy as air links and airport infrastructure have mushroomed. The volume of activity at Dubai International Airport is staggering: in 2006; the airport served nearly 29 million passengers, with 113 airlines flying from the airport to 194 destinations.[1] Given the airport's rapid growth—13 to 18 percent in recent years—in 2007 it looks to enter the ranks of the top 30 busiest airports worldwide. There are direct flights to Dubai from most of the world's major business cities, including a highly popular route from New York. Business-class seats on the route are a hot commodity and often sell out weeks in advance. Dubai's central location also places it within direct flying distance of major Asian and African cities such as Beijing, Sydney, and Johannesburg, as well as all cities in Europe.

As passenger volume in Dubai has steadily increased, investment in upgrading the airport and its facilities has grown as well. Authorities are investing over $4 billion in expanding Dubai International Airport[2] and have established a "fuel farm" to support the needs of aircraft transiting in and out of the hub. This enhancement has seen the airport's fuel storage capacity swell to nearly 450,000 barrels—enough to ensure that flights can take off 24 hours a day and be refueled around the clock.[3] The fuel farm was a far more modest investment—about $30 million—but a crucial one in maintaining the airport's global standing. In the longer term, Dubai is planning a new Jebel Ali Airport 40 kilometers from the current airport and the size of London Heathrow and Chicago O'Hare combined. The airport will be able to accommodate an astonishing 120 million passengers per year—30 times the population of the UAE—making it far busier than Atlanta Hartsfield, currently the world's busiest airport.[4]

Dubai is not the only city investing heavily in its airport. Abu Dhabi International Airport—whose passenger volume was 3.25 million (about one-eighth of Dubai's) in 2004—is in the midst of an ambitious $6.8 billion expansion, the first phase of which is expected to be completed in 2010. The expanded airport will have the capacity to serve 40 million passengers—a number equivalent to the population of all the GCC countries. In addition to the passenger facilities, the airport will have a cargo capacity of 2 million tons per year—similar to the current volume at the UPS hub in Louisville. Duty-free shopping in the airport is being heavily marketed—in fact, Abu Dhabi Duty Free has repeatedly been recognized with the Frontier Marketing Award for the "Best Marketing Campaign by a Retailer."[5] The airport is being expanded largely to support the growth ambitions of Etihad Airways, the UAE's national carrier launched in 2003 by Abu Dhabi.

Etihad Airways is itself a major infrastructure investment for Abu Dhabi and the UAE. In 2004, the government-backed start-up airline signed a memorandum of understanding with Airbus for 24 aircraft, including the new superjumbo A380 and the ultra-long-range

A340-500—which will enable direct flights from Abu Dhabi to virtually any inhabited area in the world. Etihad also has options to buy 12 additional aircraft, bringing the total value of the deal to over $7 billion.[6] Insiders report that the very creation of Etihad Airways represents Abu Dhabi's aspiration to assert its leadership in the UAE and demonstrate its ability to outshine its "junior" emirate Dubai. The increase in airline and airport capacity in the UAE, assuming all expansion plans proceed as envisioned, could have far-reaching implications for pricing and consumer choice. There is also speculation that such substantial capacity would lead to bargain-priced agreements that would entice global carriers to use the UAE even more as a layover stop for long-haul flights. Abu Dhabi and Dubai are, after all, only 90 minutes apart by road, and having both airports act as major hubs should require a large increase in flight volume.

Travel Tip: Abu Dhabi Airport and the Three-Minute Rule

As Dubai's role as a major business and tourist destination has increased, the volume of passengers stretches the capacity of even the cavernous Dubai International Airport. The main terminal, which includes retail outlets, 24-hour duty-free shopping, a round-the-clock food court, an airport hotel, and numerous airline lounges, is not always easy to navigate. The walk from the gate to the immigration and arrival hall can be substantial, and lines at passport-control stations (especially for passengers traveling coach without access to the fast-track premium lanes) can be lengthy. All in all, one needs to budget about an hour for the arrival process: from landing to exiting the airport.

Arriving at Abu Dhabi, however, is a very different experience. Like Dubai, there is no paperwork to complete and US and EU passport holders simply have their passports stamped on arrival. But unlike Dubai, travel time from gate to passport control (in the present, preexpansion terminal) is minimal. A colleague with whom I traveled frequently from the United States to Abu Dhabi once timed the process from airplane door to airport sidewalk (assuming no bags to claim and nothing to declare at customs) to be a mere three minutes. In those three minutes, passengers at the front of the plane could complete the entire landing and immigration process.

We dubbed this phenomenon the "three-minute rule" and found that, while not always repeatable, the Abu Dhabi arrival process was consistently a breeze.

When traveling to the UAE, even if your business is in Dubai, it can often make sense to land at Abu Dhabi. Flights are less likely to be sold out or crowded, the airport is far easier to manage, and the drive to Dubai is a comfortable, traffic-free 90 minutes. As I have shared this tip over the years with other business travelers, they have come to appreciate the merits of Abu Dhabi's "three-minute rule." As the airport expands and Etihad's traffic grows, I hope the charm will not be completely lost.

Qatar, too, is investing heavily in its airport and its airline. Its new airport, built by the American engineering giant Bechtel, will have a layout similar to Hong Kong's airport and a yearly capacity of 24 million passengers in its first phase, and ultimately 50 million (its current volume is around 10 million). Check-in and retail spaces will be 12 times the size at the current airport. The airport will have an oasis theme, with flowing water and oasis plants as decoration. Energy conservation is also planned to be state-of-the-art, with carbon dioxide sensors and other monitoring devices placed around the terminal to limit the amount of air-conditioning used—a very important matter in a sweltering desert climate.[7] Qatar has also been aggressively expanding its road infrastructure, building its first freeway and a strategic highway network (the latter has won worldwide recognition, in the form of the prestigious the International Road Federation's prize for best transportation projects, among other awards).[8]

There are several implications for multinationals of such substantial investments in airport capacity. Most directly, firms whose businesses have to do with airport-linked services such as engineering, project management, maintenance, and duty-free retail can find ample opportunity to market their services to Gulf airports. More broadly, business and leisure travelers to the region can expect greater ease and comfort as carriers and airports vie with one another to be the most accommodating in the region. This ease of travel is one of several reasons why the Gulf has been a natural location for Middle East regional headquarters for the bulk of leading multinationals. As related projects such as conference centers continue to expand, the GCC countries become an even better place for international seminars and training events—especially events involving participants from both Asia and Europe.

While ease of transporting people is generally a strength of the GCC infrastructure, there are some notable exceptions to this norm. Saudi Arabia's airports and immigration processes are notoriously difficult and frustrating, involving extensive paperwork and frequent hassles. All non-GCC-region citizens need to apply for visas at Saudi consulates and embassies in their home countries, and business visas require letters of invitation endorsed by the local Saudi chamber of commerce. Women traveling alone face additional hurdles, such as needing to be met at the airport by the party they are visiting. Even the "direct" flight from Riyadh to New York stops once in Jeddah and requires a tedious security process. These obstacles to easy travel cause major frustration for businesspeople and are one reason why multinationals prefer flying elsewhere for meetings, even if the meetings relate to deals or products in Saudi Arabia.

Another transportation problem is daily traffic in Dubai. As Dubai is built on two sides of a creek, the creek crossings and other narrow roads create huge delays for drivers. It is customary for people's commute to be one hour or more each way, especially if they reside in the nearby emirate of Sharjah, as many expatriates do. When there are accidents or other additional delays, commuters can be stuck for hours. Dubai is investing heavily in easing traffic as part of a $6 billion surface transport infrastructure plan. The plan includes roads, a tunnel, a bridge, and a light-rail system that seeks to ease automobile congestion considerably.[9] One practical challenge will be laying out the stations in convenient locations, as Dubai currently has little to no pedestrian culture. The daytime heat can be oppressive, and walking on exposed sidewalks is done only for short distances and out of necessity. Traffic problems in Dubai are likely to persist in the medium term, and the inconvenience of traffic delays is one drawback to holding meetings or stationing staff in the city. Many residents view traffic as a major quality-of-life issue in Dubai.

FLOW OF GOODS: THE BACKBONE OF DUBAI'S DEVELOPMENT

To many, Dubai's rise in prominence seems like a recent phenomenon, traceable to policies of the 1990s and early 2000s. Insiders, however, recognize the seeds of Dubai's development in a far earlier policy decision: the initiative, launched by the late Sheikh Rashid in 1969, to create a deep-water harbor in order to pursue his vision of making Dubai a competitive shipping location. The goal of the project was to attract leading shipping companies from around the world to Dubai, which was a natural transition point between East and West. The massive Jebel Ali port was built 10 years later, and ever since Dubai has been at the heart of shipping in the Gulf. By 1995, there were 930 companies from 72 countries operating in the Jebel Ali Free Zone, including Sony, Samsung, General Motors, Heinz, and IBM. By 2004, it was among the top 10 busiest ports in the world.[10]

Compared with other leading ports of the world, Dubai has several advantages. One is its location at the crossroads of Europe, Asia, and Africa. Dubai is, for example, about equidistant between London and Hong Kong—a perfect place for goods from China to be stored, inventoried, and distributed to Europe. Jebel Ali's status as the world's largest man-made harbor and the vast scale of its facilities allow for huge amounts of general and temperature-controlled storage, available for short- or long-term rental. Jebel Ali has also been a leader in applying state-of-the-art technology, including systems that enable the visual tracking of containers and loading and discharging within minutes. The systems can even load and discharge a ship at the same time, getting it on its way much faster than other ports can do.[11] This is like having departing passengers board an airplane from one side while arriving passengers are still exiting from the other side. Imagine how much more efficient airlines would be if they could attain the same capability.

Growth in Dubai's shipping throughput has been both phenomenal and sustained. Between 2001 and 2005, Dubai's port throughput more than doubled. Figure 9.2 shows the growth in Dubai's throughput compared with that of Singapore (the world's largest throughput port in 2005) and Los Angeles (the largest throughput port in the United States).

Dubai's annual growth rate has been twice that of Singapore and Los Angeles. This difference in growth rates has allowed Dubai to overtake Los Angeles in the throughput rankings: in 2001, Los Angeles' throughput was over 60 percent higher than Dubai's; by 2005 Dubai had slightly more throughput than LA.

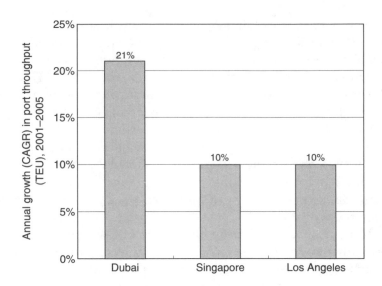

Figure 9.2 Dubai port throughput growing twice as fast as others
(Source: Port of Hamburg database, author analysis)

[12] While Singapore and Hong Kong still hold the top spots, Dubai is catching up fast—Dubai's container flow was less than a quarter of Singapore's in 2001, but grew to a third as large by 2005.

As Dubai's ports have grown in volume and sophistication, the expertise of the firm managing them has become increasingly competitive. It is not surprising, then, that one of the companies with GCC origins that has been most successful in competing worldwide is Dubai Ports World. Through organic growth and acquisitions, the company's operations now span five continents and would have included the United States if not for congressional intervention.

Dubai Ports World: Exporting Operational Excellence

The firm known as Dubai Ports World (DPW) was formed in 2005 through a merger of the Dubai Ports Authority (DPA), which managed the ports of the emirate, with Dubai Ports International (DPI), which managed ports outside the UAE. The evolution of the entities that formed DPW and of DPW itself is instructive in showing how core competencies can be nurtured and scaled internationally. The DPW story is also useful in understanding how Gulf-based companies have the potential to become serious global competitors when they combine deep expertise with capital and ambition.

DPA, in managing Dubai's own Port Rashid and Jebel Ali, was a leader in technology and became increasingly expert in advanced port operations as it built on its success.[13] DPI was created in 1999 as a platform for taking this expertise abroad and growing into other markets. Its first international partnership was in Saudi Arabia, with the Jeddah Islamic Port. With DPI's support, Saudi Arabia's first 1 million TEU (a standard unit for measuring shipping volume) terminal was achieved. Thereafter, DPI began operating ports in relatively obscure but important locations such as Djibouti (2000) and Vizag, India (2002). By 2005, DPI was one of the top six port operators worldwide.[14]

Through a consolidation with DPA and a 2005 acquisition of CSX World Terminals, the platform called DPW greatly expanded its presence and began managing ports in Hong Kong and China, Australia, Germany, and Latin America.[15] DPW was now a major force in the port management sector and a truly global establishment. When it acquired the British ports management giant P&O (the Peninsular and Oriental Steam Navigation Company) in 2006 for $6.8 billion, DPW's profile moved to a whole new level. The acquisition would make DPW the world's second-largest port manager in throughput terms and would place control of five US ports (including New York–New Jersey) in DPW's hands.[16]

Although the Bush administration supported the deal, US congressional leaders and other opinion-makers saw the move as a security risk and expressed concern about management of US ports by an Arab-based entity. Supporters of the deal pointed out DPW's solid track record, as well as that under P&O these ports were already under foreign management. Through a tumultuous process dubbed a "debacle" in a Harvard Business School case,[17] DPW agreed not to take control of the US assets and instead to spin them off to a US-based entity. Ultimately the American insurer AIG took the assets for an undisclosed sum.

DPW today manages 51 terminals in 24 countries. Its staff exceeds 30,000. It operates terminals in Hong Kong, Shanghai,

Tianjin, India, Germany, Australia, Latin America, and even Vancouver. Its capacity is in excess of 50 million TEU.[18] DPW's experience on the global stage provides many lessons and may set a trend for other Gulf-based businesses looking to expand. A first lesson is how DPW's success is founded on genuine competitive advantage and superior skill in an area of relevance (port management) beyond the Gulf market. Second, DPW began its expansion organically and in nearby ports such as Jeddah and Djibouti: testing grounds that were safe and natural extensions of its home market. Only after this more modest expansion did the firm seek acquisition-driven entry to the Far East, Western Europe, and the Americas. Third, DPW's political struggle in the United States illustrates how GCC-based firms need to tread carefully when acquiring American assets and how the United States needs a more nuanced understanding of the Gulf and businesses therein. Nobody likes debacles.

While Dubai has clearly taken the lead among GCC ports, other countries are building their shipping and transportation capabilities to compete for international traffic. Abu Dhabi's Port Zayed has larger covered and open storage facilities than Dubai's ports do,[19] although its throughput is far lower. Port Zayed's location is also farther from the Strait of Hormuz, making it less convenient for most major routes. And while Abu Dhabi has invested heavily in its port information technology, Dubai enjoys a longer reputation in the market for innovation and world-class systems. Dubai's Logistics City, which provides access to value-adding services such as light assembly and connections between sea and air links, is another facility the emirate uses to position itself as the UAE's premier shipping location.[20]

Saudi Arabia, as part of its massive, $27 billion King Abdullah Economic City project, plans to build the world's tenth-largest seaport. SAGIA, the Saudi Arabian General Investment Authority, has estimated that the country needs $100 billion worth of investment in ports, highways, and rail transportation in the coming years.[21] Large-scale and well-managed ports in Saudi Arabia could pose a serious competitive challenge to Dubai, as Saudi Arabia's national market is many times larger and therefore domestic (i.e., not for reexport) volume would be much higher. If Saudi Arabia could also serve as a viable relay point for goods to the broader region, its proposition would be bolstered significantly.

The other Gulf states, similarly keen to expand their shipping capabilities, are expanding or building out ports. Bahrain is building a new port at Hidd, with capacity for the world's largest container and bulk vessels.[22] Kuwait is pursuing a leadership role in global logistics—the Kuwaiti firm Agility (formerly PwC Logistics) is poised for expansion through both organic growth and acquisitions.[23] Kuwait's many ports are undergoing continual enhancement and improvement. Oman's Port of Salalah benefits significantly from its location along the southern coast of the Arabian Peninsula. The port has drawn leading firms such as China Shipping Container Lines (CSCL), Maersk, CMA-COM, and American President Line (APL.)[24]

As port facilities expand and improve throughout the Gulf, multinationals can benefit by incorporating the region more deeply into their logistics strategies. Leading American (e.g., Colgate-Palmolive, Xerox, and Black and Decker), Asian (Fuji, Tata, and Hyundai), and European (Nokia, Adidas, and Shell) firms have long had a presence in Dubai's Jebel Ali Free Zone. As Gulf markets become inherently more attractive and logistics capabilities continue to improve, the case for using GCC ports strengthens further. The large capacity that would be created if all port expansion plans play out as envisioned may also lead to very attractive pricing and financial incentives to draw more multinationals in and secure a greater level of port utilization.

ALL THE INGREDIENTS: SUPPORT FOR INDUSTRY AND MANUFACTURING

Gulf economies have long had abundant access to some of the key ingredients for heavy industry and manufacturing. Not surprisingly, energy costs are remarkably low, especially for oil and gas. Capital is abundant, and the currencies of nearly all GCC countries are pegged to the dollar. Labor costs—drawing on expatriates for most low-skill work—are also quite attractive. Access to waterways, for transporting raw materials and finished goods, is plentiful. What has held back the manufacturing sector, from a multinational's perspective, is the matter of property rights. Historically, foreign entities have not been allowed to own factories and manufacturing facilities without local partners. The risks associated with relying on partners, as well as the less favorable economics, have kept most multinationals away.

The creation of free-zone industrial parks has changed the situation significantly. As discussed earlier, the Jebel Ali Free Zone—Dubai's first and most industrial free zone—has attracted hundreds of international firms over more than a decade of operations. Nestlé, for example, which has been operating in Jebel Ali since 1997, has announced plans to begin manufacturing in Dubai by the end of 2007.[25] Other free zones in the UAE, such as those linked with airports, also draw industrial firms.

King Abdullah Economic City in Saudi Arabia is to include a massive 8-million-square-foot industrial district.[26] Industry and manufacturing are areas in which Saudi ownership laws have been quickest to liberalize, as government appreciation of the need to expand its industrial competitiveness is acute. Qatar's Science and Technology Park, in which GE has established a training and research center, permits 100 percent foreign ownership. The Kuwait Free Trade Zone, located in Shuwaikh Port, offers similar liberties and benefits. Bahrain's International Investment Park is a single complex with zones for services- and knowledge-based firms as well as manufacturing and industrial facilities of various sizes. Like its counterparts in other countries, the park offers 100 percent foreign ownership, tax holidays, and support systems for managing government bureaucracy.[27]

One high-profile firm that has announced its plans to manufacture in the region is Kraft. Kraft is building a plant in the Gulf to serve the broader Middle East region. The facility represents a $40 million investment.[28]

Kraft-ing a Gulf Manufacturing Facility

Kraft, the global food business, has been distributing its goods in the Middle East for half a century. Known best for its cheeses, the company also owns brands in other food categories such as Oreo cookies, Maxwell House coffee, Jell-O, and Tang. Processed food is an industry whose growth is linked to population and prosperity—both of which are moving in a positive direction in the Gulf and much of the Middle East. Kraft's outlook on the region appears to be reasonably optimistic.

In the summer of 2006, Kraft unveiled plans to build a $40 million plant in the Bahrain International Investment Park. The 60,000-square-meter manufacturing facility is expected to open before the end of 2007 and, once operational, employ 250 people. The plant will produce cheese and powdered drinks (e.g., Tang), and the output will be shipped throughout the Middle East market.[29]

Kraft's decision to manufacture in Bahrain appears sound for several reasons. Input costs, including energy and labor, will be very favorable in Bahrain. The goods produced, like most foods and beverages, are quite heavy in relation to their value and therefore costly to transport. Manufacturing close to the point of sale is therefore a desirable strategy. From Bahrain, Kraft can conveniently serve the entire Middle East region—thereby achieving enough scale to justify investing in a plant. If need be, Bahrain's excess output could conceivably be shipped to other high-growth markets in Asia as well. The infrastructure and shipping facilities of Bahrain can easily meet the manufacturer's needs. And Bahrain's International Investment Park offers a friendly business environment for a foreign firm.

As multinationals increase their focus on the Gulf, some are likely to follow Kraft's lead and begin manufacturing there. For companies for whom volume and economics justify the measure, manufacturing in the Gulf makes business sense.

Across the Gulf, governments are keen to attract multinationals who will build manufacturing and industrial facilities in the region. Such facilities are seen as adding to the embedded capital of these economies, and as making the economies more competitive. Manufacturing and large-scale industry—with the exception of the energy sector, of course—is an area in which local capabilities have lagged behind other emerging markets such as China and India. While these two markets have clear cost advantages in terms of labor, the GCC's favorable tax environment, strong legal regimes, first-class infrastructure, cheap energy, relative proximity, and access to the broader Middle East are important selling points. Beyond extending tax benefits, Gulf governments are eager to view multinationals who invest in manufacturing there as genuine development partners. Such goodwill can be immensely valuable as governments review suppliers for their ongoing projects as more sectors of the economy privatize.

AT YOUR SERVICE: BUSINESS SUPPORT FACILITIES

For companies in the services sector, the GCC's business infrastructure holds great appeal, especially in contrast with facilities elsewhere in the Middle East and in Asia. From office space and telecommunications to business hotels and conference facilities, the Gulf can offer professional amenities on a par with the leading business cities of the world. Electricity runs uninterruptedly; tap water flows properly; food is abundant, safe, and of international variety. These amenities are part of the region's appeal to multinational companies—especially professional services firms—and to expatriates across all sectors.

Since the 1970s, Bahrain has been a banking hub for the region.[30] To attract global banks, the country needed to build office complexes with facilities that catered to executives' needs. Though still considered a hardship posting by many, the country did provide amenities such as modern office space, telecommunications, information technology, hotels, and conference centers that could hold their own when compared with those in other markets around the world. In the 1990s, Dubai embarked on a high-profile and aggressive campaign—with advice from top-notch global strategy consultants—to transform into a "knowledge economy" and build the infrastructure required to attract and inspire knowledge companies and workers.

Dubai's early free zones reflect the sectors that the emirate most keenly sought to promote. After Jebel Ali—which was focused on transportation, industry, and manufacturing—Dubai launched its Media and Internet Cities. These free zones attracted global media and technology firms such as CNN, IBM, and Microsoft, along with the kinds of professionals who work for and admire them. Not long after came Knowledge Village, focused on training and education, and Health Care City. Besides ownership rights, favorable tax regimes, and flexible employment policies, these free zones offer robust infrastructure and shared services. Amenities often extend beyond the basics such as technology, meeting rooms, restaurants, and common spaces. Media City, for example, offers access to freelance writers and media professionals who can be hired by occupants as needed.[31] Free zones offer on-site government services such as issuing visas and ID cards, reducing the otherwise substantial hassle of local bureaucracy. Dubai is rapidly expanding its number of free zones, creating new sectors devoted to such specialties as biotechnology, logistics, and sports, and there is even one focusing on flowers.

Other free zones and open financial centers in the region such as Qatar Financial Centre, Bahrain Financial Harbor, and Dubai International Financial Centre likewise offer world-class facilities and shared services. Leading institutions like Goldman Sachs, Deutsche Bank, and HSBC have all become tenants in one or more of these centers. As states compete to attract marquee firms, the quality and breadth of services offered in these facilities will likely remain strong and improve. Expatriate bankers find well-apportioned offices and world-class facilities well below the rent they would pay in London or New York (though the recent boom has driven up rents in some cities).

Firms considering opening offices in the GCC need not worry about finding high-quality office space and support systems. While space is scarce in some of the hottest areas (e.g., Dubai International Financial Centre), new office buildings come online each month. The caliber of business support systems is one reason why leading professional services firms such as consultancies, investment banks, and law firms tend to place their regional head offices in the Gulf and fly out to visit clients as needed.

SYNCH TO SWIM: MANAGING MISALIGNED WEEKENDS AND TIME ZONES

One operational challenge for multinational firms operating in the GCC states is managing misaligned weekends. Not only is the Gulf weekend different from the Saturday-Sunday norm in the West and in most of Asia, but even within the GCC countries the weekend is not consistent. Half the countries are on a Friday-Saturday weekend schedule and half work on a Thursday-Friday one. Table 9.1 summarizes the schedules in each country and contrasts them with the Western-Asian norm. The shaded boxes represent working days.

All Gulf countries take Friday off, as it is the day of required congregational prayer for Muslims. Although the mandatory

TABLE 9.1

Misaligned Workweeks

Market	Monday	Tuesday	Wednesday	Thursday	Friday	Saturday	Sunday
UAE	▓	▓	▓	▓			▓
Qatar	▓	▓	▓	▓			▓
Bahrain	▓	▓	▓	▓			▓
Saudi Arabia	▓	▓	▓			▓	▓
Kuwait	▓	▓	▓	▓		▓	▓
Oman	▓	▓	▓			▓	
US/EU	▓	▓	▓	▓	▓		
Asia	▓	▓	▓	▓	▓		

midday prayer itself is about an hour long and there is no religious prohibition against working at other times during the day, Friday has evolved into a customary day off for religious, family, and social activity.[32] Historically, the weekend for the GCC countries was Thursday and Friday, but half the states have switched to Friday and Saturday for easier coordination with global markets. At the time of this writing, Kuwait was considering making the shift, too.[33] If the change goes through, only Saudi Arabia and Oman will be left on the Thursday-Friday schedule.

The complications arising from these staggered schedules are significant. One challenge they create is that of finding times in which to make conference calls and meetings that don't conflict with somebody's day off. As is evident from Table 9.1, there are only three days—Monday, Tuesday, and Wednesday—when Western and all GCC markets are open. This creates a coordination window of only 60 percent of the week. The coordination challenge is made even greater by the significant time difference between the GCC and other major business cities. Table 9.2 below summarizes the time difference during standard time (not daylight savings time), when the gap is greatest.

Four of the Gulf states are three hours ahead of Greenwich mean time; the UAE and Oman are four hours ahead. During daylight savings time in the United States and the UK, the gaps are

TABLE 9.2

Time Differences

New York (EST)	London (GMT)	Saudi Arabia, Qatar, Bahrain, Kuwait	UAE, Oman	India	China, Hong Kong, Singapore, Malaysia	Japan, Korea
9:00 a.m.	2:00 p.m.	5:00 p.m.	6:00 p.m.	7:30 p.m.	10:00 p.m.	11:00 p.m.

shorter by an hour, as there is no daylight savings time change in the GCC countries.

Thus even on days when offices in both places are open, planning transglobal conversations for times during which it is possible to talk is difficult. Staff in the United States begin their day just when Gulf offices are closing—those on a 9-to-5 schedule have no overlap time in the winter and one hour of overlap in the summer. From Europe, the time difference is much more manageable, as the bulk of the working day overlaps. This convenience, along with the relatively short travel time, is one reason why many US-based multinationals have had the Gulf region overseen by their European offices rather than the global main office. Flying from New York to Dubai or Abu Dhabi, even on a direct flight, consumes an entire day when travel time and the time difference are combined. A flight leaving New York at 11 a.m. will arrive around 8 a.m. the next morning. On the way home, though, the time gained is a real blessing—leave Dubai or Abu Dhabi at 2 a.m. and you can land at JFK around 7 the same morning.

Coordinating with the GCC from the United States is therefore a logistical challenge, usually requiring one or both of the parties involved to be inconvenienced. One solution adopted by some American firms serving clients in the Gulf is to fly staff out from the United States on a Sunday, have them work 10 days straight, and then fly them back on a Thursday for a 4-day weekend. This schedule is grueling and difficult on families, but it has been one way to ensure that staff have at least two solid periods off in a month while smoothing out, to some extent, the issue of misaligned weekends.

Coordinating with the Gulf is not, of course, impossible—but it does require careful planning. Project plans should take into account the limited windows in which all offices are working, and key interaction points must be planned accordingly. Shipments and deliveries that require offices to be open need to be scheduled carefully. On the other hand, the weekend and time differences can sometimes be put to a firm's advantage for example, a Gulf office could request information or feedback from a US office on Wednesday afternoon in Riyadh (Wednesday morning US time), give the US office three full days to manage the request, and have the information e-mailed back on Friday afternoon US time. The e-mail would arrive early Saturday morning Riyadh time, just hours before the start of the Saudi workweek. In this scenario, since the US office prepares feedback during the Saudi weekend, the process works with no downtime.

MANAGING COMPLIANCE: GOVERNMENT RELATIONS IS ITS OWN DEPARTMENT

All Gulf countries are WTO members and as such are in the process of economic liberalization, but these economies remain highly regulated, and the volume of bureaucracy is substantial. Much of the paperwork relates to employment and human resources issues, as expatriates make up a bulk of the private-sector workforce. Visas for employees and their families, national health insurance forms, and various other documents take a large amount of time to process and require both patience and expertise. Human resources professionals who understand these procedures are in great demand, and those who come from outside face a challenging learning curve.

A number of government-approval forms are also required in order to conduct general business activity. Public relations events may require authorization. Construction projects will, of course, require a set of approvals and permits. Visitors coming for a business meeting may require approval from the local chamber of commerce. The procedures for obtaining these approvals can be more complex than they seem, and they can be at least partially subject to the discretion of the government agent on duty at the time when you submit your paperwork. Managing the bureaucracy is a craft—some would say an art—of its own, and GCC organizations, including multinational firms operating there, have created the position of Public Relations Officer (PRO) to handle these issues full-time.

The PRO is always a local citizen and needs to be adept at navigating the system.

The PRO Function: Navigating Bureaucracy

The role of a Public Relations Officer (PRO) in a GCC office is both unique and indispensable. An effective PRO can be the key to securing government approvals and navigating bureaucratic complexities that could otherwise impede the smooth functioning of business. Finding top-notch PROs can be a challenge, and retaining them can be even harder. Considering the volume of government paperwork that even small offices must manage, the PRO's function cannot be ignored or underestimated.

PROs are always local nationals. Their core role is to shuttle documents between the company and various government agencies in order to secure approvals like visas, building permits, forms allowing the display of public signs and events, and so on. The most basic function of a PRO is to be a kind of courier; the best ones have a skill set that makes them part messenger, part negotiator, and part detective. The PRO must be a negotiator when a request needs to be prioritized or exceptional permission is being sought. He or she must be a detective when it is necessary to figure out what approvals are required from what agencies at what level (e.g., federal, state, or municipal) and who the relevant decision makers are.

Larger firms may have multiple PROs, led by a senior member of the team who understands the local intricacies well. Often junior-level PROs will also act as drivers for executives or as protocol officers who receive guests. The PRO's workday is less intense than that of other administrative employees and involves a lot of waiting time. Companies may have PROs work in two shifts—early morning and afternoon—with a long break in the middle of the day. Alternatively, the PRO may have a shorter workday than other employees, as government offices tend to close in the early afternoon.

As an expatriate working with or overseeing the PRO, it is important to remember that although the PRO may not be high on the organization chart, PROs need to be managed differently from other administrative staff. The company needs them more, and good PROs know that. One cannot expect them to always abide by standard guidelines for administrative staff such as 15-minute coffee breaks. At the same time, PROs can be fantastic sources of information about the business community, and of other relevant information, gotten from the local rumor mill. The PRO, for example, is likely to know more about the inner workings of public-sector decision-making processes than expatriates who are far more senior. On internal matters, their job security makes them freer to speak up than most others. If you want an honest opinion about the state of the company, ask the PRO. He will rarely pull punches, as he has relatively little to lose.

The World Bank–IFC, through its "Doing Business" indicators, has tracked the number of procedures required to start businesses in countries around the world. Findings from several GCC markets, published in 2006, are summarized in Table 9.3.[34]

T A B L E   9 . 3

Procedures for Setting up Shop in the GCC States

Country	Procedures (number)	Duration (days)	Cost in US$
Saudi Arabia	13	39	$6,900
Kuwait	13	35	$400
UAE	12	63	$8,700
Oman	9	34	$400

Saudi Arabia, consistent with its reputation for onerous bureaucracy, was at the top of the list with the most procedures. The UAE, despite its general, open-for-business policies, required the longest amount of time to establish a company and had the highest associated fees. In none of the GCC countries surveyed was the time required to start a business less than one month. Such obstacles can dampen the spirit of entrepreneurship and market entry. By contrast, the time it takes to open a business in the United States is only 5 days; in the UK it is 18.

It is important to note, however, that the above figures are based on regular, onshore company registrations as opposed to those in free zones. Free zones offer, as discussed earlier, far more streamlined processes for such activity. For example, a former colleague of mine established a company in the Ras al-Khaimah Free Trade Zone in a matter of days and praised the customer service provided by staff. Insiders hope that the efficient, responsive, and business-friendly approach of free zones will soon permeate the public sector more broadly.

USING INFRASTRUCTURE EXCELLENCE TO NURTURE WORLD-CLASS COMPANIES

One outcome of investing heavily in high-quality infrastructure—and in the management capabilities required to operate such infrastructure—is the emergence of Gulf-based companies in related sectors that can compete at a global level. Dubai Ports World, as noted earlier, has emerged at the forefront of global port management operations as a result of its experience in Jebel Ali, large amounts of invested capital, and expansionist visions. Another illustration of the phenomenon is Emirates Airlines, the Dubai-based carrier that has become a major international airline through its strategic location, differentiated service, and substantial cost savings.

Emirates Airlines: Spreading Dubai's Wings

When founded in 1985, Dubai's Emirates Airlines was not able to secure the role of the UAE's national carrier. Since then, it has won over 250 awards for international excellence and has built a network spanning over 70 cities in more than 50 countries.[35] The airline flies to Asia, Europe, the Middle East, Africa, Australia, and now directly to the United States. If it begins serving São Paulo, Brazil, in late 2007 as expected, it will have the first-ever nonstop service between the Middle East and South America. Since its inception, the airline has doubled in size every three to four years.[36] In 2003, it placed the then-biggest-ever order for aircraft (71 new planes) at the Paris Air Show.[37] The airline is a remarkable success story for the GCC and is one of the few Gulf-based companies that are globally competitive and have a truly worldwide presence.

Several factors have been at work to enable the airline's success. One is the location of Dubai—almost exactly equidistant between London and Hong Kong—as a natural layover spot for long-haul flights. The airline relies heavily on the classic hub-and-spoke model of airline routing; in fact, more than half of Emirates' Dubai passengers are in transit to other destinations.[38] If the hub were less conveniently located, making the system work would have been more challenging. Another key factor has been the airline's access to capital—it is owned by the government of Dubai. The government's investment in Dubai International Airport and in the emirate overall has given Emirates Airlines the room it needed to grow so dramatically. In other markets, such cooperation between the airport authorities and leading airlines would be difficult to achieve.

Emirates Airlines also enjoys a significant cost advantage over competitors. Fuel is secured at low prices, staff costs are modest, and labor unions are nonexistent. On top of all that, there are no corporate income taxes to pay. In a 2005 analysis, the *Economist* found that the airline's costs were "closer to Ryanair, Europe's leading no-frills carrier, than to British Airways, Air France–KLM, or Lufthansa."[39] Part of the savings is passed on to customers, and part of it contributes to the firm's profits. Emirates is poised for sustained growth despite the increased competition in the region, and especially from Abu Dhabi's Etihad Airways. Its cash position is formidable: its CEO has said it could fly for six months without charging a single passenger and still be solvent.[40]

In the years ahead, expect to see more GCC-based firms in infrastructure-linked sectors emerging as global competitors. In addition to Dubai Ports World and Emirates Airlines, two more Dubai-based firms fit the mold: the real estate firm Emaar and the hospitality firm Jumeirah International. Emaar has rapidly expanded to several Middle East markets, including Egypt, Morocco, and Jordan. Emaar Saudi Arabia is the engine behind King Abdullah Economic City, and Emaar has announced plans for a project in Pakistan as well. Emaar also acquired John Laing Homes, a US homebuilder, in a 2006 deal valued at just above $1 billion.[41] Jumeirah International, whose flagship property is the sail-shaped Burj al-Arab hotel in Dubai, has multiple properties in London and owns the Essex House hotel off New York's Central Park.

These firms, and others, are likely to become more prominent worldwide as they apply their ambition, expertise—honed in the Gulf's infrastructure-friendly environment—and capital to creating an increasingly global presence. Just as established multinationals are keen to access GCC markets, GCC firms are eager to make their marks as truly world-class institutions.

KEY LESSONS

- The GCC's *infrastructure excellence facilitates business* in the Gulf states significantly and has been funded through generous government spending over several decades.
- World-class infrastructure in the region makes for the *easy flow of people, the easy flow of goods, support for industry and manufacturing, and strong business support services.*
- *Shipping, port management, and logistics have become core competencies* of the region, as demonstrated by Dubai Ports World's rise to global leadership.
- *Industrial parks and free zones* with 100 percent foreign ownership rights are attracting multinationals and enabling them to serve the broader Middle East via the Gulf.
- The GCC *weekend does not correspond* with the US, European, and Asian weekends and is not even uniform in the Gulf, creating coordination challenges.
- *Bureaucracy in the region can be sizable*, even with deregulation. Managing compliance is a function in itself.
- The GCC's *infrastructure excellence nurtures firms in related sectors*, like Emirates Airlines, with the potential to be world leaders in their industries.

CHAPTER 10

Enabled Organization: Setting Up for Success

INTRODUCTION

A few years ago, a major multinational faced a peculiar challenge with its Middle East business. The business unit and the global head office wanted the company to grow more aggressively, in line with the booming prosperity of the region. This prosperity, of course, was linked to the increased wealth of the Gulf states. The multinational's Middle East organization, however, was not positioned to capitalize on the market opportunity. The regional head office was in Egypt—the region's most populous country and once its economic powerhouse. In the 1950s and 1960s, the period when the multinational entered the region, Cairo was the natural choice for a Middle East regional office. The multinational had kept its headquarters there for decades even though the region's dynamic economies were now being driven by the Gulf.

Being far from the action in the GCC states, the multinational tended to understaff its Gulf offices, underestimate the opportunity there, and underinvest in market intelligence and competitive analysis within the Gulf. Even worse, the few executives based in the GCC countries required frequent approvals from Cairo for much of their activity, and these approvals could take weeks or even months to secure. In the meantime, the market was passing them by. The multinational, despite its strong product line and global expertise, was simply not set up for success in the Gulf. A team of external advisors was needed to prod the organization to restructure and adopt new processes that gave greater focus to the GCC.

So far in this book we've discussed market-entry strategies, marketing approaches, human resources, financial strategies, and nuts-and-bolts operations issues in the GCC. Strength in all of these areas is important for long-term business success. Equally crucial, however, is the need to ensure that the organization charged with capturing the Gulf opportunity is set up for success. Without the right organizational design, the best-laid strategies and marketing campaigns may fail to deliver results, and high-caliber talent will become frustrated. In the long term, the sustained growth and evolution of local business will be jeopardized if the team in the region is not organized appropriately.

To effectively capture the market opportunity, the Gulf organization must be both rooted and empowered. The team in the GCC region needs to have the in-country presence required to understand market realities, many of which are apparent only after spending time there and becoming connected to the local business community. The team must be empowered—within limits, of course—to make critical decisions involving such things as marketing strategies, local hiring, and bids on government tenders. Without control over the basic resources needed for the regional business, Gulf management can be severely hindered in its ability to deliver the strong results that global head offices should expect.

Within the region, Dubai (and the UAE more broadly) has emerged as the preferred location for multinationals' regional offices. This preference is rooted in Dubai's strong infrastructure, dynamic business culture, and accommodating lifestyle for expatriates. Major multinationals like Pepsi and Merck have set up their regional headquarters in Dubai, often having the broader Middle East report into the Dubai office. For consumer product companies like Procter & Gamble, however, a substantial presence in Saudi Arabia is important. Saudi Arabia is, after all, the core market, having well over half the total population of the GCC states.

In preparing their organization for entry into the GCC market, multinationals must ensure that mechanisms are in place to enforce their global standards. These standards include a high level of product and service delivery and maintenance, integrity and best practices in corporate processes such as credit and compliance, and fairness and sensitivity in human resources issues such as labor practices and gender equity. The business environment of the Gulf can, at times, differ from environments elsewhere, but firms should enforce their global principles firmly both for ethical reasons and to safeguard their reputations.

PRESENCE AND EMPOWERMENT

A GCC organization, like regional organizations elsewhere, typically needs both local presence and a meaningful degree of empowerment in order to achieve its business objectives. A natural question, however, for a multinational to ask itself is, Why should the GCC region be treated as a separate "business unit" rather than as part of a broader set (e.g., the Middle East and North Africa)?

There are two compelling reasons why the Gulf should be viewed as a distinct business unit. The first is that the economies of the GCC states are fundamentally different from other markets within the Middle East. As discussed earlier in this book, the Gulf has long been a separate economic cluster, sharing some elements with the countries of the Levant—Iraq, Syria, Lebanon, Jordan, and Israel and the Palestinian Territories—and North Africa, but being different from them in very meaningful ways. The oil booms of the 1970s and 2000s have made the differences starker, as the GCC is now far more prosperous than the other clusters—its GDP per capita is about four times that of North Africa and more than five times that of the Levant. The Gulf states have been fairly stable monarchies, or "sheikhdoms," with a capitalist orientation while the other regions have seen less stability and have exhibited a variety of political philosophies including, at times, those having socialist tendencies. Even the Arabic dialect of the Gulf can easily be distinguished from colloquial Levantine or North African speech. These and other economic and social differences have long made the Gulf a very different place, with unique commercial characteristics and dynamics.

The second reason to view the Gulf as a distinct business unit is the increasing connectivity among Gulf markets. The creation of the Gulf Cooperation Council (GCC) in the early 1980s was a major step toward creating a common market. People and goods flow far more freely within the GCC states than between the GCC states and the rest of the Middle East.[1] While substantial steps still need to be taken before the Gulf will truly be a "common market," the six GCC member countries already act as a single unit in many respects. The political and cultural commonalities, including those found in social structures and norms, are many. While each state has its unique characteristics, *khaleeji* or Gulf culture has a full set of recognizable elements. As the Gulf states, with the exception of Saudi Arabia, have populations of below 6 million people each, it makes sense for most multinationals to manage the states collectively rather than as separate units. Each country will often require local distributors and salespeople, but many of the central support functions (like finance and human resources) and senior management oversight can be best performed when the GCC states are treated as one culturally homogeneous place. It is also usually advisable to include Yemen—if the firm has business prospects there—in the Gulf cluster due to its location on the Arabian Peninsula and its cultural similarities. Despite its modest GDP per capita and lack of oil wealth, Yemen has a rich heritage of leadership in the Gulf and aspires to GCC membership one day. Some leading multinationals use the term "Arabian Peninsula" or "Arabian Peninsula States" to describe the Gulf cluster and include Yemen in the unit.

Figure 10.1 illustrates the three core elements that are needed by a multinational's Gulf organization in order to maximize business performance. First, presence, beyond merely sales and distribution, is essential. Second, considering the dynamism and uniqueness of the Gulf market, a meaningful degree of decision-making rights is also needed to ensure nimbleness and to motivate staff. And third, resources—both material and human—are necessary ingredients for the success of any venture.

Presence in Market

A presence in the market often means more than just a distributor or a small sales team. Many firms have distribution agreements

Figure 10.1 Core elements of an enabled Gulf organization

with local GCC companies—which they may or may not monitor closely—and therefore consider their firm "present" in the Gulf. While having such arrangements reflects more commitment than does just ignoring the markets entirely, there can be real drawbacks to having only distribution and sales people in the Gulf. One drawback is that such structures often provide the multinational only minimal insight into market trends, region-specific needs, and strategic opportunities. Distribution agreements often push all in-market responsibilities onto the local distributor, with the multinational having little or no hands-on experience with or awareness of local operations. Leading retailers like IKEA and Gap, however, insist on strict guidelines for the store environment and for other quality-related factors. These distribution agreements give the global firm more presence and control than other, more passive contracts.

Even firms with direct-sales people in the Gulf may not receive a full picture of the market despite their presence. One reason for this is time: salespeople are often so engaged in making pitches, finding leads, and serving clients that they have little time for market analysis and strategic planning. Another reason relates to capabilities and access: salespeople may not have access to the information, tools, and analytical approach required for in-depth market analysis. They may likewise lack access to the strategic decision makers outside the sales organization. A third, more subtle reason relates to incentives. The sales force, in many organizations, has an incentive to understate the scale of opportunity in their region in order to set more manageable sales targets and to enable "overperformance." Delivering results above the target yields significant personal rewards, while meeting the plan's objectives exactly is considered strong performance. Unless strategy, marketing, and senior management's analysis of the market as a whole are involved, sales targets can be kept artificially low and will not reflect the business's true potential in the region. If, however, the sales organization has in-house business analysts and tools assessing the market objectively, tighter performance management is possible.

Savvy multinationals with serious intentions in the Gulf states put a team on the ground that extends beyond sales. A marketing and public relations function is important in crafting propositions that are specific to the Gulf. Strategy and business development units on the ground can assess market opportunities more directly and take a more aggressive posture toward growth in the region. Having senior management present is crucial for efficient, in-market decision making and for managing resource allocation from an informed perspective. Business support functions such as finance and human resources become relevant as the scale of business managed from the GCC region warrants the incremental costs.

Professional services firms such as consulting and law firms and investment banks have come to appreciate much more in recent years the importance of an in-market presence. Top-tier firms like McKinsey & Co., BCG, Freshfields, and Goldman Sachs long served Gulf-based clients through "fly-in" teams based in London or elsewhere. The teams would spend their weeks with the client and their weekends at home, outside the GCC countries. This approach allowed firms to serve Gulf clients opportunistically, without needing to invest in building a local office or specialized practice. It also resonated with many clients who, at the time, strongly preferred "outside" experts from developed markets to come in and provide world-class advice.

Since the boom of the 2000s (and even earlier in some cases), professional services firms have begun building local offices and regional teams to serve Gulf clients from closer to home. This change is partly due to the sheer volume of GCC-based work and the logical implication that having an in-market presence would be easier for clients and for staff. Competitive pressures among firms have also contributed to the phenomenon of local offices. Eager to differentiate themselves based on both local and global credentials, firms are playing up their regional presence and using proximity to the client as a key selling point. Client preferences have also evolved, such that in-market experience—in addition to worldwide expertise—is increasingly a factor in choosing an advisor. It's no surprise, then, that investment banks and consulting firms are snatching up office space in free zones around the Gulf. For a professional services firm to be fully competitive there, a regional presence has become crucial.

Appropriate Decision-Making Rights

Once present, the GCC team needs to be empowered to make the core decisions required to run its business. The "appropriate" level of decision-making rights will, of course, vary from company to company. Often, however, GCC organizations need some control over local pricing, marketing and PR, and staffing. These decisions need to be made within guidelines set by global headquarters (e.g., an absolute minimum gross margin on products or minimum educational requirements for jobs of a certain level) but are often best made in-market. Typically the staff on the ground is best suited to understand how to position products appropriately, how to deal with the local media, and whom to hire for the local office. While none of these actions should contradict global practices and messages, local ownership of these day-to-day decisions is often crucial.

A major multinational that maintained its Middle East headquarters in Egypt, mentioned earlier in this chapter, suffered in the GCC markets because it could not make pricing decisions fast enough. Approval for bids on major institutional business was needed from Cairo and sometimes from the global head office. The delays involved in securing approvals led not only to lost business, but also to a lowering of morale. The Gulf team felt—probably rightly—that it did not have the authority it needed to run its business optimally.

Decisions concerning local staffing, though they might seem relatively minor, can be crucial to the success of an in-market office, and it is important for the local office to have significant control over such decisions. While the global head office typically will make the hiring decisions concerning the company's most senior staff, it is important to give the local office authority over middle- and junior-level staffing. In addition to the risk that the "flown-in" resource might not have the right market-specific skills, there is the risk that he or she will seek a position in the Gulf with a short-term, take-the-money-and-run attitude. Staff members without genuine concern and interest in the market are a recipe for disaster. Further, staff members who know the local market are best positioned to assess and hire GCC citizens, whose presence on the team is essential from both a strategic and a regulatory perspective.

Toyota's relationship with its local distributors is an example of highly localized decision-making rights.[2] Each distributor runs its local business, in terms of operational matters, with almost complete autonomy. The head office in Japan sets quality standards and other guidelines, such as use of the global brand. The distributor, in turn, is responsible for local promotions, marketing, and hiring. While the global head office reviews distributors' investment plans, decisions about capital allocation lie fully with the distributor. As long as the distributor operates within global guidelines, it is free to manage the business without interference. This level of empowerment has led to much creativity at the local level, including the highly successful and well-known "Tough as Ali" advertising campaign promoting the Toyota Cressida featuring the boxer Muhammad Ali. Saudi distributor Abdul Latif Jamil conceived of and executed the campaign in the 1960s and 1970s and, through it and other marketing and service campaigns, made Toyota extremely popular in Saudi Arabia.

Adequate Resources

Presence and decision-making rights can go only so far, of course, if the GCC organization is underresourced. Having too little material (e.g., financial, IT, marketing, etc.) support can prevent a Gulf business—even in a hot market—from getting off the ground. As discussed in Chapter 6, products—though not all—require some degree of adaptation in order to achieve widespread success. The adaptation can be in the form of packaging, marketing messages, product mix, or even product development specifically for the Gulf market. In the early stages of a firm's market presence, it is only natural to prefer a low-investment, minimal-risk approach. Business leaders must be sure, however, that a lack of adaptation is not costing the firm more in terms of lost sales than it would cost to make slight modifications for the region.

As a business grows, a more subtle form of underinvestment can appear. Companies that view the Gulf as an afterthought or a marginal market may treat the region as a passive source of income. They may choose to have almost all profits from the region come straight back to the global balance sheet, with few or no "retained earnings" for the local business. The danger of this approach is that it can deprive the Gulf business of any chance it might have had of flourishing by building out its product proposition, infrastructure, and staff. Especially when there are few or no staff members whose sole responsibility is for the GCC, adopting a passive approach is a real risk—there's nobody to advocate for reinvesting more of the profits in order to make the business grow.

A lack of human resources fully allocated to the region, besides having the obvious effect of limiting a firm's regional productivity, can distort the incentives of staff partly dedicated to Gulf activities. Distorted incentives have, at times, become a real issue in professional services firms such as investment banks and consulting firms. A London-based banker "stuck" on a deal with a Gulf-based client may likely view the deal as a chore and a lifestyle drain that keeps him or her away from friends and family. Building a long-term relationship with the client through outstanding service might, ironically, make his or her life more difficult, requiring the inconvenient travel to continue. Professional standards and performance reviews will, of course, keep such bankers from slacking off. The incentive to build a long-term relationship can, nonetheless, be far less for a fly-in team based elsewhere than it is for a local team responsible for building business exclusively in the region. Having worked with both fly-in and local teams, I have seen the differences firsthand.

Investment in a Gulf business, like investment in any business, cannot be made without a strong case and a visible path toward self-funding. The GCC should not have to rely on "grants" from the head office for long. Typically, the best way to build a regional business is with carefully considered up-front investment, followed by a short period of ongoing support until the business generates enough profit to cover its costs. In the boom environment of the 2000s, most multinationals with strong product propositions and brands can reach profitability very quickly. Some professional services firms have found that their GCC offices "sell out" and are stretched thin from very early on, making these offices more profitable on a per-person basis than their counterparts elsewhere.

HEADQUARTERS DUBAI

Since the late 1990s, Dubai—and, to a degree, the UAE overall—has emerged as the strongly preferred location for multinational firms' head offices in the Gulf. It has become increasingly common for the Dubai office to oversee businesses well beyond the Gulf—very often spanning all of the Middle East and North Africa and sometimes even further. The electronics firm Canon, for example, has a wide set of Middle Eastern markets reporting through Dubai, as well as a set of French-speaking African countries. In a surprising 2007 move, the prominent and controversial energy services company Halliburton announced it was moving its CEO to Dubai in order to focus on growth in the Eastern Hemisphere. All of Halliburton's global business, therefore, is envisioned to report to Dubai.

The rationale for choosing Dubai as a regional headquarters office is straightforward. One reason is the emirate's superb infrastructure: both its "hard" infrastructure like shipping links, airports, and power; and its "soft" infrastructure like the free zones allowing 100 percent foreign ownership, corporate parks, and available talent.[3] The second is Dubai's liberal-lifestyle policies that allow expatriates to maintain the lifestyle—including norms of dressing, eating and drinking, nightlife, shopping, and more—of Western countries. Dubai's permissive policy on lifestyles surprises many visitors and makes it a "fun" destination for senior management from the global head office or from other regions.

Both elements of Dubai's appeal—infrastructure and lifestyle—have stood in stark contrast with the facilities and norms of other

Gulf states. Dubai's late ruler Sheikh Rashid invested in ports and shipping infrastructure long ago and set forth the vision for the massive Jebel Ali Free Zone from which Dubai's infrastructure excellence stems. His successors have extended the infrastructure vision with free zones dedicated to knowledge economy sectors such as media, the Internet, financial services, and health care. Finding flights in and out of Dubai for business meetings has become, thanks to Emirates Airlines and the airport's "open skies" policy, extremely easy. Other emirates, and other GCC states, have adopted similar strategies, but Dubai enjoys a strong first-mover advantage. Dubai's neighbors, even those that permit alcohol and do not require conservative dress, have not gone nearly to the lengths Dubai has in terms of nightlife and "party" culture.

Table 10.1 lists a handful of prominent global companies that have chosen to place a regional head office in Dubai. The companies span heavy industry, such as GE and GM; consumer goods firms like Pepsi; and services firms like McKinsey & Co.

TABLE 10.1

Leading Companies with Regional Head Offices in Dubai[4]

Sector	Company	Non-GCC Markets Reporting through Dubai
Industry	Halliburton	All—Dubai is one of two global headquarters
	GE	Egypt, Kenya, South Africa, Jordan, Lebanon
	GM	Jordan, Lebanon, Syria, Yemen
	Canon	Egypt, Iraq, Jordan, Lebanon, Yemen, Libya, French-speaking Africa—22 countries
Consumer Goods	Pepsi	Levant, North Africa, sub-Saharan Africa
	Unilever	Yemen (Saudi Arabia excluded)
	Beiersdorf	16 countries
	Carrefour	Egypt
Services	McKinsey & Co.	None
	IBM	Jordan, Lebanon, Palestinian Territories, Yemen
	Clifford Chance	None
	Reuters	23 countries

As more companies have placed regional head offices in Dubai, the country's commercial vibrancy and importance has increased. Each firm that sets up in Dubai makes being there all the more valuable for any other firm that wishes to do business with them. A similar phenomenon occurs within expatriate communities: as the expatriate base grows, more expatriates become comfortable migrating as well. These positive "network effects" have helped Dubai build and maintain its lead as a hub despite the increasingly competitive efforts of other GCC states to attract multinational firms.

Despite its strong appeal to many multinationals—and, ironically, somewhat because of its mass appeal—Dubai does have meaningful drawbacks as a location for a regional head office. One drawback is cost—the cost of doing business in Dubai is increasing rapidly as more firms compete for space (office, residential, and hotel), staff, and other business inputs. Firms can capture significant cost savings in the nearby emirates of Sharjah and Ras al-Khaimah, and even in the UAE capital Abu Dhabi. A second drawback is congestion and traffic: rush-hour traffic in Dubai can be unbearable and many workers commute for an hour or more each way. Wider roads and public transportation are on the way, but the construction phase itself makes getting around the city quite difficult. Some professionals strongly prefer Abu Dhabi as more "livable," manageable, and traditional. Even expatriates from socially permissive countries are at times put off by the "party" culture in certain areas and the flashy tourist attractions that some liken to Las Vegas.

An additional risk of being based in Dubai, especially if the firm has no other offices in the GCC region, is that of losing touch with typical Gulf consumers. Remember, Dubai's population is overwhelmingly expatriate, and the city's social norms differ significantly from those of the rest of the Gulf states. Firms whose customer base is largely outside of Dubai, and who benefit from being close to typical or everyday consumers, need a strong presence away from Dubai to remain grounded in the market.

SAUDI PRESENCE: ESSENTIAL FOR CONSUMER GOODS

Saudi Arabia is, without a doubt, the core consumer market of the GCC. The Saudi population is two-thirds of the Gulf total and yet constitutes a very "local" market. Expatriates make up only about 20 percent of the total population, and many expatriates are from other Arab and Muslim countries with social norms somewhat similar to (though usually less conservative than) those of Saudi Arabia. Figure 10.2 illustrates the dominance of Saudi Arabia in the GCC's consumer base:

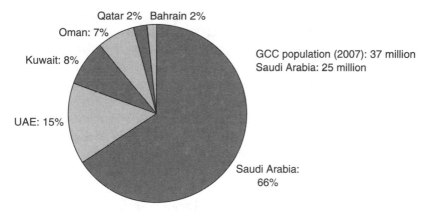

Figure 10.2 Saudi Arabia is the GCC's core consumer market (Source: IMF, 2007 estimates)

Considering these figures, it is no surprise that consumer goods companies naturally seek a significant presence in Saudi Arabia. In addition to its sheer size, however, there are other reasons why Saudi Arabia warrants an in-market presence. Like the rest of the Gulf, Saudi Arabia's population is young—70 percent are below the age of 30—and highly concentrated in urban areas. Three-quarters of the people live in urban areas, principally Jeddah, Riyadh, and Dammam.[5] The Saudi lifestyle is modern: 92 percent of households own cars and televisions, and washing machines and other appliances are pervasive.[6] Relative to other Gulf populations, however, the Saudi market has a huge number of middle-class and lower-middle-class consumers: the Saudi GDP per capita (in purchasing power terms) is $16,500—60 percent that of the UAE and half that of Qatar.[7] Like all markets with large middle classes, the Kingdom is ripe for the mass-marketing of everyday goods of reasonable quality at modest prices. Luxury goods are, of course, important for higher-income segments, but Saudi Arabia is by no means a market only of millionaires.

Conservative social regulations also differentiate Saudi Arabia from some of its neighbors. Women are still not allowed to drive and, therefore, often shop with their families or send someone else to the store to make purchases on their behalf. In certain product categories, this may limit the potential for "impulse" purchases. Print and billboard advertising must conform to conservative social norms, as ads are screened by the Ministry of Information and Culture.[8] Satellite television has given Saudi households access to a much broader range of programming and ads, but local media is far more constrained. The Internet is also carefully censored. Marketers, intent on ensuring that materials produced for the Gulf can reach the widest possible audience, will often design print ads in a manner that conforms to Saudi norms and regulations to avoid needing to create multiple versions.

Recognizing the importance of the Saudi market, multinational consumer goods companies have allocated significant resources to bolster their in-market presence. Procter & Gamble's Arabian Peninsula head office is in Saudi Arabia, giving the firm's senior management direct access to the region's core consumer base.[9] Unilever, another massive consumer goods company, treats Saudi Arabia as a market separate from the other GCC markets. The other five GCC states and Yemen report through a Dubai head office, while Saudi Arabia has its own reporting line.[10] For both firms, Saudi Arabia represented their very first foray into the Middle East, as early as the 1930s. Placing senior executive, marketing, and business support teams in Saudi Arabia helps ensure that the country receives adequate focus. Even firms that choose to maintain their head office in Dubai will often have large market-facing teams in the Kingdom to keep a finger on the market's pulse.

A presence is Saudi Arabia can be a real challenge, especially for expatriate staff and visitors. Travel in and out of the country is difficult, with a lengthy visa application process requiring a letter of invitation certified by a local chamber of commerce. The infrastructure is modern, but built less recently than those of the UAE, Qatar, or Kuwait. Government bureaucracy is tedious, with less customer orientation than is found in the UAE and other states. Female visitors, like all women, cannot drive and must dress conservatively in public. Postings in Saudi Arabia are generally considered by expatriates to be far less attractive from a lifestyle perspective than postings in the UAE, making it all the more difficult to attract global talent to a regional head office if it is in Riyadh or Jeddah. Visits by overseas management to a Saudi office require far more planning, including visa formalities that are not required in the UAE. For these reasons and others, a large number of consumer goods leaders like Pepsi maintain regional head offices outside Saudi Arabia despite Saudi Arabia's far greater sales volume.

Saudi authorities are, of course, eager to make their business environment friendlier and easier to deal with for multinationals. King Abdullah Economic City, with its first-rate infrastructure, is one important initiative aimed at enhancing the business environment for all. Other Economic Cities are planned around the Kingdom. Saudi Arabia's tremendous scale advantage and status as the region's core market make it a natural place for firms to increase their presence, as soon as the business environment becomes more competitive with that of other states in the region.

MAINTAINING GLOBAL STANDARDS

In designing and enabling their Gulf organizations, global firms should ensure that their global standards—for quality, business processes, and people management—are stringently maintained. Fortunately, Gulf business norms in many of these areas exceed or meet global standards. Service quality, for example, tends to be very high. This is especially true in the hospitality sector, where hotels are managed at world-class standards with eager staff recruited through highly competitive processes.

Corruption in the Gulf exists to a far smaller degree than in other emerging markets. Bribery is rare. All GCC countries, in fact, score better than both China and India in transparency ratings conducted by global organizations.[11] A strength of the GCC's business environment is its rule of law and the enforcement of contracts. Central banks have introduced regulations in line with global best practices to prevent money laundering and adhere to strict know-your-client requirements. Regulators are sensitive to the risk of being seen as "loose" or soft on terrorist financing and have proactively tightened their controls. Corporate governance standards are rapidly evolving as public listings become more common and family businesses bring on outsiders as professional management.

One advantage that multinationals often have relative to local firms is robust business processes tried and tested in other markets. In financial services, for example, international banks often have rigorous credit approval processes that help maintain greater discipline in corporate and consumer lending. These sorts of controls proved very helpful in keeping international banks from excessive margin lending during the stock market boom of the early 2000s and the bust of 2006. Proven business processes of multinationals have also exerted a positive influence in such other sectors of the GCC economies as manufacturing, inventory control, and the retail environment. Savvy multinationals maintain strict guidelines in these areas in order to manage risk and optimize performance. After setting the guidelines, they then empower local management to grow the business within the given parameters.

Where firms may feel especially challenged in maintaining their global standards is in the sensitive area of people management. A common practice in many local firms, for example, is to pay different wages to individuals employed in the same function depending on their nationality. American and European expatriates, for instance, can be paid more for doing the same job than expatriates from the Arab world, Asia, or Africa. Such discrimination is unacceptable according to the policies and core values of most leading firms. Although the local market may tolerate such practices, multinationals should uphold their global principles and provide equal pay for equal work. Doing so not only protects their international reputation but also sends a strong signal to the talent market about ethical employment practices.

Gender issues have historically been similarly challenging, but the situation is improving. Most multinationals embrace principles by which all staff members, irrespective of gender, have equal opportunity for advancement and promotion. The same should apply in the local companies operating within the GCC states.

Thankfully, public-sector and business leaders across the region are embracing this principle and encouraging women to rise in the ranks. As discussed earlier in the book, the UAE's minister of economy is a woman, and she is a role model for many women in the region. More women are entering local universities than men, and female graduates are a critical component of the local workforce. Multinationals should capitalize on these trends and take all steps needed to ensure that the local organization and line managers provide female staff equal access to leadership roles and promotions.

Labor practices and the rights of low-income workers in the Gulf is a matter of concern to many principle-driven organizations worldwide. Human Rights Watch, for example, published a report in 2006 entitled "Building Towers, Cheating Workers,"[12] which detailed unjust—and illegal—practices in the UAE construction industry such as not paying workers for months on end. Visitors to Dubai need only take a taxi ride during the day to see workers toiling in sweltering heat in order to enable the massive real estate boom and development spree. There are labor laws on the books to protect workers' rights, yet adherence and enforcement of these laws have not been consistent. Labor conditions in construction and other sectors are—and should be—a serious ethical concern for firms and investors. While most multinationals are not directly engaged in the sectors most known for labor abuses, they should nonetheless make known their concerns about workers' rights to local contractors and service providers whom they engage. Would any firm want its GCC office to be built through exploitative labor practices? Even worse, would they want that known worldwide? Taking an ethical stance early and proactively can both reflect the firm's values and engender awareness and change within the broader market.

Business in the Gulf offers an attractive and growing commercial opportunity. In pursuing this opportunity, global firms must retain the robust quality, process, and people management principles that have made them successful worldwide. Compromising a global reputation for a regional business is simply not an option, and standards must always be upheld. Besides being the right thing to do, it makes business sense.

KEY LESSONS

- To be effective, the GCC organization typically needs *presence in the market, appropriate decision-making rights, and adequate resources.*
- Dubai, and the UAE more broadly, have emerged as the *strongly preferred location for multinationals' head offices* in the region.
- The attributes that make Dubai an appealing place for many head offices also have *some negative side effects* (inflation, crowding, etc.) that need to be considered.
- Consumer product companies need a *strong presence in Saudi Arabia* to stay close to the core market.
- Global firms must ensure they *maintain their global quality, business processes, and people management practices in the Gulf* as they do everywhere.

PART 3

Conclusion: The GCC at Global Headquarters

CHAPTER 11

Bringing It Home: Fostering GCC Awareness in the Head Office

INTRODUCTION

In a 2007 survey, 50 students on an Ivy League campus were asked to identify what a set of international abbreviations stand for. The university is home to one of America's top five business schools, and the bulk of the randomly selected participants were students of management. Nearly everyone, as expected, could correctly say that the "EU" stands for the European Union. About 90 percent recognized the "WTO" as the World Trade Organization. Far fewer could identify what "OPEC" and "ASEAN" precisely stand for, although their links to oil and to Asia were understood somewhat better. When asked about the "GCC," awareness was extremely low. Less than 10 percent of students at this Ivy League university could link "GCC" to the Gulf Cooperation Council and to the six up-and-coming economies of which it consists.[1]

Despite the economic importance and commercial potential of the GCC, awareness of the region remains low. Had a similar survey been conducted among senior managers at leading global firms, awareness would likely have been better, but not stellar. To be fair, the very term "GCC" did not exist until the early 1980s, and the commercial relevance of the region is relatively recent. Many senior managers have had little interaction with the region in their careers. Business leaders being trained today, however, need a far more solid grounding in the markets of the Gulf than their predecessors had. Today's young business minds need exposure to the GCC in order to develop a truly comprehensive view on global business.

In this book's earlier chapters, we discussed the background of the Gulf markets and what makes them different from other parts of the Middle East. We discussed the substantial opportunity the GCC represents for multinational businesses, as well as the significant risks and drawbacks that must be considered when evaluating these markets. In Part 2, we turned our attention to how individual firms should approach the Gulf. We reviewed market-entry strategies, marketing, human resources, finance, operations, and organization. By now, you know that the GCC is a promising growth market, and you have some ideas about how to approach it. Hopefully, you have more clarity about how your firm might expand there, and you're eager to make something happen.

Translating enthusiasm to action, however, requires more than just a strategy. It requires support from the global organization and, typically, a fair degree of consensus from colleagues at the head office. Most likely, you can't make the plan come alive by yourself, and you don't want to be the sole voice calling for change. That's precisely why you need this chapter.

In this, our final chapter, we explore the challenge of building awareness of the GCC at the global head office. We discuss a range of strategies, including one-time events like senior management visits, regular events like a dedicated business planning cycle, and structural changes in how the GCC businesses report to the head office. Often the region is so deeply buried within a broader cluster that it receives little or no senior management attention. In some cases, a more direct reporting line is appropriate. Broad-based awareness of the GCC, attainable through the measures we will discuss, is a final essential element in integrating the Gulf more deeply into a firm's global strategy.

LOW AWARENESS IS THE NORM

When we conducted our survey of Ivy League students, we expected GCC awareness to be low. What we didn't expect, however, was that awareness would be in the single digits. The finding adds all the more urgency to broadening the collective understanding of the Gulf region. Consider the state of affairs in your own company or organization. How many professionals—even those without direct responsibility for European business—would know what the EU stands for? How many would identify the GCC? How many of those who would correctly identify it are not directly involved with Middle East business?

The good news is that awareness is on the rise. Prominent investments by Gulf-based investors, and especially Dubai Ports World's acquisition of P&O, have turned executives' attention to the region. Dubai's reputation for commerce and tourism grows stronger each year. Qatar, the "upstart" of the Gulf, is making head-lines as well. Saudi Arabia, long known more for political and secu-rity matters than for commerce, is making its way more frequently into the business section of the newspaper. However, scattered news reports need to be supplemented with more comprehensive materials that connect the dots and form a strategic profile of the Gulf region.

Although most senior executives today have little firsthand experience managing business in the Gulf, there are notable excep-tions. Coca-Cola's Chief Customer and Commercial Officer,[2] a British national, was once regional sales manager for the Gulf and later general manager for the GCC.[3] HSBC's Chief Operating Officer was previously chief executive of HSBC Bank of the Middle East, before which he led HSBC's joint-venture bank in Saudi Arabia.[4] McDonald's regional head for Asia-Pacific, the Middle East, and Africa was formerly managing director of the firm's Middle East Development Company, where he oversaw 300 restau-rants in 11 Middle Eastern countries.[5] These executives bring Gulf awareness to the senior management teams of their organizations and help the firm, at the global level, make more informed decisions about the region.

In the energy industry, as one would expect, senior managers tend to have a more intimate understanding of the GCC. The CEO of the French oil major Total, for example, spent much of his career in the Middle East and was formerly Total's Executive Vice President for the Middle East.[6] In 2007, the energy services giant Halliburton announced it was moving its CEO to Dubai in order to focus more on Eastern Hemisphere business. The move was questioned by many observers, including members of the US Senate. While there are substantial—and understandable—doubts regarding the firm's decision, a robust senior management presence in the Gulf makes a great deal of business sense for firms in the energy sector.

Move to Dubai: Interpreting Halliburton's Motives

In March 2007, Halliburton, the energy services firm once led by US Vice President Dick Cheney and historically a key contractor for the US government, announced that its CEO, David Lesar, would "move to Dubai to lead the company's efforts in growing Halliburton's business in the Eastern Hemisphere."[7] As the Eastern Hemisphere had come to represent about 40 percent of Halliburton's global oil-field services revenue, the firm believed shifting the head office to Dubai was both a reflection of its evolving business and a strategic move to capitalize more effectively on the regional opportunity.

Some members of Congress, however, saw the matter differently. Senator Byron Dorgan openly questioned whether the move was for the purpose of tax evasion, circumvention of US law, or "to run away from bad publicity on their contracts."[8] The firm has been under investigation for its contracts in a slew of countries, most notably Iraq. Senator Patrick Leahy criticized the move strongly, calling it "an insult to US soldiers and taxpayers who paid the tab for their no-bid contracts and endured their overcharges for all these years."[9] Revenue from the US government did, after all, account for over a quarter of Halliburton's total earnings in 2006.[10]

While there are likely tax benefits to Halliburton's move, and while we may never fully know the firm's motives, there is a fundamental business case for looking east. As Gulf states and other countries invest heavily in their energy infrastructure, there is much opportunity for service providers looking to expand their business. Companies need not move their head office to the region like Halliburton did in order to increase GCC awareness. Increasing senior management presence there, however, can be a critical step in ensuring adequate strategic focus on the Gulf.

As more executives with Gulf experience take global leadership roles, the strategies of firms in the region will naturally receive more insightful attention. Executives without firsthand experience in the GCC markets or deliberate study of the region are far more likely to hold dangerous misconceptions that can lead to poor strategic decisions and stifle sound initiatives put forth by regional management.

RAISING AWARENESS AT THE HEAD OFFICE

There are three ways in which awareness of the GCC is raised within an organization: one-time events, regular events, and systemic changes. Depending on your firm's circumstances, culture, and overall business norms, one or more of these ways will work best for raising its awareness. There is no one method or prescription, no magic bullet that will work for all organizations. Figure 11.1 illustrates and describes, in order of increasing intensity, the three categories of awareness-building measures.

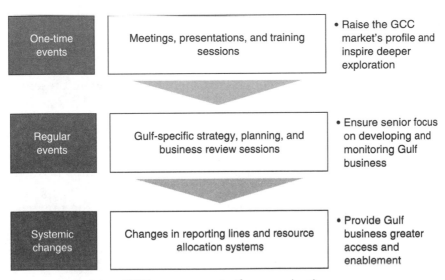

Figure 11.1 Raising GCC awareness in the organization

One-Time Events

One-time events can be a simple, yet powerful, method for bringing attention to the GCC business without disrupting business processes or structures. Events such as a visit to the region by the CEO, an off-site meeting of senior management in one of the Gulf states, presentations to main-office staff or corporate training events on the region can have a meaningful impact on how seriously the organization thinks about its Gulf business. Drawing attention to the region will likely inspire at least some members of the global staff to consider more deeply the opportunities and challenges of business there.

CEO visits to the region have become increasingly common. John Mack of Morgan Stanley, for example, toured the region in 2006 when officially inaugurating the firm's office at the Dubai International Financial Centre. He called the new office "clear evidence of our commitment to developing our presence" in the region, and his personal involvement in the inauguration reinforced the message internally and to the public.[11] GE's Jeff Immelt made a similar trip to Dubai in 2007, launching a regional head office in Dubai Internet City. He asserted that the region "has all the key growth drivers that are favorable for growth of GE businesses."[12] Analysts and staff interpret such statements and visits as a sign of ongoing focus and investment in the Gulf. Even in private firms without analyst scrutiny, senior management visits to the GCC countries send an important message to local and global staff. When the law firm DLA Piper opened its Dubai office, its chairman—former senator George Mitchell—and all three chief executives of the firm were present.[13] After such a high-profile launch, one can be assured that phone calls from the Dubai office will be returned promptly.

Staff presentations and corporate training events are another tool for raising awareness among staff who do not work directly with the region. Presentations by staff based in the Gulf, scheduled to coincide with an already planned visit to the head office, are easy enough to arrange. Considering the excitement in the business press about the region, reasonable attendance can be expected at a lunchtime or early-evening presentation. Outside experts or advisors can be drawn in for additional perspective or to underscore the importance of the region.

Educational programs on China and India for senior managers have become more common in recent years. The Harvard Business School, for example, runs a "Senior Executive Program for China" in conjunction with two Chinese institutions. The University of Pennsylvania's Wharton School has at least four education programs dealing with China or India designed exclusively for executives, along with Web sites dedicated to probing analyses of Chinese and Indian business topics. Programs on the Middle East, though not as well established, are growing. In early 2007, the London Business School announced it would begin offering Executive MBA and Executive Education programs in conjunction with the Dubai International Financial Centre (DIFC).[14] Another British business school plans an Executive MBA program with DIFC as well.[15] At the same time, other programs have been designed especially for executives who have spent their careers working in the Gulf; the Wharton School offers two such programs aimed at training Gulf professionals in law and business.[16] All of these programs boost Western managers' awareness of the Gulf (and Gulf managers' understanding of the West) and give both groups a well-rounded view of the market before they plunge into the details of assessing their own firms' businesses.

One-time events can boost GCC awareness rapidly and are advisable for firms as they begin integrating the region more fully into their global business. As companies become more serious about the region, a progression from one-time to more regular events and even to systemic changes in the organization's design is a natural evolution.

Regular Events

Regular events keep the GCC consistently on an organization's agenda and help foster a more permanent awareness of the region. The kinds of events described as "one-time," such as senior management visits to the GCC region and corporate training sessions, can, of course, be repeated regularly. A firm may choose, for example, to hold one of its quarterly senior management summits in the Gulf every two years (one out of eight meetings), as a reflection of the strategic importance of the region. The most effective regular events, however, are those linked to the company's corporate processes: events related to strategic planning and business reviews. Ensuring a GCC voice in these corporate events keeps the Gulf from being a management fad and helps it become an integral part of the firm's overall strategy development process.

Figure 11.2 provides an illustrative view of a Gulf planning cycle, from developing a multiyear GCC strategy to performing annual reviews of the regional business. Depending on a firm's organizational structure and planning processes, different parts of the cycle will occur within the region and at the head office. What matters most is that the GCC-specific cycle takes place, and that both the region and the head office share responsibility for the process and for the results.

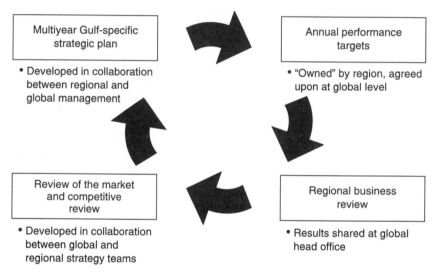

Figure 11.2 The Gulf strategy cycle

The strategy cycle begins with a multiyear plan for the firm's growth in the region. Like most medium-term strategies, the plan needs to be directional and aspirational in nature, rooted in both external trends and internal capabilities. Growth and contribution figures can be projected based on assumptions about the market size, growth, and potential share. A packaged-food company that has around 10 percent market share in other emerging markets, for example, can aspire to a more modest 5 percent share in the Gulf in the medium term, ramping up to 10 percent over time. The strategic measures required to reach that goal (e.g., stronger distribution partners, market-specific products, etc.) would need to be identified and tested for viability. To ensure the right level of input and global commitment, the plan would need to be developed through collaboration between regional and local management.

It is crucial that the plan be specifically for the GCC, not the broader MENA region. While the GCC plan would naturally feed into—and likely drive—the broader Middle East plan, the unique attributes of the Gulf market call for a region-specific plan. Narrower, country-level views, especially for Saudi Arabia and the UAE, also have their place and inform the "Gulf" plan. It is important, however, that the GCC be seen as a unit and that cross-market opportunities be explicitly discussed within the strategic plan. Irrespective of how the GCC reports to the head office, the global CEO and strategy team should insist that a Gulf-specific plan be created.

The next two steps of the cycle—annual performance targets and a regional business review—are standard practices in large corporations and will be familiar to most organizations. What is important in our case is that the business be reviewed and considered through a set of documents distinct from the analysis of other Middle East clusters. The head office should be asking: "How are we doing in the Gulf?" as well as "How are we doing in the Middle East overall?" Savvy organizations have already made such a distinction for China, posing the "China questions" as separate from general questions on Asia.

The fourth step of the cycle is a review of the market and competitors that is as objective as possible. Strategy leaders from the head office, along with counterparts in the region, should refresh their knowledge of market trends and competitive dynamics on a regular basis. With dynamic change—competitive and regulatory—occurring in the region each year, firms run the risk of adhering to outdated strategies unless external monitoring is continual. While the local strategy team is best positioned to monitor the changes, support from the head office is important in validating the analyses and ensuring that global resources are allocated appropriately in line with the evolving strategy.

Systemic Changes

One-time events raise the profile of the GCC and signal the firm's seriousness about the region. Regular events reinforce that profile and ensure attention for the region on an ongoing basis. As the Gulf becomes an increasingly important part of a global company's business, there often is value in codifying GCC awareness even more deeply by making systemic changes to how the organization works. The most common type of systemic change, both powerful in its effect and lasting in its impact, is to change the reporting line by which the GCC business reports to the head office. A more direct line generally ensures greater ongoing focus from the CEO and from the global strategy team.

Typically, the Gulf business is included in a global firm's "Middle East" or "Middle East and North Africa" region. This region, in turn, often reports to what might be called a "megacluster" of regions: an amalgamation such as "Europe, the Middle East, and Africa" or "Asia-Pacific, the Middle East, and Africa." When used, these megaclusters tend to be referred to in the organizations through acronyms (EMEA or APMEA, for example). Figure 11.3 illustrates three basic models through which the GCC typically reports to the head office.

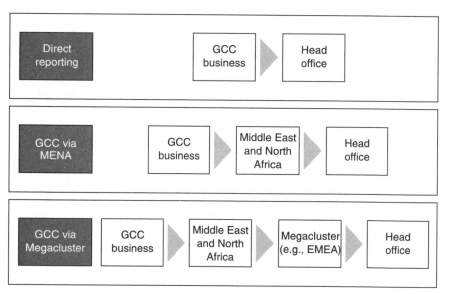

Figure 11.3 Reporting lines from the Gulf to the head office

Under a "Direct Reporting" model, the head of the GCC business reports directly to the global head office, typically to the CEO. This model is uncommon within large multinational firms, for good reason. Usually the Gulf's revenues and strategic importance, even if significant, are too small to warrant so much of the chief executive's attention. The model does, however, have benefits for firms for which the Gulf is a major contributor and an important growth driver. Halliburton is one such firm, and having its head office in Dubai facilitates significant senior attention to the region. The German engineering and industrial giant Siemens, for which the Gulf is an important market, has a direct reporting line from Saudi Arabia to the head office.[17] The US Department of Defense, a non-corporate entity for which the Gulf and broader region are an utmost strategic priority, has a direct reporting line from the Gulf-focused US Central Command to the secretary of defense.[18]

A direct line to the chief executive can help greatly in assuring that the Gulf has access to resources and has its pressing decisions made quickly. Also, having the head of the Gulf region serve on the company's executive committee assures that global issues brought to the group benefit from a GCC-sensitive perspective. With a presence at senior gatherings, Gulf executives are able to introduce ideas with global consequences such as looking to the GCC as a source of capital, a channel for diversifying the company's shareholder base, or a distribution hub between Europe and Asia. As most global firms' Gulf revenues do not yet justify a direct reporting line, such suggestions today need to work their way up through other channels.

The "GCC via MENA" model is more common. In this model, the GCC business reports to a head of the Middle East and North Africa region, who in turn reports to the head office. Such a structure is a natural fit for many organizations, as the MENA region shares certain characteristics and has scale—certainly from a consumer perspective—to justify a direct reporting line to the head office. Having the Gulf business report closer to home can also help minimize turnaround time on key decisions, although the head of MENA may need to refer some issues up to the head office in any case. The challenge in such a structure is to ensure that the Gulf is not lost in the broader Middle East cluster, which may spend much of its time concerned about non-GCC issues such as political risk in

Iraq and Lebanon or focused on the more populous markets of North Africa. As already discussed, managing the Middle East collectively is appropriate only if its various clusters (the Gulf, the Levant, and North Africa) are not painted with the same broad brush. As many firms place their MENA head office in Dubai, the risk of overlooking the GCC becomes far smaller. Having senior regional resources based in the Gulf gives them firsthand appreciation of the area's opportunities and challenges. The MENA head therefore becomes a natural advocate for the GCC business.

A third, and often problematic, structure frequently used by global companies is to have the Gulf report into MENA and then have MENA report into one of the megaclusters described above. The head offices for these megaclusters tend to be in the largest market within the group—EMEA structures, for example, tend to be led from Europe. Within a megacluster there can be a tendency to allocate resources and attention, especially during senior management meetings, to the biggest revenue contributors. A meeting in which the overall Asia-Pacific, Middle East, and Africa region is discussed will likely be dominated by reviews of the businesses in Japan, China, India, and Korea. Despite its promise and dynamism, the Gulf will have difficulty reaching the top of the agenda. This dilution of focus can be a major hindrance to serious investment in the GCC region.

Megacluster structures can, however, prove effective in contexts where decision-making rights are broadly distributed and front-line resources are empowered. Procter & Gamble, Coca-Cola, and Unilever, all of which rely on heavy consumer marketing and local insights, report through megacluster structures.[19] Coca-Cola's success in a market, however, relies more on the effectiveness of its local bottler and local marketing team than on support and investment from Atlanta. Similarly, Procter & Gamble and Unilever rely on in-market distribution and marketing more than on product support from headquarters. Other sectors, in which head office support is more crucial, are less suitable for megacluster reporting models.

There is no single right answer to the question of what is the best way for the GCC to report to the main office. The appropriate model depends on a number of factors, including the GCC's revenue contribution and strategic importance, the degree to which decision making is centralized at the head office, the Gulf business's need for access to senior management, and the overall structure and norms of the organization. As a firm becomes more serious about its Gulf business, shortening the reporting distance between the GCC and the main office is a natural—and empowering—evolutionary step.

BRINGING IT HOME: CLOSING THOUGHTS

Integrating the GCC into your global strategy is one of the most interesting—and challenging—imperatives in business today. The economies of Dubai & Co. are prosperous and dynamic, with economic, demographic, and regulatory changes rapidly transforming the business environment. The Gulf countries share much in common, but each has its unique history and challenges. The region has become a highly attractive place in which to do business, but it does have significant risks and drawbacks. Failing to understand them can lead to seriously flawed strategies and business models.

This book has introduced you to strategies in the Gulf across a wide range of business functions: market entry, marketing, human resources, finance, operations, and organization. You have seen that the unique dynamics of the region affect the full range of corporate activity. Whether your firm has yet to enter the market or has been in the Gulf for decades, you are now better prepared to assess your GCC strategy and to ask probing questions on how it could be improved.

It's hard to say when you will next come across the Gulf. Perhaps, like GE or Morgan Stanley, you will see the GCC as a major growth market with highly attractive customers. Or, like McDonald's and Zara, you may find yourself considering customized products or product mixes for the Gulf region. Then again, your next encounter with the Gulf could be like those of the Four Seasons or Aston Martin—in an M&A situation, with a GCC investor making a bid. Considering the growing importance of the region, your next encounter is more likely to be sooner than later.

Not every business will see the Gulf as a growth opportunity, and clearly there is no one way to engage the region. Savvy firms will reflect on the issue, consider their options, and explore ways to integrate the GCC more tightly into the overall enterprise. The wisest firms may embrace the region or choose to proceed with caution—but they certainly will not ignore it. No corporate strategy is truly global without attention to Dubai & Co.

Notes

INTRODUCTION

1 www.transparency.org/policy_research/surveys_indices/cpi/2005 (accessed October 18, 2006). Of the GCC nations, only Saudi Arabia has a mediocre score in Transparency International's Corruption Perceptions Index, but even its performance is superior to China's or India's. All the other GCC nations rival well-known emerging markets such as Taiwan and South Korea in being relatively uncorrupt places to do business.

2 US Treasury, Major Foreign Holders of Treasury Securities, www.ustreas.gov/tic/mfh.txt (last accessed May 16, 2007). Figures as of March 2007.

3 "Kuwait to invest $720 million in IPO of China's ICBC," Yahoo! Singapore, September 24, 2006, sg.biz.yahoo.com/060924/ 3/43mep.html (last accessed May 18, 2007).

4 IMF and the *Economist*, 2005 data (accessed 2006).

5 Ibid.

6 Qatar National Bank, 2006.

7 *Wall Street Journal*, October 2005.

8 Yahoo Finance, accessed 2006.

9 *International Herald Tribune*, March 2006.

10 Dubai Municipality, Census, official figures.

11 www.ameinfo.com/28375.html.

12 ACNielsen, 2006.

13 Ibid.

14 "Swiss lead the GCC banking boom," www.ameinfo.com/ 48503.html (last accessed May 16, 2007).

CHAPTER 1

1 Roger Adelson, *London and the Invention of the Middle East* (New Haven, Conn.: Yale University Press, 1995).

2 "White House Broader Middle East and North Africa Initiative," White House Factsheet, November 6, 2003.

3 *CIA World Factbook, 2007.*

4 Ibid.

5 Ibid.

6 Ibid.

7 Ibid.

8 Ibid.

9 Ibid.

10 "Country Report: Algeria," Economist Intelligence Unit, December 2006.

11 IMF World Economic Outlook Database, September 2006.

12 HSBC Gulf Economic Outlook, December 2006.

13 Ibid.

14 Kuwait and Bahrain ratified in 1981; the others ratified in 1982.

15 J. E. Peterson, "The GCC and Regional Security," *The Gulf Cooperation Council*, John A. Sandwick, ed. (Colorado: Westview Press, 1987), 171.

16 Since its formation, no new states have been admitted to the GCC. Yemen, in centuries past the Gulf's leading civilization but now an economic laggard, is seeking negotiations and hopes to join by 2016. Its relatively low standard of living poses major challenges in making Yemen "fit" within the GCC, much like the tensions that exist between new Eastern European members of the EU and the wealthy nations of Western Europe.

17 GCC Charter, 1981.

18 "Country Report: Bahrain," Economist Intelligence Unit, December 2006.

19 Ibid.
20 Ibid.

CHAPTER 2

1 *BP Statistical Review of World Energy*, June 2007.
2 HSBC published research, 2006.
3 Central bank projections, 2006.
4 Economic Analytical Unit, Department of Foreign Affairs and Trade, Australian Government, "More Than Oil: Economic Developments in Bahrain, Kuwait, Oman, Qatar and the United Arab Emirates," 2005.
5 IMF, 2006.
6 UNCTAD, World Investment Report, 2005.
7 *BusinessWeek* Special Advertising Section, 2006, www.businessweek.com/adsections/2006/pdf/121802_saudi.pdf.
8 Dubailand: guide.theemiratesnetwork.com/living/ dubai/dubailand.php

World Project: realestate.theemiratesnetwork.com/ developments/dubai/world_islands.php

Palm Island: realestate.theemiratesnetwork.com/developments /dubai/palm_islands.php

Durrat al-Bahrain: realestate.theemiratesnetwork.com/ developments/bahrain/durrat_al_bahrain.php

King Abdullah Economic City: www.emaar.com/MediaCenter/ PressReleases/December20.asp

Amwaj Islands: www.designbuild-network.com/projects/amwaj/

Omagine: www.primenewswire.com/newsroom/ news.html?d=111145
9 *UAE Yearbook 2007*, 126.
10 Copyright (c) 2007 The Emirates Network (TEN), guide.theemiratesnetwork.com/living/dubai/dubailand.php.
11 RetailME, November 2006.
12 Dubai Shopping Festival, www.mydsf.com/dsf/cng/ dsf_statistics.aspx.
13 "More Than Oil."
14 *Hawaa* literally means "Eve," that is, the female name. In this context, however, it is a synecdoche referring to women in general, just as Kleenex is a particular brand of tissue but can refer to tissues in general.

15   Danish national statistics and BBC, "Cartoons Row Hits Danish Exports," September 9, 2006, news.bbc.co.uk/2/hi/europe/5329642.stm.

16   Anthony Browne, "Denmark Faces International Boycott over Muslim Cartoons," *The Times* (UK), January 31, 2006, www.timesonline.co.uk/tol/news/world/europe/article723266.ece.

17   Danish national statistics and the BBC, 2006.

18   Ford Corporation Web site, February 2006.

19   Mickey Meece, "What Do Women Want? Just Ask," *New York Times*, October 29, 2006.

20   The Cooperation Council for the Arab States of the Gulf, Secretariat General, library.gcc-sg.org/gccstat/educstat/ed31.htm.

21   `Izzat Sund, "Al-Mazhariyya Wafid Jadid `Ala Suluk al-Imaratiyya: Muwatinat Ghariqat fi 'Dulmat' al-Duyun," ("The appearance of a new trend in Emirati behavior: Emirati women drown under loans") *Kul Al Usra* 688 (December 2006) 38.

22   Forbes.com, August 2006.

23   In Chapter 7, we will discuss the strategic initiatives undertaken by GCC governments to reduce dependence on expatriate workers and the impact of these initiatives on multinational businesses. Multinationals must understand this trend, appreciate its importance, and genuinely partner with local governments to help build the local talent base.

CHAPTER 3

1   EIU and *CIA World Factbook, 2007*.

2   *CIA World Factbook, 2007*.

3   World Economic Forum on the Middle East, May 22, 2006.

4   *Economist*, June 10, 2006.

5   Stanley Reed, "The New Middle East Oil Bonanza," *BusinessWeek*, March 13, 2006.

6   "Recycling Petrodollars," *Economist*, November 12, 2005.

7   Reed, "The New Middle East Oil Bonanza."

8   Associated Press, "Qatar Airways Raises Airbus Order," May 31, 2007.

9   Reed, "The New Middle East Oil Bonanza."

10   Andrew Ross Sorkin and Michael J. de la Merced, "G.E. Nears a Deal to Sell Plastics Unit," *New York Times*, May 18, 2007.

11 ACNeilsen, cited in Retail ME, November 2006.

12 Directory of Major Malls, 2006.

13 Robert Ditcham, "81% of Retail Space Sold at Mall of Arabia," *Gulf News*, March 20, 2007.

14 "Playing by Unfair Rules," *Economist*, November 25, 2006.

15 "Capturing Opportunities in the Gulf's Financial Sector," *McKinsey Quarterly*, March 2007.

16 Retail ME, November 2006.

17 Retail ME, November 2006.

18 James J. Zogby, "Shedding Light on the Gulf's Middle Class," *McKinsey Quarterly*, February 2007.

19 Cited in *Economist*, December 16, 2006.

20 The Heritage Foundation Web site,www.heritage.org.

21 Unweighted average of the six member countries' scores.

22 These abbreviations stand, respectively, for the General Agreement on Tariffs and Trade, the General Agreement on Trade in Services, and Trade-Related Aspects of Intellectual Property Rights.

23 The World Trade Organization.

24 "Report of the Working Party on the Accession of the Kingdom of Saudi Arabia, Addendum: Part II—Schedule of Specific Commitments in Services, List of Article II MFN Exemptions," WT/ACC/SAU/61/Add.2, 1 Nov 2005.

25 Oman Chamber of Commerce & Industry, "Oman's Commitments under WTO Agreements," www.chamberoman.com/doing_occi_opportunities7.asp (accessed March 19, 2007).

26 US Department of State, "Middle East Free Trade Area Initiative," June 21, 2006, usinfo.state.gov/mena/img/assets/4756/062206_mefta_1.pdf

27 "Gulf Expects EU Trade Deal by June," Reuters, March 5, 2007.

28 www.bilaterals.org/article.php3?id_article=6574.

29 Heather Timmons, "A Middle East Equity Giant with a Small Global Footprint," *New York Times*, December 8, 2006.

30 "Report of the Working Party on the Accession of the Kingdom of Saudi Arabia to the World Trade Organization," WT/ACC/SAU/61, 1 November 2005.

31 Since 1999, non-GCC foreigners, wherever resident, have been allowed to invest indirectly in the Saudi stock market through mutual funds. Foreign participation is capped at 10 percent of the value of the fund. GCC nationals can invest in Saudi stocks without

restriction. Saudi Arabian General Investment Authority, www.sagia.gov.sa/printpage.asp?ContentID=551&Lang=en; U.S. Trade Representative, www.ustr.gov/assets/Document_Library/ Reports_Publications/2007/2007_NTE_Report/ asset_upload_file211_10978.pdf.

32 Achmed Al- Shahrabani and Kito de Boer. "Modernizing the United Arab Emirates: An Interview with Minister of Economy Lubna Al Qasimi," from The McKinsey Quarterly Web exclusive, February 2007.

33 Kito de Boer and Jaap B. Kalkman. "Meeting Bahrain's Challenges: An Interview with Crown Prince Salman bin Hamad Al-Khalifa," from The McKinsey Quarterly Web exclusive, January 2007, www.mckinseyquarterly.com/article_page.aspx?ar=1907.

34 Transparency International 2005 ratings.

35 William Wallis, "Gulf Arab Holidaymakers Travel Closer to Home," *Financial Times*, September 29, 2004.

36 Associated Press, "Crowd Trashes Offices of Red Sea Ferry Firm," February 6, 2006, www.msnbc.msn.com/id/11157659/.

37 Henry T. Azzam, "Remittances Are Major Asset for Some Arab Countries," *Daily Star*, December 11, 2006.

38 "Senior Bush Urges Students to 'Seek Out, Understand Cultures,'" *Gulf Times*, March 20, 2007.

39 www.answers.com/topic/arab-league (last accessed March 20, 2007).

40 Although OPEC's headquarters is in Vienna, its most influential members are in the Gulf.

41 Helene Cooper, "Aid Conference Raises $7.6 Billion for Lebanese Government," *New York Times*, January 26, 2007.

42 Statement by H.E. Ambassador Abdulaziz Nasser R. Al-Shamsi, The Permanent Representative of the United Arab Emirates to the United Nations, before the 61st Session of the General Assembly on Item "Strengthening of the coordination of humanitarian and disaster relief assistance of the United Nations, including special economic assistance; Assistance to the Palestinian people," November 13, 2006, www.un.int/uae/E13-11-06.htm.

43 Terry Carter and Lara Dunston, "Lonely Planet Dubai," Footscray, Vic.: Lonely Planet Publications, 2004, p. 12, and other sources.

44 Vimala Vasan, "NRIs Account for Chunk of UAE Remittances," The Hindu Business Line, February 23, 2005.

45 "Indian Investments in UAE to Reach USD 5 bn," IRIS, December 12, 2006.

46 Ministry of Hajj, KSA, www.hajinformation.com/main/1.htm.

47 Jasim Husain Ali, "The Economy of Holy Places," *Oman Economic Review*, February 2007, www.oeronline.com/php/2007_feb/gcc_dairy.php.

48 Hassan M. Fattah, "The Price of Progress: Transforming Islam's Holiest Site," *New York Times*, March 8, 2007.

49 "Turk Telekom Privatisation Succeeds? *Southeast European Times*, July 19, 2005.

50 Rafi-uddin Shikoh, "Is Intra-OIC Trade Finally Taking Off?" *Dinar Standard*, April 15, 2005, www.dinarstandard.com/current/intraoic041505.htm.

51 UK Foreign and Commonwealth Office, "Country Profile: United Arab Emirates," March 5, 2007.

52 "Saudi Arabia's Foreign Workforce," BBC News, May 13, 2003.

53 City Mayors, www.citymayors.com/gratis/uk_topcities.html.

54 AME Info, "Britons Prefer Dubai as Second Home," November 13, 2006, www.ameinfo.com/101675.html.

55 Daniel Bardsley, "Here's to Life," *Gulf News*, November 30, 2005, archive.gulfnews.com/indepth/uae_national_day_2005/more_stories/10001575.html.

56 Piers Gladstone, "A Dacha in Dubai," *Passport Magazine*, n.d.,www.passportmagazine.ru/article/619/.

57 "Dubai Hosts Natalie Tours Congress," *Dubai Weekly Newsletter*, September 28, 2006, www.dubaitourism.ae/newsletter/arrow/ar_ArchivesWeb.asp?uID=3&nID=79.

58 Heather Timmons, "Asia Finding Rich Partners in Mideast," *New York Times*, December 1, 2006.

59 Ibid.

60 Iqbal Khan, "The Arched Gateway," Khazanah Megatrends Conference, 2006.

61 US Energy Information Administration, International Energy Outlook 2006, www.eia.doe.gov/oiaf/ieo/figure_32.html (last accessed May 17, 2007).

62 Since the Agency's prediction, oil prices have in fact gone well above their 2006 high, scraping $80 per barrel in September 2007.

63 Jad Mouawad, "Oil Innovations Pump New Life into Old Wells," *New York Times*, March 5, 2007.

64 US Energy Information Agency, www.eia.doe.gov/oiaf/ieo/figure_26.html.

65 Ibid.

66 Pepe Escobar, "Dubai Lives the Post-Oil Arab Dream," *Asia Times*
    June 7, 2006, www.atimes.com/atimes/Middle_East/
    HF07Ak01.html.

67 "Swiss Lead the GCC Banking Boom," November 8, 2004,
    www.ameinfo.com/48503.html.

CHAPTER 4

1   Quoted by Prince Amr bin Mohammad Al Faisal, PBS *Frontline,*
    2003.

2   Ras al-Khaimah did not join until 1972. Had the UAE included Qatar
    and Bahrain, as originally envisioned, the GCC landscape might
    have been quite different today.

3   "Emirati" denotes UAE nationals.

4   Library of Congress, "A Country Study: United Arab Emirates,"
    1993.

5   BP, *Statistical Review of World Energy 2006.*

6   Sudip Roy, "Adia Unveils Its secrets," *Euromoney,* April 1, 2006.

7   www.sheikhmohammed.co.ae/english/dubai/
    dubai_almaktoum.asp (last accessed May 16, 2007).

8   www.ameinfo.com/93650.html, AME Info, August 2006.

9   www.rakftz.com/en/index.php, Ras al-Khaimah FTZ Web site, 2007.

10 Ownership restrictions and deregulation are discussed in much
    greater detail in a later chapter.

11 "Doing Business in the UAE: Free Zones," UAE Federal
    Government e-Portal, 2007.

12 RAK FTZ Web site, March 2007, www.rakftz.com/en/
    news_details.php?id=46.

13 IMF, 2007 estimates, www.imf.org/external/country/SAU/
    index.htm.

14 Ibid.

15 BP, *Statistical Review of World Energy 2006.*

16 Library of Congress, "A Country Study: Saudi Arabia," 1993.

17 *CIA World Factbook, 2006.*

18 "Questions About the World's Largest Gas Field," *The Oil Drum
    Online,* June 9, 2006.

19 AME Info, 2006.

20 British Embassy, Bahrain, "UK-Bahrain Relations," www.
    britishembassy.gov.uk/servlet/Front?pagename=OpenMarket/
    Xcelerate/ShowPage&c=Page&cid=1035898708295 (last accessed
    May 16, 2007).

21 "Bahrain: Background Notes" US State Department, October 2006.

22 Library of Congress, "A Country Study: Bahrain," 1993.

23 "Bahrain: Background Notes" US State Department, October 2006.
    CIA World Factbook 2007, Luxembourg.

24 BP, *Statistical Review of World Energy 2006*.

25 *CIA World Factbook, 2006*.

26 Forbes.com, August 2006.

27 "Kuwait: Background Notes." US State Department, 2006.

28 "Oman: Background Notes," US State Department, 2006.

29 *CIA World Factbook, 2006*.

30 Ibid.

31 Ibid.

CHAPTER 5

1 Expert interviews; corporate history; and www.rootsweb.com/
    ~sauwgw/Jamil.htm.

2 The firm's full name is the Fawaz Abdul Aziz Al-Hokair Group.

3 Fashion Retail," Al-Hokair corporate Web site, www.alhokair.com.sa/
    Pages/Page.aspx?PageId=7 (last accessed January 15, 2007).

4 "Another Growth Year—Retail International's Review of the Year,"
    Retail International, Winter 2006, www.retailcity.ae/upl_images/files/
    RI-Survey_winter_2006.pdf (last accessed January 15, 2007).

5 Ibid.

6 "Gap Inc. Expands International Reach with Franchise Agreements for
    Middle East," Al-Tayer Group corporate Web site, April 18, 2006,
    www.altayer.com/whatsnew/view_article.asp?article_id=114 (last
    accessed Jan 15, 2007).

7 Louise Lee, "Gap Goes Global," *BusinessWeek*, April 18, 2006,
    www.businessweek.com/bwdaily/dnflash/apr2006/nf20060418_583
    5_db016.htm (last accessed January 15, 2007).

8 "Carrefour—The Group—Franchisees," Carrefour corporate Web
    site, www.carrefour.com/cnglish/groupecarrefour/franchise.htm
    (last accessed February 11, 2007). Interestingly, three other MENA

countries—Tunisia, Egypt, and Algeria—have also been entered through franchises or partnerships.

9   Al-Futtaim corporate Web site and press releases.

10 "Inter IKEA Systems B.V.—Ikea Concept," IKEA corporate Web site, franchisor.ikea.com/showContent.asp?swfId=concept2 (last accessed February 11, 2007).

11 "Inter IKEA Systems B.V.—Ikea Franchising," IKEA corporate Web site, franchisor.ikea.com/showContent.asp?swfId=franchise2 (last accessed February 11, 2007).

12 Abdulla Al-Futtaim, The World's Richest People—Forbes," www.forbes.com/lists/2006/10/Y6MM.html (last accessed February 11, 2007).

13 "Al Futtaim Seeks to Double Retail Value," *Zawya*, February 7, 2007, www.zawya.com/Story.cfm/sidGN10102989 (last accessed February 11, 2007).

14 "Dell Middle East Resellers," Dell corporate Web site, www1.euro. dell.com/content/topics/topic.aspx/emea/contact/edb/arae? c=ae&l=en&s=gen&~ck=mn (last accessed May 16, 2007).

15 It should be noted, however, that Dell Partners are not exclusively dedicated to Dell; they may sell or service the products of other computer makers as well. Later in this chapter, we will review some of the challenges presented by conflicts of interest in distributorship agreements.

16 This perspective assumes, of course, that the multinational feels confident in its ability (or its potential) to manage the business directly. As the Middle East has long appeared an enigma to many managers, some multinationals prefer to take the risk that a distributor not perform well rather than bear the operating risk of doing the job themselves.

17 This issue is not uncommon. Beverage distributors in the United States, for example, often pose such challenges to small manufacturers who need them for their capabilities but realize the distributor represents other comparable or competitive products.

18 Boomberg (ranked according to Q4 2006 total assets).

19 Abdulrahman Al-Hamidi, "Banking Sector Issues in Saudi Arabia," Bank of International Settlements Web site, www.bis.org/publ/bppdf/ bispap28v.pdf, pg 4(last accessed Jan 14, 2007).

20 www.wto.org/English/news_e/pres05_e/pr420_e.htm.

21 One exception to this rule is at Dubai's huge Mall of the Emirates, which boasts an indoor ski slope. Not to be outdone, a competitor is building Dubai's second indoor ski slope.

22 World Bank Group, "Economy Rankings," www.doingbusiness.org/ EconomyRankings/ (last accessed January 13, 2007).

23 Thomson Banker, Thomson Financial, accessed May 2007.

24 Saudi Arabian General Investment Authority, "The Foreign Investment Act: Statute for the General Investment Authority, Executive Rules," www.sagia.gov.sa/Downloads/Pub/Act%20-%20English.pdf (accessed December 26, 2006).

25 "Report of the Working Party on the Accession of the Kingdom of Saudi Arabia, Addendum: Part II—Schedule of Specific Commitments in Services, List of Article II MFN Exemptions," WT/ACC/SAU/61/Add.2, November 1, 2005.

26 Free zones are discussed in greater depth in Chapter 3 of this book.

27 DIFC marketing presentation, www.fsc.bg/events/proqvi/ prezentacii/DIFC%20Presentation%20-%20General%2029% 20JUN%202006.pdf.

CHAPTER 6

1 Matt Blackborn, CEO of Publicis Group Media, quoted in Christiana Passariello, "Chic Under Wraps: Elle's Middle Eastern Edition Balances Fashion and Tradition; Wearing Designer Labels Indoors," *Wall Street Journal*, June, 20, 2006.

2 Quoted in "Strategic Brand Management," www.etstrategicmarketing. com/smNov-Dec1/stra_brand_br2.htm (last accessed May 14, 2007).

3 Research team photograph, December 2006.

4 Sprite's case is especially interesting, as the Arabic language has no "P" sound. Therefore the company's logo reads—and is often pronounced—as "Sbrite." The same phenomenon leads to "Bebsi" and "bizza."

5 Translations by author.

6 Kiran Karande, K. Al-Murshidee, and F. Al-Olayan, "Advertising Standardization in Culturally Similar Markets: Can We Standardize All Components?" *International Journal of Advertising* 25, no. 4 (2006): 489–512.

7 F. S. Al-Olayan, and K. Karande, "A Content Analysis of Magazine Advertisements from the United States and the Arab World," *International Journal of Advertising* 29, no. 3 (2000): 69–82.

8 "Chic Under Wraps: Elle Magazine Launches Middle East Edition," *Wall Street Journal*, June 20, 2006, online.wsj.com/article/ SB115075929382184604.html?mod=todays_us_marketplace.

9 Research team interview with marketing executive, Saudi Arabia, March 2007.

10 Business Intelligence Middle East, April 5, 2006, www.bi-me.com/ main.php?id=173&cg=9&t=1&PHPSESSID=68682d1e0649d68f013939 a5b195bbef.

11 "Working Knowledge," Harvard Business School, hbswk.hbs.edu/ archive/4652.html.

12 Ibid.

13 *Chicago Sun-Times*, March 19, 2003.

14 www.mcdonaldsarabia.com/english/ksa/about_impact.asp (last accessed May 14, 2007).

15 www.mcdonaldsarabia.com/english/uae/about_story.asp (last accessed May 14, 2007).

16 www.mcdonaldsarabia.com/english/kuwait/about_story.asp (last accessed May 14, 2007).

17 www.mcdonaldsarabia.com/english/bahrain/about_story.asp (last accessed May 14, 2007).

18 www.mcdonaldsarabia.com/english/oman/about_story.asp (last accessed May 14, 2007).

19 www.mcdonaldsarabia.com/english/qatar/about_story.asp (last accessed May 14, 2007).

20 *Restauranta and Institutions Magazine*, December 1, 2006, www.rimag. com/archives/2006/12/business-china.asp.

21 "Arab Advertising Comes of Age," AMEInfo, www.ameinfo.com/ 31160.html.

22 Middle East Media Guide (2006), Lexis Nexis, Zawya.com.

23 Bloomberg, www.bloomberg.com/apps/ news?pid=20601102&sid=auosJ3C.yfnA&refer=uk.

CHAPTER 7

1 *CIA World Factbook, 2006.*

2 Figure 7.2 is illustrative—clearly, GDP per capita has been more volatile than the chart suggests. The point is to contrast more classic development models with the experience of the GCC.

3 Onn Winckler. "The Demographic Dilemma of the Arab World: The Employment Aspect," *Journal of Contemporary History* 37, no. 4 (October 2002): 617–36. Page 623 for this citation.

4 Saudi Aramco corporate Web site, May 2007, www.saudiarmco.com.

5 One exception to this phenomenon is for owners of freehold properties in UAE "free zones" such as the Palm Islands. Freehold

ownership comes with resident status for the owner and his or her family. Such properties tend to be expensive and thus out of reach for most expatriates.

6 The naturalization process for citizens of Arab countries is sometimes more manageable than the process for non-Arabs, but is onerous in any case.

7 Robert Looney, "Saudization and Sound Economic Reforms: Are the Two Compatible?" *Strategic Insights* 3, no. 2, (February 2004), www.ccc.nps.navy.mil/si/2004/feb/looneyFeb04.asp (last accessed March 5, 2007).

8 Fragomen, Del Rey, Bernsen & Loewy, LLP. "United Arab Emirates— 'Emiritization' of Workforce Bars Work Permits for Human Resource Managers and Secretaries," pubweb.fdbl.com/news1.nsf/d1cfb387 f152cd6188256aa9004f93e8/1abddcf6291ba3f8852571a900777dce? OpenDocument (last accessed May 15, 2007).

9 Ibid.

10 Achmed Al- Shahrabani and Kito de Boer. "Modernizing the United Arab Emirates: An Interview with Minister of Economy Lubna Al Qasimi," *McKinsey Quarterly* Web exclusive, February 2007, www.mckinseyquarterly.com/article_page.aspx?ar=1919&L2=7&L3= 10&srid=17&gp=0 (last accessed March 4, 2007).

11 "Mission Statement," from Qatarization online, www.qatarization. com.qa/qatarization/qat_web.nsf (last accessed March 5, 2007).

12 Economic Development Board, "Reforming Bahrain's Labour Market," September 23, 2004.

13 Ibid.

14 Kito de Boer and Jaap B. Kalkman, "Meeting Bahrain's Challenges: An Interview with Crown Prince Salman bin Hamad Al-Khalifa," *McKinsey Quarterly* Web exclusive, January 2007, www. mckinseyquarterly.com/article_page.aspx?ar=1907 (last accessed March 4, 2007).

15 "IMF Executive Board Concludes 2006 Article IV Consultation With Kuwait," International Monetary Fund's Public Information Notice, March 10, 2006, www.imf.org/external/np/sec/pn/2006/pn0635. htm (last accessed March 5, 2007).

16 Gassan Al-Kibsi, Claus Benkert, and Jorg Schubert. "Getting Labor Policy to Work in the Gulf," *McKinsey Quarterly* Web exclusive, February 2007, www.mckinseyquarterly.com/article_abstract_visitor. aspx?ar=1930&L2=7&L3=8&srid=246 (last accessed March 3, 2007).

17 Oman Chamber of Commerce and Industry, "Oman's Commitments under WTO Agreements," www.chamberoman.com/doing_occi_opportunities7.asp (last accessed March 19, 2007).

18 Ugo Fasano and Rishi Goyal. "Emerging Strains in GCC Labor Markets," IMF Working Paper, WP/04/71, April 2004.

19 Ibid.

20 Al-Kibsi, Benkert, and Schubert. "Getting Labor Policy to Work in the Gulf."

21 Ibid.

22 DIFC FAQ, www.difc.ae/base/faq/ (last accessed May 13, 2007).

23 I am indebted to Iqbal Khan, Founding CEO of HSBC Amanah, for introducing me to the term "embedded franchise."

24 Hiring local staff also, of course, lets firms comply with quota systems and other nationalization policies discussed earlier.

25 Dubai Knowledge Village Web site, www.kv.ae/en/default.asp# (last accessed May 2007).

26 Cass Business School Web site, www.cass.city.ac.uk/mba/dubai/index.html (last accessed May 2007).

27 Qatar Foundation Web site, www.qf.edu.qa/output/page307.asp (last accessed May 2007).

28 Claire M. Guehenno, "Arabic Courses Draw Higher Enrollment," Harvard Crimson online, October 5, 2005, www.thecrimson.com/article.aspx?ref=508807 (last accessed April 24, 2007).

29 "United Arab Emirates: Citibank UAE Wins Human Resources Development Award for Second Year," Citigroup Web site, www.citigroup.com/citigroup/press/2003/030305a.htm (last accessed March 5, 2007).

30 "GE to Open Technology Center at Qatar Science and Technology Park," Qatar Foundation News, December 2005, www.qf.edu.qa/output/page1079.asp.

31 Ibid.

32 Quoted in ibid.

CHAPTER 8

1 "All That Glisters . . . Dubai," *Economist*, December 16, 2006.

2 Shuaa Capital, March 2007.

3 *BP Statistical Review of World Energy,* June 2007.

4 While the Dubai government has a more diversified income stream, the UAE overall is still heavily reliant on oil.

5 Peter Garnham, "Kuwait Ends Peg against Dollar," *Financial Times*, May 21, 2007.

6 "An Oasis of Opportunity," Strategy focus, Deutsche Bank, December 4, 2006.

7 Shuaa Capital, March 2007.

8 Library of Congress Country Studies; *CIA World Factbook*, December 1992, www.photius.com/countries/saudi_arabia/economy/saudi_arabia_economy_economic_policy_duri~1411.html.

9 "The New Middle East Oil Bonanza," *BusinessWeek*, March 13, 2006, www.businessweek.com/magazine/content/ 06_11/ b3975001.htm.

10 "MENA Region: 2006 Economic Developments and Prospects—Financial Markets in a New Age of Oil," World Bank, 2006.

11 *Abu Dhabi Factbook, 2006.*

12 *Economist*, May 24, 2007, www.economist.com/finance/displaystory.cfm?story_id=9230598.

13 "Money and Mystery: ADIA Unveils Its Secrets," *Euromoney*, 2006.

14 KPMG Corporate Tax Survey 2006, 209.85.165.104/search?q=cache: 2XJVQQdrXF4J:www.stern.nyu.edu/~adamodar/pdfiles/articles/KPMGtaxratesurvey.pdf+corporate+taxes+gcc&hl=en&ct=clnk&cd=1&gl=us&client=firefox-a.

15 *Arab News*, March 2007, www.menafn.com/qn_news_story_s.asp?StoryId=1093147692.

16 Ibid.

17 DIFC Website: Media Enquiries, February 2007.

18 David Ignatius, "Where's the Oil Money?" *Washington Post*, December 9, 2005, www.relocalize.net/node/1723.

19 Waleed Khalil Rasromani, "Financial Executives Foresee Weaker Correlation with Gulf Stock Markets," *Daily Star* (Egypt), July 12, 2006, www.dailystaregypt.com/article.aspx?ArticleID=2235.

20 Mushtak Parker, "Saudi Banking and Industrialization," *Arab News*, December 6, 2006, www.arabnews.com/?page=15&section=0&article=89608&d=10&m=5&y=2007.

21 Reuters, "Gulf Markets 'Cannot Afford a Crash,'" *Gulf News*, April 3, 2006, archive.gulfnews.com/articles/06/03/04/10022969.html.

22 Jia Lynn Yang, "Saudi Arabia's Stock Collapse," *Fortune*, January 17, 2007, money.cnn.com/magazines/fortune/fortune_archive/2006/12/11/8395382/index.htm.

23 Investment Company Institute, "Half of American Households Own Equities," 2002, www.ici.org/shareholders/dec/02_news_equity_ownership.html.

24 Interestingly, the required first-year finance course at the Harvard Business School begins with a lecture that includes a discussion of how interest had been frowned upon for centuries in the West.

25 For more on Islamic finance, refer to the Web sites of HSBC Amanah—www.hsbcamanah.com—and publications of the Harvard Islamic Finance Program—www.ifp.harvard.edu.

26 Z. Iqbal and H. Tsubota, The World Bank (2006).

27 Oman is an outlier when it comes to Islamic finance: there is no Islamic finance in the country, despite significant consumer demand. Bahrain, by contrast, has positioned itself as a global hub for Islamic finance and is home to several industry associations. In Saudi Arabia, the UAE, Qatar, and Kuwait, the phenomenon has been consumer driven.

28 Central banks data, author analysis, expert interviews.

29 Gillian Tett, "Islamic Bonds Used to buy 007's Wheels," *Financial Times*, March 16, 2007, www.ft.com/cms/s/7461bd9c-d40a-11db-83d5-000b5df10621.html.

30 Standard & Poor Report (April 24, 2007)—sourced from Bloomberg.

31 "Japan Holds 1st Seminar On Islamic Finance," Bernama.com, January 23, 2007, www.bernama.com.my/finance/news.php?id=242814.

32 Bemo Securitisation SAL, "East Cameron Gas Sukuk," June 19, 2006 (press release), www.securitization.net/pdf/content/BSEC_19Jun06.pdf.

33 Securities Exchange Act of 1934 ß 13(d)(1); Japan Securities and Exchange Law (2002), Chapter II-3, Article 27-33; Dechert LLP, "Implementation of the Transparency Directive Changes Shareholder Notification Requirements across Europe," February 2007, www.dechert.com/library/FSG_Update3_2-07.pdf; Hong Kong Securities and Futures Ordinance (2003), Part XV.

34 As of May 30, 2007.

35 www.msnbc.msn.com/id/18896026/.

36 Ibid.

37   select.nytimes.com/gst/abstract.html?res=F60612FC3B550C748
      DDDAC0894DF404482&n=Top%2fNews%2fBusiness%2fCompanies
      %2fDeutsche%20Bank%20A%2eG%2e.

38   www.washingtonpost.com/wp-dyn/content/article/2007/03/05/
      AR2007030501369.html.

39   www.khaleejtimes.com/DisplayArticleNew.asp?xfile=data/
      business/2007/May/business_May65.xml&section=business.

40   www.msnbc.msn.com/id/18686163/.

41   www.forbes.com/facesinthenews/2007/04/16/saudi-hsbc-maan-
      face-cx_po_0416autofacescan01.html.

42   www.khaleejtimes.com/DisplayArticleNew.asp?xfile=data/
      business/2007/May/business_May65.xml&section=business.

43   www.ft.com/cms/s/0d9b64c6-ec80-11db-a12e-000b5df10621.html.

44   news.bbc.co.uk/2/hi/business/6755497.stm.

45   Saudi banking joint ventures are discussed in more detail in Chapter 5.

46   Information drawn from Shuaa Capital, "Raising Capital in the GCC:
      A Comparative Analysis," November 21, 2005.

CHAPTER 9

1   "DIA Registers 16.17 Per Cent Growth in 2006," January 11, 2007,
     www.dubaiairport.com/DIA/English/TopMenu/News+and+Press/
     Airport+News/DIA+registers+16.17+per+cent+growth+in+2006.htm
     (last accessed May 15, 2007).

2   Ibrahim Al Abed, ed., United Arab Emirates, UAE Ministry of
     Information and Culture, *United Arab Emirates Yearbook 2006*
     (London: Trident Press, 2006), 199.

3   "Fuel Farm Development," December 31, 2006, uaeinteract.com/
     news/default.asp?ID=26.

4   John F. O'Connell, Air Transport Group, "The Changing Dynamics of
     the Arab Gulf Based Airlines and an Investigation into the Strategies
     That Are Making Emirates into a Global Challenger."

5   *UAE Yearbook 2006*, 200.

6   *UAE Yearbook 2005*, 207.

7   New Doha International Airport Web site, January 2007,
     www.ndiaproject.com.

8   Qatar Embassy, January 2007, www.qatarembassy.net/
     major_projects.asp#Petrochemicals.

9   Al Abed, *UAE Yearbook 2006*, 182.

10 Andrew P. Mcafee, Karen Ooms-Walls, Lubna Al Qasimi, "Dubai Ports Authority (A)," Harvard Business School, February 5, 2003, 3.

11 Alex Abraham, "Dubai Ports Authority: Creating Competitive Advantage," Business Line, Monday, March 25, 2002, www.thehindubusinessline.com/2002/03/25/stories/2002032500080900.htm.

12 Port of Hamburg database, author analysis, www.hafen-hamburg.de/en/index.php?option=com_content&task=view&id=58&Itemid=91.

13 It is noteworthy that Sheikha Lubna Al Qasimi, who later became the UAE's minister of economy, once held responsibility for IT within the Dubai ports system.

14 Corporate Web site, portal.pohub.com/portal/page?_pageid=761,248333&_dad=pogprtl&_schema=POGPRTL.

15 "Dubai Port International Completes Acquisition of CSX World Terminals," February 22, 2005, www.csx.com/?fuseaction=media.news_detail&i=46857.

16 Julio J. Rotemberg, "The Dubai Ports World Debacle and Its Aftermath," Harvard Business School, October 24, 2006.

17 Ibid.

18 Corporate Web site, January 2007.

19 "Airports and Seaports," January 2007, www.uae.gov.ae/Government/ports.htm.

20 Corporate Web site, www.dubailogisticscity.com.

21 "The Saudi Economy at Mid-Year 2006," Samba, August 2006.

22 Bahrain Economic Development Board, www.bahrainedb.com/default.asp?action=category&id=7 (last accessed January 1, 2007).

23 HSBC Research: Gulf Weekly, November 20, 2006.

24 Salalah Port Web site: www.salalahport.com/frame-operations.htm.

25 "Nestlé to Set Up Manufacturing Facility in Techno Park," Dubai City Guide, www.dubaicityguide.com/geninfo/news_dtls.asp?newsid=3258 (last accessed May 15, 2007).

26 "The Saudi Economy at Mid-Year 2006."

27 Park Web site, www.biip.com.bh/.

28 "Kraft to Build $40 Million Manufacturing Plant in Bahrain," July 16, 2006, business.maktoob.com/foodnew.asp?id=20060716131304.

29 Ibid.

30 See our discussion of Bahrain's development in Chapter 4.

31 Media City Web site: www.dubaimediacity.com/.

32 Although Muslims worldwide observe the mandatory Friday prayers, not all Muslim-majority countries take the day off. Turkey and Malaysia, for example, operate on a Monday–Friday week consistent with international practice. People take an extended midday break for prayers and lunch. Muslims in the West and in Muslim-minority states do the same.

33 *Kuwait Times*, May 8, 2007, www.kuwaittimes.net/read_news.php? newsid=MTMyMzQ4OTU3MA==.

34 World Bank and IFC, Doing Business indicators, www.doingbusiness.org. Cost figures rounded to nearest hundred.

35 "Emirates Group Case Study: Global Branding and Communication Delivered by Tridion," March 6, 2007, www.tridion.com/Images/TridionCS_Emirates_tcm6-2979.pdf.

36 Matthew Maier, "Rise of the Emirates Empire," CNN online, October 1, 2005, money.cnn.com/magazines/business2/business2_archive/2005/10/01/8359251/index.htm (last accessed March 6, 2007).

37 "Airlines in India," Profile of Emirates Airlines, www.iloveindia.com/airlines-in-india/international/emirates-airline.html (last accessed May 15, 2007).

38 John F. O'Connell, Air Transport Group, "The Changing Dynamics of the Arab Gulf Based Airlines."

39 EasyOz; Emirates Airlines, *Economist*, October 29, 2005.

40 "Wie eine Fluglinie aus Dubai die Branche auf den Kopf stellt," *Wirtschaftswoche*, September 7, 2006, www.wiwo.de/pswiwo/fn/ww2/sfn/bm_artikel/bmpara/1567/bmpara/41525420556e7465726e e65686d656e20575733/id/126/id/210077/fm/0/artprint/1/SH/0/depot/0/index.html (last accessed May 15, 2007).

41 Emaar corporate Web site, www.emaar.com/International/usa/Index.asp.

CHAPTER 10

1 The common elements of GCC markets and rapid deregulation in these markets are discussed extensively in earlier chapters of this book.

2 Source: Press review and expert interviews.

3 Dubai's infrastructure is discussed at length in Chapter 9.

4 Sources: Corporate Web sites, annual reports, and press releases.

5 "Doing Business in Saudi Arabia: A Country Commercial Guide for U.S. Companies," www.buyusa.gov.

6   A. John Quelch, *Introduction to Cases in Strategic Marketing Management: Business Strategies in Muslim Countries* (Upper Saddle River, N.J.: Prentice-Hall, 2001).

7   IMF, 2007 estimates.

8   "Doing Business in Saudi Arabia."

9   www.pg.com/company/who_we_are/worldwide_operations.jhtml.

10 www.unileverme.com/our-company/about-unilever/middleeast.asp.

11 For example, on Transparency International's Corruption Perceptions Index 2005, the GCC nations scored an average of 5.38 (higher scores indicate less corruption), better than Italy or South Korea. The lowest-ranked GCC country, Saudi Arabia, had a score of 3.4, ahead of China (3.2) and India (2.9).

12 "Building Towers Cheating Workers," *Human Rights Watch Report 18*, no. 8(E) (November 2006), hrw.org/reports/2006/uae1106/index.htm.

CHAPTER 11

1   Research team survey, 2007.

2   Executive profiles are current as of June 2007.

3   Corporate Web site, www.thecoca-colacompany.com/ourcompany/bios/bio_92.html.

4   Corporate Web site, www.hsbc.com/hsbc/news_room/news/news-archive-2006?cp=/public/groupsite/news_room/2006_archive/hsbc_appoints_new_chief_operating_officer.jhtml&isPc=true.

5   www.mcdonalds.com/corp/about/bios/tim_fenton0.html.

6   *BusinessWeek*, Total Company Profile: People, investing. businessweek.com/research/stocks/people/person.asp?personId=506878&symbol=TOTF.PA.

7   Press release, "Halliburton Opens Corporate Headquarters in the United Arab Emirates," March 11, 2007, www.halliburton.com/default/main/halliburton/eng/news/source_files/news.jsp?newsurl=/default/main/halliburton/eng/news/source_files/press_release/2007/corpnws_031107.html.

8   Quoted in Stephanie Kirchgaessner, "Halliburton under Fire over Dubai Proposal," *Financial Times*, March 12, 2007, www.ft.com/cms/s/977df3ac-d0ce-11db-836a-000b5df10621.html.

9   Quoted in ibid.

10 Halliburton 2006 Annual Report.

11 Press release, www.morganstanley.com/about/press/articles/ 3745.html.

12 Quoted in AME Info, February 12, 2007, www.ameinfo.com/ 122071.html.

13 Andrew Longstreth, "Dubai Dreams," *American Lawyer*, October 2006, www.law.com/jsp/tal/PubArticleTAL.jsp?hubtype= Inside&id=1159434325166.

14 www.london.edu/assets/documents/PDF/ Dubai_press_release_ 2006_final.pdf.

15 www.iedp.info/news/07-feb22.htm.

16 www.dubaileaders.ae/HomePage/tabid/36/ctl/Details/mid/ 366/ ItemID/0/Default.aspx; executiveeducation.wharton.upenn.edu/ resources/pr_0703-MEPI.cfm.

17 Corporate Web site, www.siemens.com/index.jsp?sdc_p= ft4mls7uo1032895i1328954pcz2&sdc_bcpath=1327903.s_7,1328954.s_ 7,&sdc_sid=15024242314&.

18 Department of Defense Directive 5100.1, § 2.2.3, November 21, 2003, www.dtic.mil/whs/directives/corres/pdf/510001p.pdf.

19 Coca-Cola, www.thecoca-colacompany.com/ourcompany/ seniormanagement_operating_group_leadership.html; Procter & Gamble, www.pg.com/company/who_we_are/ worldwide_ operations.jhtml; www.pg.com/content/pdf/01_about_pg/ 01_about_pg_homepage/about_pg_toolbar/download_report/ factsheet.pdf; Unilever: www.unileverme.com/our-company/ about-unilever/middleeast.asp; www.unilever.com/ourcompany/ aboutunilever/companystructure/unileverexecutive/default.asp.

INDEX

Formerly the global head of strategy for HSBC Amanah, Aamir A. Rehman has extensive expertise in both strategy development for multinationals and the Middle East/GCC region. Aamir is responsible for strategy development and implementation across global markets, including the UAE, Saudi Arabia, and the broader GCC. HSBC is one of the world's largest banks, and HSBC Amanah serves over 300,000 customers worldwide. Prior to joining HSBC, Aamir was a strategy consultant to Fortune 500 and other leading businesses since 1999. He has worked with the Boston Consulting Group and with the Monitor Group.

Aamir has written several articles on business strategy in the Middle East, including two pieces—"Dubai, Inc." and "The Business of Ramadan"—for the Harvard Business School's *HARBUS* publication. His general management commentary has been featured in the Harvard Business School's *Working Knowledge*, in the *New York Times*, and on National Public Radio. Aamir is on the advisory panel of *Dinar Standard*, and he is also a contributor to that publication. He and colleagues are currently founding an investment holding company focused specifically on investing in the Gulf states and other emerging growth markets.

Aamir is a native of Staten Island, New York, and lives in New York City. He may be reached at aamir.rehman@rehman-institute.com.